LONDON

HOTELS & MORE

LONDON

HOTELS & MORE

Angelika Taschen
Photos David Crookes
Text Christine Samuelian

TASCHEN

HONG KONG KÖLN LONDON LOS ANGELES MADRID PARIS TOKYO

7.4 million residents and 32 boroughs over 1,579 square kilometres: London is so confusingly huge that it has taken me many years to even begin to find my way around this truly cosmopolitan city. The aim of this book is to assist the visitor to find the most attractive and interesting places and hotels quickly and reliably.

I recommend hotels primarily when they provide the guest with some inkling of the history and individuality of London. It may well be that hotel chains such as the Mariott and the Hilton have cheaper rooms which are less dusty, but it is my view that the atmosphere and local colour of a hotel are much more relevant.

The right choice of district for accommodation is extremely important for the visitor. Soho is the best place for those who love night life with clubs and fashionable pubs. Those who prefer a little more peace and quiet should choose South Kensington. Solid, traditional England is to be found in Mayfair (also the best place for shopping), the creative live in East Central, and

7,4 Millionen Menschen und 32 Stadtbezirke auf 1579 Quadratkilometern: London ist so verwirrend groß, dass ich viele Jahre gebraucht habe, um mich in dieser wahrhaften Weltstadt einigermaßen zurecht zu finden. Dieses Buch soll dem Besucher helfen, schnell und zuverlässig die schönsten und interessantesten Plätze und Hotels zu finden.

Hotels empfehle ich vor allem dann, wenn sie dem Gast etwas über die Geschichte und die Eigenheiten Londons erzählen. Es kann schon mal sein, dass in Kettenhotels wie Mariott und Hilton die Zimmer preiswerter sind und weniger staubig, aber ich meine, dass Atmosphäre und Lokalkolorit eines Hotels viel entscheidender sind.

Extrem wichtig für den Besucher ist die Wahl des Viertels, in dem man übernachten möchte. Liebt man das Nachtleben mit Clubs und Szene-Kneipen, ist man in Soho gut aufgehoben. Hat man es gern etwas beschaulicher, ist South Kensington die richtige Wahl. In Mayfair erlebt man das traditionsreiche, gediegene England (und die beste Shopping-Gegend), in East Central leben die

7,4 millions de personnes et 32 arrondissements sur 1579 kilomètres carrés : Londres est si vaste que l'on si perd, et il m'a fallu de nombreuses années pour apprendre à m'y orienter. Le présent ouvrage est conçu pour aider le visiteur à trouver rapidement et facilement les sites et les hôtels les plus beaux et les plus intéressants.

Je mentionne surtout des hôtels qui peuvent transmettre à leurs clients un peu de l'histoire et de l'originalité de la métropole. Les chambres seront peut-être moins chères et moins poussiéreuses dans des hôtels de chaîne comme le Mariott et le Hilton, mais ce qui compte selon moi, ce sont l'atmosphère et la couleur locale d'un établissement.

Le choix du quartier où l'on désire séjourner est capital. Ceux qui aiment la vie nocturne, les clubs et les bars apprécieront Soho, alors que South Kensington est le bon choix pour les amateurs de calme et de méditation. A Mayfair, la bonne vieille Angleterre riche en traditions est au rendez-vous (et c'est aussi le meilleur endroit pour faire des achats). Les créatifs vivent à East

the trendy in Notting Hill. The cultural range in London is so enormously varied and exciting that this book has deliberately decided against presenting the classic sites like Buckingham Palace, Big Ben, the Houses of Parliament, the National Gallery, Trafalgar Square, Portobello Road and Carnaby Street. I'd rather recommend a visit to the Wallace Collection, for example, which, besides its porcelain and furniture collection, also has some of the most beautiful paintings of the Rococo period. Or the Hauser & Wirth Gallery at Piccadilly, housed in a building by Edwin Lutyens, one of England's most renowned architects (thus killing two birds with one stone: classical architecture and contemporary art).

If Paris is defined by fashion, perfume and luxury, it's the pubs, parks and picnics of London that spring to my mind. Again and again the recurrently bad air and traffic noise drive me into the wonderful, rambling parks to relax on a bench or a hired deckchair and read. It can even be a pleasure to walk in the drizzle – if you have previously

Kreativen, in Notting Hill die Hippen. Das Kulturangebot in London ist so immens vielfältig und aufregend, dass dieses Buch bewusst darauf verzichtet, Klassiker vorzustellen wie Buckingham Palace, Big Ben, Houses of Parliament, National Gallery, Trafalgar Square, Portobello Road und Carnaby Street. Lieber möchte ich zum Beispiel den Besuch der Wallace Collection empfehlen, die neben ihrer Porzellan- und Möbelsammlung einige der schönsten Gemälde des Rokoko besitzt. Oder die Hauser & Wirth Gallery am Piccadilly, die in einem Haus von Edwin Lutyens untergebracht ist, einem der wichtigsten Architekten Englands (so schlägt man zwei Fliegen mit einer Klappe: klassische Architektur und zeitgenössische Kunst).

Wenn Paris durch Mode, Parfum und Luxus geprägt wird, fallen mir für London Pubs, Parks und Picknicks ein. Der Verkehrslärm und die oft schlechte Luft treiben mich immer wieder in die wunderbar großzügigen Parks, um dort auf einer Bank oder in einem gemieteten Liegestuhl zu lesen. Sogar ein Spa-

Central, les hippes à Notting Hill. L'offre culturelle est si vaste, si variée et si excitante à Londres, que ce livre renonce à présenter des classiques tels le Buckingham Palace, Big Ben, le Parlement, la National Gallery, Trafalgar Square, Portobello Road et Carnaby Street. Je préfèrerais vous proposer de visiter la Wallace Collection par exemple ; à côté de ses porcelaines et de ses meubles, elle possède quelques-uns des plus beaux tableaux de l'ère rococo. Ou, à Picadilly, la Hauser & Wirth Gallery qu'abrite une maison d'Edwin Lutyens, un des plus grands architectes anglais (on fait ainsi d'une pierre deux coups : architecture classique et art contemporain).

Si Paris est la ville de la mode, des parfums et du luxe, Londres est pour moi celle des pubs, des parcs et des pique-niques. Voulant fuir la circulation bruyante et l'air souvent vicié, je me réfugie dans les parcs merveilleusement vastes, où je lis sur un banc ou une chaise-longue de location. Même une promenade sous la bruine peut être un délice – lorsqu'on a acheté auparavant un splendide parapluie chez James

bought a stylish umbrella at James Smith & Sons. (see p. 106)
In summer it's a good idea to enjoy a picnic in the park with sandwiches – two English inventions. In no other town do British chains, such as E.A.T., Pret-a-manger, Café Nero and Benugo, provide such tasty products.
England was considered a culinary wilderness for many years (rightly so, in my opinion), but today there are countless excellent restaurants in London. I mainly recommend places which offer good, classic English cuisine. Best of all are the pubs, I find, and there are more than five thousand of them in London. The "gastropubs" also serve hearty meals, such as fish & chips, and stews, and there is serious competition as to who makes the best batter and the best home-made salad cream.

Sincerely

Angelika Taschen

ziergang im Nieselregen kann ein Genuss sein – wenn man vorher stilvoll bei James Smith & Sons einen Regenschirm gekauft hat (s.S. 106). Im Sommer empfiehlt es sich, im Park ein Picknick mit Sandwiches zu zelebrieren – beides englische Erfindungen. In keiner anderen Stadt bieten britische Ketten wie E.A.T., Pret-a-manger, Café Nero und Benugo so wohlschmeckende Produkte. Nachdem England lange als kulinarisches Sibirien galt (zu Recht, wie ich meine), gibt es in London heute unzählige exzellente Restaurants. Ich empfehle vor allem Lokale mit guter, klassisch englischer Küche. Am tollsten finde ich die Pubs, von denen es in London mehr als fünftausend gibt. Die „Gastropubs" servieren dazu noch herzhaftes Essen wie Fish & Chips und Stews, und es herrscht ein regelrechter Wettbewerb, wer die beste Panade (Batter) und die beste hausgemachte Remoulade hinkriegt.

Ihre

Angelika Taschen

Smith & Sons (cf. p. 106). L'été, c'est le temps de pique-niquer, et les sandwiches, autre invention anglaise, s'imposent. Dans aucune autre ville du monde des chaînes comme chez E.A.T., Pret-a-manger, Café Nero et Benugo ne proposent des produits aussi goûteux.
L'Angletere a été longtemps considérée – non sans raison – comme un désert culinaire, mais aujourd'hui les bons restaurants sont légion à Londres. Je recommande surtout ceux qui proposent la cuisine britannique classique. A mon avis les meilleurs sont les pubs, et ils sont plus de 5000 à Londres. Les gastropubs servent en plus des plats simples et savoureux, fish & chips et stews par exemple, et c'est à celui qui réussira la meilleure pâte à frire et la meilleure rémoulade maison.

Votre

Angelika Taschen

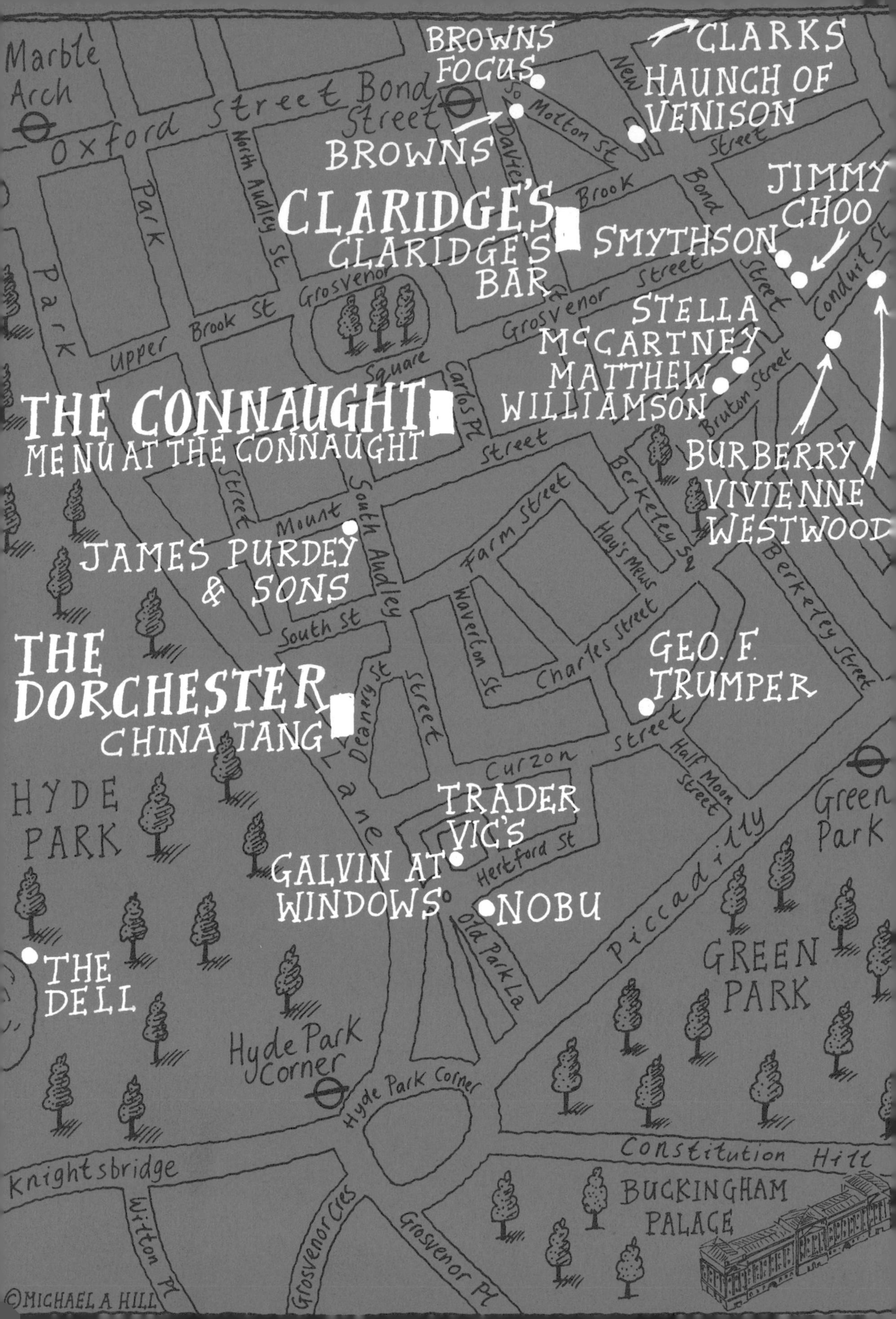

Marble Arch

Oxford Street

Bond Street

BROWNS FOCUS

CLARKS

HAUNCH OF VENISON

New Bond Street

Motton St.

Davie's St.

North Audley St.

BROWNS

CLARIDGE'S

CLARIDGE'S BAR

Brook

Brook St.

SMYTHSON

JIMMY CHOO

Conduit St.

Grosvenor

Grosvenor Street

STELLA McCARTNEY

MATTHEW WILLIAMSON

Bruton Street

THE CONNAUGHT

MENU AT THE CONNAUGHT

Square

Carlos Pl.

Carlos Street

BURBERRY

VIVIENNE WESTWOOD

Bond Street

Berkeley Street

Upper Brook St.

Park

Park

Mount

South Audley

Street

Mount

JAMES PURDEY & SONS

South Audley

Street

Farm Street

Hay's Mews

Berkeley St.

Berkeley Street

THE DORCHESTER

CHINA TANG

South St.

Deanery St.

Park Lane

Waverton St.

Charles Street

Charles street

GEO. F. TRUMPER

HYDE PARK

Curzon

Street

Half Moon Street

Green Park

TRADER VIC'S

GALVIN AT WINDOWS

NOBU

Hertford St.

Old Park La.

Piccadilly

GREEN PARK

THE DELL

Hyde Park Corner

Hyde Park Corner

Constitution Hill

Knightsbridge

Witton Pl.

Grosvenor Cres.

Grosvenor Pl.

BUCKINGHAM PALACE

©MICHAEL A HILL

W1

Mayfair

1 Romantic Sunset/Romantischer Sonnenuntergang/
Coucher de soleil romantique
The Dell

2 Cocktail Bar & Restaurant/Cocktail Bar & Restaurant/
Cocktail Bar & Restaurant
Trader Vic's

3 Japanese Restaurant/Japanisches Restaurant/
Restaurant japonais
Nobu

4 Barbers & Perfumers/Herren-Salon/Barbier & Coiffeurs
Geo. F. Trumper

5 Guns & Hunting Fashion/Gewehre & Jagdmode/Armurerie &
tenues de chasse
James Purdey & Sons

6 Bar/Bar/Bar
Claridge's Bar

---

1 Restaurant & Bar/Restaurant & Bar/Restaurant & Bar
China Tang at The Dorchester

2 Bar/Bar/Bar
Galvin at Windows

3 Fashion/Mode/Mode
Matthew Williamson

4 Fashion/Mode/Mode
Stella McCartney

5 Iconic British Fashion/Britische Mode/Mode Britannique
Burberry

6 Fashion/Mode/Mode
Vivienne Westwood

---

1 Restaurant/Restaurant/Restaurant
Menu at The Connaught

2 Gallery/Galerie/Gallerie
Haunch of Venison

3 Leather Goods/Schreib- und Lederwaren/Articles en cuir
Smythson of Bond Street

4 Shoes/Schuhe/Chaussures
Jimmy Choo

5 Fashion/Mode/Mode
Browns & Browns Focus

6 Shoes/Schuhe/Chaussures
Clarks

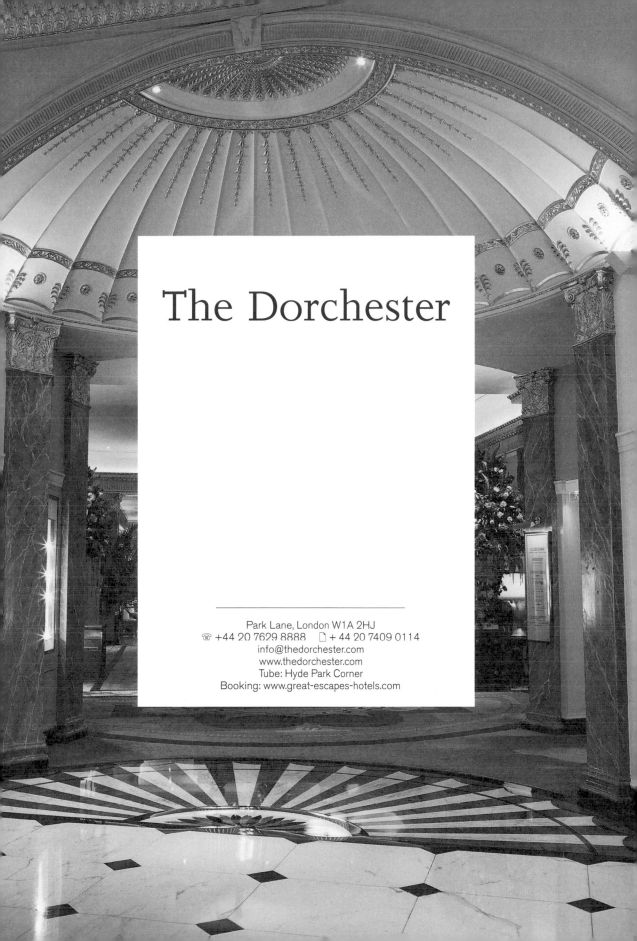

The Dorchester

Park Lane, London W1A 2HJ
☎ +44 20 7629 8888   📠 + 44 20 7409 0114
info@thedorchester.com
www.thedorchester.com
Tube: Hyde Park Corner
Booking: www.great-escapes-hotels.com

The Dorchester

The Dorchester dominates London's Park Lane with its yellow and white awnings blinking like giant eyelids. If you can navigate your way through the Bentleys parked out front and make it through the door, then be braced: the décor at The Dorchester is seriously over the top. Sit on one of the plump sofas at the Promenade lobby restaurant, sip tea accompanied by a plate of macaroons and spy on the weird and wonderful mix of big-haired American belles; English families nibbling finger sandwiches; cigar-smoking men and their veiled wives; and the sugar daddies accompanied by women tottering around in vertiginous heels. Pick a luxe English-style room with views of Hyde Park and enjoy the space: many rooms come with walk-in wardrobes, and the bathtubs are meant to be the deepest in London. If hunger strikes, head down to The Grill Room: the Scottish-themed tartan décor will either destroy your appetite or whet it for the traditional roasts served.

Mit seinen gelb-weißen Markisen ist das Dorchester der Blickfang der Park Lane. Wer durch die unzähligen Bentleys den Weg ins Innere findet, dem stockt zunächst der Atem: Das Dekor ist fast zuviel des Guten. Die Szenerie eignet sich allerdings bestens für Feldstudien: Man lässt sich dazu auf einem der üppigen Sofas im Lobby-Restaurant Promenade nieder, nippt an Tee, nascht „Macaroons". Und schon flanieren sie an einem vorbei, die Amerikanerinnen mit Superfrisur, die britischen Familien, die an Finger-Sandwiches knabbern, die Zigarren schmauchenden Herren und die Sugar Daddys in Begleitung von Damen auf Schwindel erregenden Absätzen. Nicht zu vergessen: Die Deluxe-Zimmer in englischem Dekor sind geräumig, die meisten verfügen über einen begehbaren Schrank und supertiefe Badewannen. Eine Kuriosum ist das Restaurant The Grill Room mit schottischem Karomuster-Dekor: Hier bekommt man unsäglich Lust auf einen traditionellen „Roast".

Le Dorchester domine Park Lane avec ses dais à rayures jaunes et blanches qui claquent au vent. Si vous parvenez à vous glisser jusqu'à la porte entre les cheiks arabes et leurs Bentley, préparez-vous à un choc : le décor est chargé. Installez-vous sur les canapés douillets du restaurant Promenade et, devant un thé accompagné de macarons, savourez l'étrange mélange de belles Américaines aux crinières de lionne, de familles british grignotant des mini sandwichs, de fumeurs de cigare suivis de leurs épouses voilées et de vieux messieurs offrant le bras à de jeunes femmes perchées sur des talons vertigineux. Choisissez une spacieuse chambre « de luxe » décorée à l'anglaise avec vue sur Hyde Park ; la plupart sont équipées de grands dressings et les baignoires sont réputées les plus profondes de Londres. Un petit creux ? Descendez à la rôtisserie : si le décor tout en tartans écossais ne vous coupe pas l'appétit, vous vous régalerez avec les grillades traditionnelles.

Rates: From 525 € (360 GBP) excl. VAT.
Rooms: 250 (53 suites).
Restaurants: The Grill Room, The Promenade, China Tang.
History: The Dorchester opened its doors in 1931 and such luminaries as Alfred Hitchcock, Elizabeth Taylor, Barbra Streisand and General Eisenhower have all stayed here.
X-Factor: The gorgeous Floris products in the bathrooms.
Internet: Broadband access at 18.50 GBP per day.

Preise: Ab 525 € (360 GBP) exkl. VAI.
Zimmer: 250 (53 Suiten).
Restaurants: The Grill Room, The Promenade, China Tang.
Geschichte: The Dorchester eröffnete 1931 und beherbergte so illustre Gäste wie Alfred Hitchcock, Elizabeth Taylor, Barbra Streisand und General Eisenhower.
X-Faktor: In den Badezimmern stehen Beauty-Produkte von Floris.
Internet: Breitbandanschluss für 18,50 GBP pro Tag.

Prix : À partir de 525 € (360 GBP). TVA non comprise.
Chambres : 250 (53 suites).
Restauration : The Grill Room, The Promenade, China Tang.
Histoire: Le Dorchester a ouvert ses portes en 1931 et a accueilli des célébrités telles qu'Alfred Hitchcock, Elizabeth Taylor, Barbra Streisand et le général Eisenhower.
Le « petit plus » : Les fabuleux produits Floris dans les salles de bains.
Internet : Accès haut débit à 18,50 GBP par jour.

1

2

3

1   Romantic Sunset/Romantischer Sonnenuntergang/Coucher de soleil romantique

The Dell
Hyde Park
Eastern side of Serpentine
Tel: +44 20 7706 0464
Tube: Hyde Park Corner

Not only can you stroll, play games, ride a bike or a horse, rollerblade and row a boat in Hyde Park, but you can also stop off at The Dell for refreshments. It's right on the Eastern side of Hyde Park with the best views of Hyde park by the lake Serpentine so you can perch on one of the seats on the outdoor terrace, watch the sunset and forget you are in one of the busiest cities in the world.

Im Hyde Park kann man spazieren, spielen, sich auf ein Fahrrad oder Pferd schwingen, Rollschuhe anschnallen, in einem Boot rudern – und man kann einen Erfrischungs-Halt im Dell machen. Vom Restaurant, auf der Ostseite des Hyde Park, gleich am Serpentine Lake, hat man einen fantastischen Blick auf den Park. Am besten setzt man sich an einen Tisch auf der Terrasse, beobachtet den Sonnenuntergang und vergisst die Großstadt rundherum.

Hyde Park vous offre, outre ses promenades, ses jeux, ses tours en bicyclette, à cheval ou en barque, des lieux comme The Dell où prendre un verre. Situé le côté gauche du parc, on y a la meilleure vue sur les jardins et le lac. Assis sur la terrasse, vous pouvez contempler le coucher de soleil et oublier que vous êtes dans une des capitales les plus animées du monde.

2   Cocktail Bar & Restaurant/Cocktail-Bar & Restaurant/Bar & Restaurant

Trader Vic's
The London Hilton on Park Lane
22 Park Lane
London W1Y 4BE
Tel: +44 20 7208 4113
www.tradervics.com
Tube: Hyde Park Corner

There are some restaurants and bars you dare not enter for fear you are not cool enough. Before venturing into Trader Vic's in the basement of the London Hilton on Park Lane, you will check your attitude in at the door and walk in with the knowledge that tacky Tiki can sometimes be far more fun than trendy. Don't let the faux South Pacific style put you off: go with good friends, order a Mai Thai and relax.

Manchmal steht man vor einem Restaurant oder einer Bars und traut sich kaum hinein, so cool sind sie. Bei Trader's Vic im London Hilton on Park Lane ist es genau umgekehrt. Kaum drinnen, wird man jedoch feststellen, dass kitschiger Tiki-Stil viel mehr Spaß machen kann als eine supercoole Attitüde. Man lasse sich also vom südpazifischen Imitations-Dekor nicht abschrecken. Ein Mai Thai zusammen mit ein paar guten Freunden ist hier ein toller Spaß.

Il y a des restaurants et des bars où l'on n'ose à peine entrer de peur de faire tache. Avant de descendre au sous-sol du London Hilton on Park Lane, où se trouve Trader Vic's, laissez vos appréhensions à la porte et plongez-vous sans vergogne dans l'atmosphère Tiki pur toc. Allez-y avec des amis, commandez un Mai Thai et détendez-vous.

3   Japanese Restaurant/Japanisches Restaurant/Restaurant japonais

Nobu
19 Old Park Lane
London W1K 1LB
Tel: +44 20 7447 4747
www.noburestaurants.com
Tube: Hyde Park Corner/Green Park

Mustn't mention the certain things that took place in the Nobu broom cupboard because this restaurant is serious about sushi. It is one of many Nobu restaurants in the world, of course, but its location in The Metropolitan Hotel means that everyone who is anyone has eaten here. The black cod is a favourite but there are few things on the menu that don't appeal to those who love fish.

Eigentlich schade, dass Nobu nur wegen seiner Besenkammer so berühmt wurde. Das Essen hier ist nämlich wirklich erstklassig. Es ist zwar nur eines von vielen Nobu-Restaurants weltweit, doch da es im mondänen Metropolitan Hotel liegt, hat hier so ziemlich jeder bedeutende Name gespeist. Der „black cod" gehört zu den beliebtesten Gerichten. Doch fast alle Gerichte sind für Liebhaber von Fisch gedacht.

On taira ce qui s'est passé dans le placard à balais de Nobu car ce restaurant ne badine pas avec les sushis. C'est l'une des nombreuses enseignes de la chaîne, certes, mais son emplacement dans le Metropolitan Hotel signifie que tout le gratin cosmopolite y a dîné. La morue charbonnière y est exquise mais la carte a largement de quoi ravir tous les amateurs de poisson cru.

4   Barbers & Perfumers/Herren-Salon/ Barbiers & Coiffeurs

Geo. F. Trumper
9 Curzon Street
London W1J 5HQ
Tel: +44 20 7499 1850
www.trumpers.com
Tube: Green Park/Hyde Park Corner

British men have a secret love of good grooming and products. Lucky, then, that Geo. F. Trumper has been on Curzon Street since 1875 and provides some of the best toiletries for men in the world. There is also a wonderful old-fashioned barbershop here that does not only haircuts, but also offers shaves. If you want to refine your own technique, sign up for the shaving school.

Britische Männer haben eine geheime Vorliebe für gepflegte Rasuren und Toilettenartikel. Für sie ist das Geschäft von Geo. F. Trumper, seit 1875 an der Curzon Street, ein Glücksfall. Hier gibt's Toilettenartikel vom Allerfeinsten, und im wunderbar altmodischen Barbershop kann man sich nicht nur die Haare schneiden, sondern auch rasieren lassen. Wer die höhere Kunst des Rasierens lernen will, kann sich in die Rasurschule einschreiben.

4

5

6

Les hommes anglais sont réputés pour être particulièrement soignés. Heureusement pour eux, Geo F. Trumper existe sur Curzon Street depuis 1875 et fabrique parmi les meilleurs produits de toilette pour hommes dans le monde. On y trouve également un merveilleux salon de coiffure et de rasage. Si vous voulez peaufiner votre technique, inscrivez-vous à l'école de rasage.

---

5 Guns & Hunting Fashion/Gewehre & Jagdmode/Armurerie et tenues de chasse

James Purdey & Sons
Audley House
57–58 South Audley Street
London W1K 2ED
Tel: +44 20 7499 1801
www.purdey.co.uk
Tube: Hyde Park Corner/Green Park

Hunting may not be a palatable activity to some of us, but there are still plenty of Brits who take the sport very seriously, and Purdey has been around to indulge them since 1814 (the store has been on this site since 1882). Who knew there were so many types of game guns and rifles? Those with a weak stomach can leave the guns on the shelves and instead buy lots of tweed and some Wellingtons.

Nicht jedem sagt die Jagd zu. Doch viele Briten nehmen diesen Sport sehr ernst, und für sie ist Purdey das Paradies schlechthin. Seit 1814 gibt es dieses Geschäft bereits, allerdings erst seit 1882 an dieser Adresse. Man wird hier staunen, wie viele verschiedene Pistolen und Gewehre es überhaupt gibt. Achtung: Wer schwache Nerven hat, sollte unverzüglich zu der zeitlosen Tweedbekleidung und den Gummistiefeln weiterziehen.

Tout le monde n'apprécie pas la chasse mais de nombreux Britanniques prennent encore ce sport très au sérieux. Purdey est leur fournisseur depuis 1814 (la boutique actuelle existe depuis 1882). Qui aurait imaginé qu'il puisse y avoir une telle variété de fusils de chasse ? Les âmes sensibles préféreront sans doute se concentrer sur les beaux tweeds et les bottes en caoutchouc.

---

6 Bar/Bar/Bar

Claridge's Bar
Davies Street
London, W1A 2JQ
Tel: +44 20 7629 8860
www.claridges.co.uk
Tube: Bond Street

Claridge's Bar hosts the most stylish and interesting people in the media, business and arts world. It was designed by David Collins, which means that it is glamorous and has beautiful details such as a silver-leafed ceiling and rich red banquettes. Languish in the gorgeous Art-Deco surroundings and sip Champagne: it is the drink of choice with a great list of special and rare ones for the chic clientele.

Die Claridge's Bar ist Treffpunkt gestylter und interessanter Leute aus der Medien- und Kunstszene. Interior-Designer David Collins hat der Bar mit glamourösen, wunderschönen Details, wie der versilborten Decke und den satt-roten Sitzbänken, seinen Stempel aufgesetzt. Hier kann man in traumhaftem Art-Deco-Dekor schwelgen und dabei an einer der außergewöhnlichen Champagner-Raritäten nippen.

Le Claridge's Bar est l'antre des personnalités les plus chics et intéressantes des médias et du monde de l'art. L'élégant décor Art Déco signé David Collins inclut de superbes détails tels que le plafond à la feuille d'argent et les banquettes en cuir rouge. Prélassez-vous devant une coupe de champagne, la carte propose à sa clientèle sélecte une magnifique liste de cuvées rares et spéciales.

Personal Finds/Eigene Entdeckungen/ Découvertes personnelles:

The Connaught

Carlos Place, London W1K 2AL
☎ + 44 20 7499 7070   📠 + 44 20 7495 3262
info@the-connaught.co.uk
www.the-connaught.co.uk
Tube: Bond Street
Booking: www.great-escapes-hotels.com

The Connaught

It's worth staying at The Connaught if only to float down the magnificent mahogany staircase. It dates back to 1897 and is looked after daily by a French polisher. A famous American designer once asked to buy the stairs – whole – to ship to New York but his request was declined. The old-fashioned, clinking keys used to open room doors are also charming; not only are they rare and precious, but this is one of the only remaining hotels in London not to succumb to using plastic. Sample the cuisine at Menu or The Grill; Angela Hartnett is one of the most highly respected chefs in the UK. These venues really come into their own in the evenings when candles burn and diners are treated to a warm and intimate eating experience. Cocktails are also essential and no trip here is complete without checking out the old-world charm of The American Bar or The Red Room, both of which attract Mayfair locals as well as guests. Especially deliciouris also the Scotish beer.

Allein dafür, die prächtige Mahagoni-Treppe von 1897 hinunter schweben zu können, lohnt es sich, im Connaught abzusteigen. Für die tägliche Politur des edlen Holzes ist übrigens ein französischer Fachmann verantwortlich. Ein bekannter amerikanischer Designer war vom Prachtsstück derart angetan, dass er es nach New York verschiffen wollte. Sein Kaufangebot wurde allerdings abgelehnt. Zu den Preziosien des Hauses gehören auch die altmodischen Zimmerschlüssel – ein stilvoller Widerstand gegen den allgegenwärtigen Plastik-Trend. Feinschmecker sollten unbedingt einen Tisch im Menu oder The Grill reservieren: Küchenchefin Angela Hartnett zählt zu den besten Kochkünstlern des Landes. Besonders stimmungsvoll ist ein Dinner bei Kerzenlicht. Zu den Musts gehört auch ein Abstecher in die charmant-altmodische American Bar oder den Red Room. Die Cocktails sind legendär und das Publikum ein lockerer Mix aus Mayfair-Bewohnern und Hotelgästen. Besonders köstlich ist auch das schottische Bier.

Le Connaught mérite un séjour ne serait-ce que pour descendre son majestueux escalier en acajou. Datant de 1897, il est poli chaque jour par un spécialiste français. Un célèbre couturier américain a proposé de l'acheter pour le faire remonter aux États-Unis, en vain. Les vieilles clefs cliquetantes des chambres sont un autre détail charmant : elles sont non seulement rares et précieuses mais le Connaught est un des rares hôtels londoniens à ne pas avoir succombé au plastique. Goûtez la cuisine du Menu ou du Grill. Le chef Angela Hartnett est une sommité au Royaume-Uni. Les deux restaurants sont particulièrement agréables le soir pour un dîner intime aux chandelles. Un détour par l'American Bar ou la Red Room s'impose ; les cocktails y sont légendaires et une clientèle très Mayfair s'y mêle aux clients de l'hôtel. La bière écossaise est aussi particulièrement délicieuse.

Rates: From 470 € (320 GBP) excl. VAT.
Rooms: 92 (24 suites).
Restaurants: The Grill Room, Menu, The American Bar, The Connaught Bar.
History: The Connaught was opened in 1897 and originally called The Coburg Hotel. It was renamed in 1917, during the Great War, after Queen Victoria's third son, Prince Arthur, the first Duke of Connaught.
X-Factor: The gym at The Connaught will appeal to even the least athletic guest.
Internet: Broadband in all rooms at 20 GBP per day.

Preise: Ab 470 € (320 GBP) exkl. VAT.
Zimmer: 92 (24 Suiten).
Restaurants: The Grill Room, Menu, The American Bar, The Connaught Bar.
Geschichte: Das Connaught wurde 1897 als The Coburg Hotel eröffnet. 1917, während des 1. Weltkriegs, wurde es nach Königin Victorias drittem Sohn, Prinz Arthur, Duke of Connaught, umbenannt.
X-Faktor: Die Fitnessanlage im Connaught ist auch für weniger Sportliche attraktiv.
Internet: Breitbandanschluss in allen Zimmern für 20 GBP pro Tag.

Prix : À partir de 470 € (320 GBP), TVA non comprise.
Chambres : 92 (24 suites).
Restauration : The Grill Room, Menu, The American Bar, The Connaught Bar.
Histoire : Inauguré en 1897 sous le nom de Coburg Hotel, il fut rebaptisé en 1917 durant la Grande Guerre en l'honneur du troisième fils de la reine Victoria, le prince Arthur, premier duc de Connaught.
Le « petit plus » : La salle de gym tentera même le client le plus apathique.
Internet : Accès haut débit à 20 GBP par jour.

1

2

1   Restaurant & Bar/Restaurant & Bar/
     Restaurant & Bar

China Tang at The Dorchester
Park Lane
London W1A 2HJ
Tel: +44 20 7629 9988
www.thedorchester.com
Tube: Hyde Park Corner

China Tang (a David Tang creation) is all-
together charming and as glamorous as
The Dorchester is flashy. Opt for one of
the low banquettes, order a Cosmopolitan
(avoid the wine list which is sadly lacking)
and watch the wonderfully mixed crowd.
Rupert Everett is as likely to be there with
a gaggle of beautiful men as is a grand
American dame with her facelift and ap-
propriately suave husband.

China Tang, das jüngste Projekt von Life-
style-Unternehmer David Tang, ist so
glamourös, dass selbst das Dorchester
erblasst. Von einem der Sitzbänke lässt sich
die buntgemischte Szenerie schön beobachten. Gut möglich, Rupert Everett mit seiner Entourage anzutreffen oder aber eine
der eleganten, gelifteten Amerikanerinnen
mit entsprechend gepflegtem Gatten an
der Seite. Da die Weinliste nicht beindruckt,
besser einen Cosmopolitan bestellen.

Le China Tang (créé par David Tang) est
aussi charmant et chic que le Dorchester
est clinquant. Préférez les banquettes
basses, commandez un cosmopolitan (la
carte des vins n'est pas à la hauteur) et
observez la clientèle bigarrée. Vous y croi-
serez peut-être Rupert Everett entouré de
jolis garçons ainsi que des grandes dames
américaines liftées accompagnées de
leurs maris dociles.

2   Bar/Bar/Bar

Galvin at Windows
The London Hilton on Park Lane, 28th Floor
22 Park Lane
London W1K 1BE
Tel: +44 20 7208 4021
www.hilton.co.uk/londonparklane
Tube: Hyde Park Corner

Galvin at Windows closely follows brothers Chris and Jeff Galvin's successful
launch of Galvin Bistrot de Luxe on Baker
Street earlier in 2006. Go for the views
from the 28th floor of the London Hilton
on Park Lane, they are unbeatable at
night. Drink a cockail while you gaze out
the window towards Hyde Park and
Buckhingham Palace. You may even catch
a glimpse of the Queen.

Die Brüder Chris und Jeff Galvin haben
mit dem Galvin Bistrot de Luxe an der Baker
Street bereits eine Erfolgsformel gefun-
den. Das Galvin at Windows wurde Anfang
2006 im 28. Stockwerk des London Hilton
auf der Park Lane eröffnet. Die Aussicht
hier ist spektakulär, vor allem nachts. Tipp:
An einem Cocktail nuckeln, dabei Richtung
Hyde Park und Buckhingham Palace guk-
ken, und dabei vielleicht einen Blick auf
die Queen erhaschen.

Galvin at Windows a ouvert peu après
l'inauguration en 2006 du très branché
Galvin Bistrot de Luxe des frères Chris
et Jeff Galvin sur Baker Street. Les vues
depuis le 28e étage de London Hilton de
Park Lane sont imprenables. Prenez un
cocktail en contemplant Hyde Park et le
palais de Buckingham. Vous apercevrez
peut-être la reine.

3   Fashion/Mode/Mode

Matthew Williamson
28 Bruton Street
London W1J 6QH
Tel: +44 20 7629 6200
www.matthewwilliamson.com
Tube: Bond Street/Green Park

Matthew Williamson is one of the darlings
of the British fashion landscape. He burst
onto the scene in the late 1990s with his
Indian-inspired colourful fabrics worn by
model friends such as Jade Jagger. His
look has moved on but his popularity
hasn't. His jewel box of a store with his
rich colours and striking details is an ode
to his particular – and lasting – sense of
beauty.

Matthew Williamson gehört zu den Lieblin-

gen der britischen Modeszene. Auf ihn
aufmerksam wurde sie in den späten
1990ern, als Leute wie Jade Jagger an-
fingen, seine bunten, damals indisch angehauchten Kreationen zu tragen. Sein Look
hat sich weiterentwickelt, angesagt ist er
genau so wie damals. Seine farbenfrohe
Boutique mit vielen interessanten Details
erinnert an eine Schmuckschatulle und ist
eine Ode an seine eigenwillige Ästhetik.

Matthew Williamson est un des chouchous
de la mode anglaise. Il a fait sensation à
la fin des années 90 avec ses tissus aux
couleurs indiennes portés par ses amies
mannequins comme Jade Jagger. Son
style a changé mais pas sa popularité. Sa
boutique, un petit bijou rempli de couleurs
et de détails, est un hommage à son sens
esthétique unique.

4   Fashion/Mode/Mode

Stella McCartney
30 Bruton Street
London W1J 6LG
Tel: +44 20 7518 3100
www.stellamccartney.com
Tube: Bond Street/Green Park

She is the cool princess of the London
fashion scene and what Stella McCartney
sells in her shop is very much a reflection
of her own personal style: a little bit sassy,
a bit eclectic and very, very London. Her
flattering tailored suits are hugely popular
as are her feminine chiffon dresses, which
normally come in very pale pinks and other
neutrals. Also great are the leather-free
handbags and shoes designed by the french
vegetarian.

Sie ist das Coolste, was die Londoner
Modeszene zu bieten hat. Die Kleider und
Accessoires, die Stella McCartney in ihrer
Boutique verkauft, entsprechen genau
ihrem persönlichen Stil: frech, eklektisch
und typisch für London. Genau so beliebt
wie die figurschmeichelnden Anzüge sind
die femininen Chiffonkleider in Blassrosa
und andern hellen Tönen. Fantastisch
auch die Taschen und Schuhe, die Vege-
tarierin McCartney ohne Leder herstellen
lässt.

4

5

6

Dans sa boutique londonienne, la petite princesse de la mode anglaise présente les vêtements qui reflètent son propre sens du style : un peu provocants, éclectiques et très, très british. On s'arrache ses tailleurs impeccables et flatteurs ainsi que ses robes ultra féminines en mousseline de soie rose pâle ou dans d'autres couleurs neutres. Ses sacs et souliers sans cuir valent aussi le détour.

6   Iconic British Fashion/Britisch Mode/Mode Britannique

Burberry
21–23 New Bond Street
London W1S 2RE
Tel: +44 20 7968 0000
www.burberry.com
Tube: Bond Street/Oxford Circus/
Green Park

In the past ten years Burberry has resurrected itself from a tired brand trying, in vain, to peddle Britishness to the world, to a label that pretty much took over the world. Like the Burberry check or not, most people around the globe identify it with British luxury. The New Bond Street store is vast and is great for gorgeous leather handbags, accessories and, of course, beige trench coats.

Burberry hat es in den letzten zehn Jahren geschafft, von einem verstaubten Kleiderhersteller zu einem der angesagtesten Labels der Welt zu werden. Mit Burberry ist britischer Stil und Luxus cool geworden, ob man nun das Burberry-Karomuster mag oder nicht. Im großzügigen Geschäft an der New Bond Street gibt's wunderschöne Lederhandtaschen, Accessoires und natürlich auch die beigen Trench-Coats.

Au cours des dix dernières années Burberry, éponyme du chic british, est rené de ses cendres pour prendre le monde d'assaut. Qu'on aime le célèbre imprimé ou non, il symbolise le luxe anglais aux quatre coins de la planète. La vaste nouvelle boutique sur Bond Street vaut le détour pour ses magnifiques sacs et accessoires en cuir, sans oublier naturellement, ses fameux trench-coats beiges.

6   Fashion/Mode/Mode

Vivienne Westwood
44 Conduit Street
London W1S 2YL
Tel: +44 20 7439 1109
www.viviennewestwood.co.uk
Tube: Bond Street/Oxford Circus/
Green Park

If Stella McCartney is the princess of British fashion, then Vivienne Westwood is its queen. Westwood made a name for herself in the 1970s with her then-love, Malcolm McLaren, and they defined the Punk fashion of Kings Road. While she is a bit more low key these days, Westwood still has a loyal following for her brilliant suits for men and quirky but highly wearable dresses for women.

Vivienne Westwood gilt als die Queen der britischen Modeszene. In den 1970ern erfand sie an der Kings Road, zusammen mit ihrem damaligen Geliebten, Malcom McLaren, die Punk-Mode und sorgte damit für einiges Aufsehen. Auch wenn Westwood heute nicht mehr modisch an vorderster Front steht, so hat sie immer noch eine loyale Kundschaft. Ihre Herrenanzüge sind vom Feinsten und die Damenkleider sind zwar unkonventionell, doch sehr tragbar.

Si Stella McCartney est la princesse de la mode britannique, Vivienne Westwood en est indubitablement sa reine. Elle s'est fait un nom dans les années 70 en définissant la mode Punk de Kings Road avec son compagnon d'alors, Malcom MacLaren. Elle s'est un peu assagie depuis mais ses superbes costumes masculins et ses robes, excentriques mais très portables, continuent de faire recette.

Personal Finds/Eigene Entdeckungen/
Découvertes personnelles:

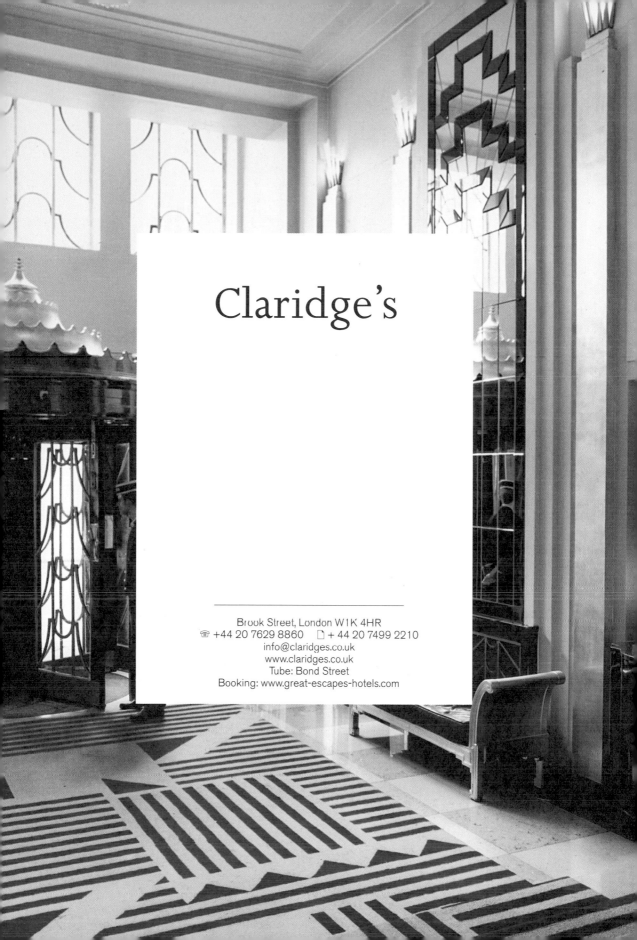

Claridge's

Brook Street, London W1K 4HR
☎ +44 20 7629 8860   📠 + 44 20 7499 2210
info@claridges.co.uk
www.claridges.co.uk
Tube: Bond Street
Booking: www.great-escapes-hotels.com

Claridge's

If there is a hotel in London that embodies English gentility and glamour, it is Claridge's, right in the heart of Mayfair. The lobby has a rich golden glow, gleaming black-and-white floors, swooping chandeliers and a dramatic winding staircase. In the Foyer and Reading Room at high tea, you may see the handsome Tom Ford sipping his tipple while a gaggle of Saudi wives and children take tea (one of 30 different kinds) at another table, munching cucumber sandwiches. Claridge's Bar is also a hive of activity, with London's suited financiers and intellectuals gathered for drinks and fashionable gossip. Claridge's draw, of course, is that it is slightly stuffy and a bit old-fashioned, as all very charming British things are. Rooms are either decorated in a Victorian fashion or with authentic 1930s detailing. Don't leave without visiting the original Art-Deco public bathroom, and say hello to the nice lady who turns on the taps so you can wash your hands.

Kein Hotel verkörpert den Stil und Glamour der britischen Upper Class besser als das Claridge's mitten in Mayfair. In der golden-schimmernden Lobby glänzen die schwarz-weißen Böden wie Lack. Dazu sorgen imposante Leuchter und eine dramatisch geschwungene Treppe für standesgemäßen Prunk. In den Zimmern bestimmt der viktorianische Stil den Look, manchmal sind auch Dekors aus den 1930ern zu finden. Es ist diese leicht verstaubte, typisch englische Atmosphäre, die den Charme des Hotels ausmacht. Es kann gut sein, dass man beim High Tea im Foyer oder Lesezimmer auf Tom Ford trifft. Am Nebentisch sitzen dann ziemlich sicher saudische Ehefrauen mit ihrem Nachwuchs, trinken Tee (30 verschiedene Sorten) und vertilgen dazu Gurken-Sandwiches. Die Bar des Claridge's hingegen ist Treffpunkt für Londons Financiers und Intellektuelle. Nicht verpassen: die öffentlichen Art-Deco-Toiletten. Hier muss man zum Händewaschen nicht einmal den Wasserhahn öffnen. Dafür sorgt eine freundliche Angestellte.

Aucun hôtel à Londres ne personnifie mieux la distinction et le chic anglais que le Claridge's, au cœur de Mayfair, avec son hall aux tons dorés, ses sols en damier noir et blanc étincelants, ses grands lustres et son escalier spectaculaire. L'après-midi, vous pourrez voir Tom Ford dans le Foyer ou la Reading Room sirotant un verre pendant que quelque épouses saoudiennes et leurs enfants goûtent une des quelques trente variétés de thé accompagnée de sandwiches au concombre. Le bar est une vraie ruche, les banquiers de la City et les intellectuels s'y retrouvant pour boire un verre et échanger des potins mondains. Le principal attrait du Claridge's, c'est son atmosphère légèrement désuète et guindée, tout ce qui fait le charme anglais. Le décor des chambres est victorien ou années 30. N'oubliez pas de faire une visite aux toilettes publiques Art Déco et de saluer la dame charmante qui vous ouvre le robinet pour que vous vous laviez les mains.

Rates: From 670 € (460 GBP) excl. VAT.
Rooms: 203 (67 suites).
Restaurants: Gordon Ramsay at Claridge's, The Foyer, Reading Room.
History: James Mivart first opened a hotel in a house on the current site in 1812, but Claridge's as it is today was built in 1898. Many areas and rooms were re-designed in Art-Deco style in the early 1930s.
X-Factor: The Claridge's "C" monogrammed towels.
Internet: Broadband in all rooms at 20 GBP per day.

Preise: Ab 670 € (460 GBP) exkl. VAT.
Zimmer: 203 (67 Suiten).
Restaurants: Gordon Ramsay at Claridge's, The Foyer, Reading Room.
Geschichte: James Mivart eröffnete 1812 auf diesem Grundstück ein Hotel. Das heutige Claridge's wurde allerdings erst 1898 gebaut. In den frühen 1930ern wurde ein Teil des Hotels im Art-Deco-Stil umgebaut.
X-Faktor: Die Badetücher sind mit dem „C" für Claridge's bestickt.
Internet: Breitbandanschluss in allen Zimmern für 20 GBP pro Tag.

Prix : À partir de 670 € (460 GBP), TVA non comprise.
Chambres : 203 (67 suites).
Restauration : Gordon Ramsay at Claridge's, The Foyer, Reading Room.
Histoire : James Mivart a ouvert un hôtel en 1812 mais le Claridge's actuel a été construit en 1898. De nombreux espaces et chambres ont été redécorés dans le style Art Déco au début des années 30.
Le « petit plus » : Les serviettes de bain ornées du monogramme « C ».
Internet : Accès haut débit dans toutes les chambres pour 20 GBP par jour.

1

2

3

1   Restaurant/Restaurant/Restaurant

Menu at The Connaught

16 Carlos Place
London W1K 2AL
Tel: +44 20 7592 1222
www.gordonramsay.com
Tube: Bond Street

Angela Hartnett, a protégée of Gordon Ramsay's, joined The Connaught in 2002 and has since turned "Menu" into one of the most respected restaurants not just in London, but in the entire country. The French-inspired menu features fish, duck and foie gras, amongst other things. The restaurant is wonderful in the evening with the lights dimmed and the candles on. Perfect for a romantic dinner a deux.

Angela Hartnett gehört zu den Protégés von Starkoch Gordon Ramsay. 2002 übernahm sie das „Menu" im Connaught und hat daraus eines der renommiertesten Restaurants Londons und ganz Englands gemacht. Auf der Karte stehen französisch inspirierte Gerichte mit Fisch, Ente, Foie Gras und vielem Anderem. Am Schönsten ist es hier abends bei gedämpften Kerzenlicht: perfekt für ein Dinner zu zweit.

Angela Hartnett, une élève de Gordon Ramsay, est arrivée au Connaught en 2002 et a fait du « Menu » un des restaurant les plus respectés du Royaume-Uni. D'inspiration française, la carte propose des poissons, du canard et du foie gras, entre autres. Le restaurant est merveilleux le soir avec ses lumières tamisées et ses chandelles. Idéal pour un dîner en tête à tête.

2   Gallery/Galerie/Galerie

Haunch of Venison

6 Haunch of Venison Yard
(off Brook Street)
London W1K 5ES
Tel: +44 20 7495 5050
www.haunchofvenison.com
Tube: Bond Street

Rachel Whiteread launched the inaugural exhibit at Haunch of Venison in 2001 and

the caliber of the contemporary art here has remained just as illustrious. This light-filled gallery is housed in a Georgian building that was once home to Admiral Lord Nelson and the street is named after a tavern that served venison. Artists who have shown here include M/M, Mark Alexander, Dan Flavin and Nathan Coley.

Gleich mit der Eröffnung 2001 wurden mit den ausgestellten Werken von Rachel Whiteread die Erwartungen hoch angesetzt, die Haunch of Vension bisher mit großen Namen der Kunstszene erfüllte: M/M, Mark Alexander, Dan Flavin und Nathan Coley. Die lichtdurchflutete Galerie befindet sich in einem Gebäude im Georgian- Stil, in dem einst Admiral Lord Nelson lebte. Der Name der Galerie und der Straße stammt von einer lokalen Taverne, die auf Wild spezialisiert war.

Depuis son inauguration en 2001, la qualité de l'art présenté à Haunch of Venison n'a jamais faibli. La galerie de Raquel Whiteread, inondée de lumière, se trouve dans une maison du XVIIIe siècle où habitait autrefois l'amiral Nelson. La rue porte le nom d'une ancienne taverne qui servait du gibier. M/M, Mark Alexander, Dan Flavin et Nathan Coley comptent parmi les artistes qui ont exposé ici.

3   Leather Goods/Schreib- und Lederwaren/Articles en cuir

Smythson of Bond Street

40 New Bond Street
London W1S 2DE
Tel: +44 20 7629 8558
www.smythson.com
Tube: Bond Street/Oxford Circus

Started in 1887, Smythson of Bond Street has been the purveyor of fine products for those who love stationery. It is the most quintessentially English place in London to get your thank-you cards, personal stationery, beautiful pens and leather diaries. Do not leave the premises without a Classic Travel Wallet. It's as beautiful as it is practical.

Smythson of Bond Street ist seit 1887

Lieferant für edle Schreibwaren und Briefpapiere. Hier kann man Kärtchen, persönlich bedrucktes Briefpapier, edle Schreibfedern und in Leder gebundene Tagebücher beziehen – alles in feinster englischer Tradition. Unbedingt eine der Classic-Travel Brieftaschen erstehen: Sie sind nicht nur schön zum Anschauen, sondern auch äußerst praktisch.

Depuis 1887, Smythson of Bond Street approvisionne les amateurs de beau papier. C'est l'endroit à Londres où acheter ses cartes de remerciement, son papier à en-tête, de beaux stylos et des agendas en cuir. Ne repartez pas sans un portefeuille de voyage, ils sont aussi beaux que pratiques.

4   Shoes/Schuhe/Chaussures

Jimmy Choo

27 New Bond Street
London W1S 2RH
Tel: +44 20 7493 5858
www.jimmychoo.com
Tube: Bond Street/Oxford Circus

Jimmy Choo has come to define everything glamorous about footwear. Whether it's a strappy stiletto or a sky-high boot, Tamara Mellon, a former accessories editor, society girl and head of the company, knows what her chic clientele are looking for. She started the company in 1996 with East End shoemaker Jimmy Choo and her empire just keeps growing.

Jimmy Choo ist die Verkörperung glamourösen Schuhwerks schlechthin. Tamara Mellon, Society-Girl, ehemalige Modejournalistin für Accessoires und Besitzerin des Schuhimperiums, weiß mit Riemchen-Stilettos und endlos langen Stiefeln ihre todschicke Klientel glücklich zu machen. Den Grundstein für das erfolgreiche Unternehmen setzte sie 1996 zusammen mit dem East-End-Schuhmacher Jimmy Choo.

Jimmy Choo incarne le glamour de la chaussure. Qu'il s'agisse de talons aiguilles à lacets ou de cuissardes, Tamara Mellon, ancienne directrice des accessoires et

4

5

6

grande mondaine, sait ce que veut sa clientèle ultra chic. Depuis qu'elle a créé la société en 1996 avec Jimmy Choo, chausseur issu du East End, son empire ne cesse de grandir.

---

5 Fashion/Mode/Mode

Browns

23–27 South Molton Street
Tel: +44 20 7514 0000

Browns Focus

38–39 South Molton Street
Tel: +44 20 7514 0063
London W1K 5RN
www.brownsfashion.com
Tube: Bond Street

Browns and Browns Focus are widely considered two of the best shops in London for getting the best-edited fashion collections around, thanks to Joan Burstein who started the company in the 1970s (she made stars of John Galliano and Alexander McQueen.) The five connecting townhouses are a lovely place to wander while Browns Focus, which opened opposite in 1997, is the more cutting-edge version of the original.

In London findet man nirgends eine so fantastische Auswahl an Fahion-Labels wie bei Browns und Browns Focus. Dahinter steckt Joan Burstein, die das Unternehmen 1970 gegründet hatte und Designern wie John Galliano und Alexander McQueen zum Durchbruch verhalf. Browns ist in fünf nebeneinander liegenden Stadthäusern untergebracht und lädt zum Flanieren ein. 1997 eröffnete Burstein genau gegenüber Browns Focus mit jüngeren, angesagten Labels.

Browns et Browns Focus sont considérés par beaucoup comme les enseignes londoniennes où l'on trouve le meilleur choix de collections de designer, grâce à Joan Burstein qui a créé la société en 1970 (elle a lancé John Galliano et Alexander McQueen). Se promener dans les cinq bâtiments communicants est un vrai bonheur. Brown Focus, inauguré en 1997, présente une mode plus avant-garde.

---

6 Shoes/Schuhe/Chaussures

Clarks

260 Oxford Street
London W1C 1DN
Tel: +44 20 7629 9609
www.clarks.co.uk
Tube: Oxford Circus

This company has been around since 1825 when Cyrus and James Clark founded a sheepskin slipper company in the village of Street, Somerset. In the 1950s, the company created the classic Desert Boot and in the 1960s, the iconic Wallabee. These days, Clarks is more stylish with footwear that is cool as well as comfy. A Wallabee is still a must-have.

1825 von Cyrus und James Clark im kleinen Dorf Street in Somerset gegründet, stellte Clarks ursprünglich Slipper aus Schafsleder her. In den 1950ern wurde der Klassiker Desert Boot lanciert und in den 1960ern der Kultschuh Wallabee. Clarks hat sich ein schickeres Image verpasst und man findet hier Schuhe, die sowohl cool als auch bequem sind. Und: ein Wallabee gehört immer noch zu den Dingen, die man haben muss.

En 1825, Cyrus et James Clark fabriquaient des chaussons en peau de mouton à Street, un village du Somerset. Les années 50 ont vu le lancement de la Desert Boot, un classique, les années 60, celui des légendaires Wallabee, qui continuent d'être un must. Aujourd'hui, dans ses boutiques décorées par Richard Found, Clarks propose une gamme de chaussures cool et confortables.

Personal Finds/Eigene Entdeckungen/
Découvertes personnelles:

_____

_____

_____

_____

W1

Mayfair
St James's

ALISON
JACQUES

SADIE COLES HQ

New Bond St

Maddox St

Grosvenor St

Conduit Street

Clifford St

Regent Street

Carnaby St

Beak Street

Lexington St

Brewer Street

Old C

Savile Row

Shaft

BROWN'S
HOTEL

Berkeley Sq

Old Bond Street

Burlington Gans

OZWALD
BOATENG

Sackville St

Piccad
Circ

Swallow St

Brewer

DOVER
STREET MARKET

Dover Street

Albemarle Street

JASPER
CONRAN
ALEXANDER
McQUEEN

BENTLEY'S

BATES

Swallow St

Jermyn St

Ha

St

ROWLEY'S

Charles St

PAUL SMITH
FURNITURE
SHOP

HAUSER & WIRTH

PAXTON AND WH

Curzon Street

FORTNUM
& MASON

Duke St St James

FLORIS

JOHN LOBB

St James's

ORMONDE
JAYNE

Curzon

THE
WOLSELEY

St James's

D.R.
HARRIS
& CO.

King St

St James Square

St James's

Mall

Piccadilly

Green
Park

St James's Pl

St James's St

Pall

Carlto

DUKES
HOTEL

ST JAMES'S
PALACE

GREEN
PARK

The M

INN

Constitution Hill

BUCKINGHAM
PALACE

ST JAME
PARK

Birdcage

Queen Ann

W

Avenue
Charing Cross
Leicester Square
Long Acre
Covent Garden
COVENT GARDEN
Wellington St
Aldwych
PENHALIGON'S
RULES
Cranbourn St
New Row
St Martin's Lane
Bedford St
Maiden Lane
J. SHEEKEY
Road
Strand
William IV St
John Adam St
Savoy Pl
NATIONAL GALLERY
Embankment
Waterloo Bridge
Villiers St
Trafalgar Square
Charing Cross
TATE MODERN
Cockspur St
Embankment
THE TRAFALGAR
Northumberland Ave
Hungerford Bridge
Hungerford Footbridges
Whitehall Place
Whitehall Court
ROYAL FESTIVAL HALL
Horse Guards Road
Whitehall
Horseguards Ave
Victoria
R. THAMES
LONDON EYE
Belvedere Road
PARK
Downing Street
York Road
Parliament St
Westminster
Gt George St
Parliament
Westminster Bridge
Square
HOUSES OF PARLIAMENT
TATE BRITAIN
©MICHAELA HILL

Brown's Hotel

Albemarle Street, London W1S 4BP
☎ +44 20 7493 6020 📠 + 44 20 7493 9381
reservations.browns@roccofortehotels.com
www.roccofortehotels.com
Tube: Green Park
Booking: www.great-escapes-hotels.com

Brown's Hotel

Designed by Olga Polizzi, Brown's Hotel is a blend of contemporary and luxurious touches, such as wood floors in some rooms and one-off pieces of original Art-Deco furniture, all punctuated with spacious rooms that have super-modern amenities. More sweetly, each room has a selection of books, such as The Oxford Book of English Verse or works by Charles Dickens, DH Lawrence and William Shakespeare for guests to read. If finances allow, book into one of the Royal Suites and pretend you are staying in your own Mayfair apartment. Or go for more urban experience in one of the loft rooms with Mary Poppins-style views over London rooftops. From 3pm on the dot (not a minute earlier) join the pencil-thin, Russian blondes for High Tea in the English Tea Room, where they seek respite from a hard day's shopping. Latch on to this English philosophy: any care in the world can be erased with a scone, clotted cream and a cup of tea on fine china.

Designerin Olga Polizzi hat es verstanden, das Brown's Hotel genau so zeitgemäß wie luxuriös zu gestalten. Die meisten der großzügigen Gästezimmer sind modern eingerichtet und einige mit Holzböden und originalen Art-Deco-Möbeln gemixt. In jedem Zimmer liegt eine interessante Auswahl an Büchern aus, etwa das „Oxford Book of English Verse" oder Werke von Charles Dickens, DH Lawrence und William Shakespeare. Wer es sich leisten kann, sollte eine der Royal Suiten buchen und sich so wie ein Besitzer eines eleganten Mayfair Apartments fühlen. Für ein urbaneres Feeling wählt man eines der Loft-Zimmer mit Blick über die Dächer Londons. Punkt 15 Uhr (keine Minute früher) wird der High Tea im English Tea Room serviert. Unter den Gästen: spargeldünne, blonde Russinnen, die hier nach einem harten Shopping-Tag eine englische Weisheit auf die Probe stellen: Kleine und große Sorgen, so sagt man, lösen sich bei Scone-Gebäck, etwas „Clotted Cream" und Tee in edler Porzellantasse in Luft auf.

Décoré par Olga Polizzi, le Brown's Hotel associe les touches contemporaines et luxueuses tels que parquets et meubles Art Déco dans de spacieuses chambres au confort ultramoderne. Petite note attentionnée: dans chacune d'elle, on trouve des anthologies de poésie anglaise et des œuvres de Charles Dickens, DH Lawrence ou William Shakespeare. Si vos finances vous le permettent, réservez une des suites royales où vous vous croirez dans votre propre appartement de Mayfair. Ou optez pour une expérience plus urbaine dans un des lofts avec ses vues à la Mary Poppins sur les toits de Londres. À quinze heures pile, un troupeau de poupées russes blondes platine à taille de guêpe débarque dans le salon de thé pour souffler un peu après une rude journée de shopping. Accrochez-vous à cette devise philosophique toute britannique : tous les soucis du monde s'évaporent avec un scone, un peu de crème et un thé dans une tasse en porcelaine.

Rates: From 430 € (295 GBP) excl. VAT.
Rooms: 117 (15 Suites).
Restaurants: The Grill, English Tea Room, The Donovan Bar.
History: The hotel opened in 1837 and has a rich history. Alexander Graham Bell made the UK's first telephone call from the hotel in 1876; Rudyard Kipling penned The Jungle Book here.
X-Factor: The Spa is wonderful for de-stressing.
Internet: WiFi in public areas at 6 GBP per hour; 10 GBP per day. Broadband in all rooms at 15 GBP per day.

Preise: Ab 430 € (295 GBP) exkl. VAT.
Zimmer: 117 (15 Suiten).
Restaurants: The Grill, English Tea Room, The Donovan Bar.
Geschichte: Das Hotel wurde 1837 eröffnet, 1876 tätigte Alexander Graham Bell von hier aus den ersten Telefonanruf in Großbritannien und Rudyard Kipling schrieb im Brown's das Dschungelbuch.
X-Faktor: Das Spa ist Entspannung pur.
Internet: WiFi in allen öffentlichen Räumlichkeiten für 6 GBP pro Stunde und 10 GBP pro Tag. Breitbandanschluss in allen Gästezimmern für 15 GBP pro Tag.

Prix : À partir de 430 € (295 GBP), TVA non comprise.
Chambres : 117 (15 Suites).
Restauration : The Grill, English Tea Room, The Donovan Bar.
Histoire : Alexander Graham Bell y a passé le premier coup de téléphone en 1876. Rudyard Kipling y a rédigé Le Livre de la jungle.
Le « petit plus » : Le Spa est idéal pour destresser.
Internet : WiFi dans les zones publiques pour 6 GBP l'heure; 10 GBP par jour. Haut débit dans toutes les chambres pour 15 GBP par jour.

1

2

3

1   Perfum/Parfüm/Parfum

Ormonde Jayne
The Royal Arcade
28 Old Bond Street
London W1S 4SL
Tel: +44 20 7499 1100
www.ormondejayne.com
Tube: Green Park

Linda Pilkington founded this divine little perfumery in 2003 with an aim to sell gorgeous, luxury scents. The shop is located in the architecturally beautiful Victorian Royal Arcade built circa 1880. All of her perfumes are made in London and her perfume library boasts scents inspired by her worldwide travels. Walk out with a new signature scent or just pick up candles as delicious gifts.

Linda Pilkington bietet in dieser 2003 von ihr gegründeten reizenden, kleinen Parfumerie wunderbare Luxusdüfte an und das mitten in dem wunderschönen Bau der Victorian Royal Arcade aus den 1880ern. Alle Parfüms werden in London hergestellt; dazu gibt es eine Parfüm-Bibliothek mit Düften, inspiriert von Pilkingtons Reisen rund um die Welt. Einen der neuen Düfte zu erwerben ist ein Muss, und die Duftkerzen geben schöne Geschenke her.

Linda Pilkington a ouvert cette charmante petite parfumerie en 2003 afin d'y vendre ses fragrances luxueuses. Elle est située dans les belles Victorian Royal Arcade, une galerie bâtie vers 1880. Tous ses parfums sont fabriqués à Londres et beaucoup s'inspirent de ses voyages à travers le monde. Repartez avec votre nouveau parfum ou simplement des bougies parfumées qui font des cadeaux divins.

2   Vintage Furniture/Vintage-Möbel/
     Mobilier du vintage

Paul Smith Furniture Shop
9 Albemarle Street
London W1S 4BL
Tel: + 44 20 7493 4565

www.paulsmith.co.uk
Tube: Green Park

As with Sir Paul Smith's fashion collections, the furniture he peddles has his quirky British modern twist (and humour) all over it. He opened this funky shop opposite Brown's Hotel in 2005 and he showcases pieces of contemporary furniture jazzed up with interesting fabrics or older pieces modernised with his own textiles. Colourful china, the ones in Smith's signature stripes, are also cool.

Genau wie seine Mode ist die Möbelkollektion von Sir Paul Smith eigenwillig britisch und humorvoll. Das unkonventionelle Geschäft gleich gegenüber dem Brown's Hotel eröffnete er 2005. Hier gibt es mit interessanten Stoffen aufgepeppte Möbel, aber auch gebrauchte Stücke, die mit Smith-Textilien zu neuem Leben erweckt wurden. Cool ist auch das bunte Porzellangeschirr mit den typischen Paul-Smith-Streifen.

Comme sa mode, les meubles choisis par sir Paul Smith possèdent cette touche d'excentricité et d'humour toute britannique. Dans cette boutique ouverte en face du Brown's Hotel en 2005, il présente des meubles contemporains égayés par des tissus intéressants ou des pièces plus anciennes modernisées avec ses propres textiles. On y trouve aussi de jolies porcelaines aux rayures typiquement P. Smith.

3   Fashion/Mode/Mode

Alexander McQueen
4–5 Old Bond Street
London W1S 4PD
Tel: +44 20 7355 0088
www.alexandermcqueen.com
Tube: Green Park/Piccadilly Circus

Alexander McQueen, the son of a taxi driver, burst onto the London fashion scene in the late 1990s as a rebel. His training at Savile Row tailors such as Anderson & Sheppard as well as Gieves & Hawkes gave him his impeccable skills. No other luxury fashion brand holds a candle to the innovation and, at the same time, high quality of this man's work: his cuts are as perfect as his "Novak" bag is cult.

Alexander McQueen tauchte Ende der 1990er in der Londoner Modeszene auf. Der Sohn eines Taxifahrers hatte gerade seine Ausbildung bei erstklassigen Savile-Row-Schneidern wie Anderson & Sheppard und Gieves & Hawkes hinter sich und galt als genau so rebellisch wie talentiert. Kein anderes Luxuslabel verbindet Innovation und höchste Qualität wie Alexander McQueen: seine Schnitte sind perfekt und mit Handtaschen wie der „Novak" schafft er Kultobjekte.

Enfant rebelle de la mode, Alexander McQueen, fils d'un chauffeur de taxi, s'est fait connaître à la fin des années 1990. Formé chez des tailleurs de Savile Row comme Anderson & Sheppard et Gieves & Hawkes, son savoir-faire est irréprochable. Aucune autre marque de luxe n'associe mieux l'innovation à une telle qualité de travail. Ses coupes sont aussi impeccables que son sac « Novak » est culte.

4   Fashion/Mode/Mode

Dover Street Market
17–18 Dover Street
London W1S 4LT
Tel: +44 20 7518 0680
www.doverstreetmarket.com
Tube: Green Park

Started by Comme des Garçons in 2004, it is more like a museum where fashion is curated in various different environments, not merely hung up for customers to admire, the Raf Simons floor is f.e. designed by Jan De Cock. Brands include big names such as Lanvin and John Galliano but more obscure labels (Sacai Gem, Ronnie Loves and Tabletop) are served well too.

Eigentlich ist Dover Street Market mehr ein Museum als ein Geschäft. Von Comme des Garçons 2004 ins Leben gerufen, werden hier Kleider wie Ausstellungsstücke präsentiert. So zeigt Raf Simons seine Kreationen in einer vom Künstler

4

5

6

Jan De Cock gestalteten Umgebung. Neben andern großen Namen wie Lanvin und John Galliano findet man hier auch weniger bekannte Labels wie Sacai Gem, Ronnie Loves und Tabletop.

Lancé par Comme des Garçons en 2004, c'est plus un musée où les clients peuvent admirer la mode présentée dans différents environnements. L'étage Raf Simons a été décoré par Jan De Cock. On y trouve de grands créateurs comme Lanvin ou John Galliano mais aussi des marques plus obscures telles que Sacai Gem, Ronnie Loves ou Tabletop.

---

5   Tea & Restaurant/Teeroom & Restaurant/Salon de thé et restaurant

The Wolseley

160 Piccadilly
London W1J 9EB
Tel: +44 20 7499 6996
www.thewolseley.com
Tube: Green Park

Since its opening in 2003, the great and good of London have descended in droves. The Venetian/Florentine influences of this 1921 building (a car showroom, originally) was respected when, in 2003, designer David Collins converted it into a grand, chandeliered space. It's hard to get a dinner booking but drop in for breakfast or afternoon tea. Be nice to staff: they are British politeness personified.

Seit der Eröffnung von 2003 pilgert ganz London hierher. Designer David Collins hat die venezianischen und florentinischen Elemente des Gebäudes bewahrt und aus dem ehemaligen Auto-Showroom einen prachtvollen Raum gestaltet. Eine Reservierung für ein Dinner zu erhalten ist praktisch unmöglich; für ein Frühstück oder einen Afternoon-Tea sollte es allerdings klappen. Das Personal ist übrigens die Verkörperung britischer Höflichkeit.

Depuis son ouverture en 2003, le tout Londres s'y rue. Les influences vénitiennes et florentines de cet ancien showroom de voitures bâti en 1921 ont été préservées par David Collins qui l'a converti en espace

grandiose orné de lustres. Obtenir une table pour dîner est difficile mais passez donc prendre le petit-déjeuner ou le thé. Soyez gentil avec le personnel : ils sont la politesse anglaise incarnée.

---

6   Specialities/Spezialitäten/Épicerie fine

Fortnum & Mason

181 Piccadilly
London W1A 1ER
Tel: +44 20 7734 8040
www.fortnumandmason.com
Tube: Green Park/Piccadilly Circus

Fortnum & Mason, housed in a marvellous Georgian building right on Piccadilly, has been around since 1707 and it's the arbiter of everything to do with English food as biscuits, cakes, fish, cheese and sweets, for a start. Of course, it is also famous for its gorgeous tea and hampers, always most beautifully packaged in colourful tins and boxes both of which make perfect gifts for friends and family back home.

Fortnum & Mason ist seit 1707 eine der Institutionen Londons. Das Feinkost-Paradies liegt in einem prächtigen Gebäude im Georgian-Stil direkt am Piccadilly. Hier findet man erstklassige englische Spezialitäten wie Biscuits, Kuchen, Fisch, Käse, Bonbons und selbstverständlich auch Tee und Geschenkkörbe – alles wunderschön verpackt in farbigen Büchsen und Schachteln. Sie sind auch perfekte Mitbringsel.

Dans un beau bâtiment du XVIIIe siècle donnant sur Picadilly, Fortnum & Mason, est, depuis 1707, la référence pour tout ce qui touche aux biscuits, cakes, poissons, fromages et bonbons anglais. Naturellement, la maison est aussi connue pour ses paniers garnis et ses thés, toujours superbement présentés dans des boîtes colorées qui en font des cadeaux parfaits pour les amis et les parents.

Personal Finds/Eigene Entdeckungen/
Découvertes personnelles:

7

8

9

7 Gallery/Galerie/Galerie

Hauser & Wirth London
196A Piccadilly
London W1J 9DY
Tel: +44 20 7287 2300
www.hauserwirth.com
Tube: Piccadilly Circus

The London branch of this established Zurich-based art gallery has become as reputable as its Swiss sister since it opened in 2003. The gallery is in an historic Edwin Lutyens-designed 1920s building, a structure as gorgeous as the art it holds inside, and right across the road from the Royal Academy of Art. Artists represented here include Louise Bourgeois, Pipilotti Rist and Martin Creed.

Die Galerie Hauser & Wirth aus Zürich hat seit 2003 eine Niederlassung in London, die genau so renommiert ist wie die Schweizer Mutter. Die Galerie liegt gleich gegenüber der Royal Academy of Art in einem historischen, von Edwin Lutyens in den 1920ern entworfenen, Gebäude. Es ist genau so fantastisch wie die Künstler, die hier ausgestellt werden: Louise Bourgeois, Pipilotti Rist und Martin Creed.

Depuis son ouverture en 2003, la branche londonienne de cette galerie zurichoise n'a rien à envier à sa sœur suisse. Elle est située dans un bâtiment classé des années 20 d'Edwin Lutyens, aussi beau que l'art qu'il abrite, en face de la Royal Academy of Art. Parmi les artistes représentés : Louise Bourgeois, Pipilotti Rist et Martin Creed.

8 Fashion & Home Collection/Mode & Inneneinrichtung/Mode & Décoration

Jasper Conran
36 Sackville Street
London W1S 3EQ
Tel: +44 20 7292 9080
www.jasperconran.com
Tube: Piccadilly Circus

Jasper Conran's flagship store is a thing of beauty and taste. Housed in a Georgian building, the shop opened in 2005 and is the perfect environment in which to try on his luxurious pieces or just wander around feeling like a guest in a private home. Women can't go wrong with his flattering evening dresses while men gravitate towards the well-cut suits. His home collection is also beautiful.

Jasper Conran hat 2005 in diesem Haus im Georgian-Stil seinen Flagship-Store eröffnet, der zum Inbegriff des guten Geschmacks geworden ist. Es ist der perfekte Ort, um seine Luxus-Sachen anzuprobieren oder etwas herumzustöbern und sich dabei wie ein gern gesehener Gast in einem Privathaus zu fühlen. Die figurschmeichelnden Abendkleider und gut geschnittenen Anzüge sind immer richtig. Auch die Home-Collection ist wunderbar.

Beauté et bon goût sont les mots d'ordre de la boutique phare de Jasper Conran, ouverte en 2005 dans un bâtiment du XVIIIe siècle. On peut y essayer ses superbes vêtements ou se promener comme un invité dans une maison particulière. On ne peut pas se tromper avec ses robes du soir flatteuses et ses costumes d'hommes impeccablement coupés. Le linge de maison est également très beau.

9 Fish Restaurant/Fisch-Restaurant/ Restaurant de poissons

Bentley's
11–15 Swallow Street
London W1B 4DG
Tel: +44 20 7734 4756
www.bentleys.org
Tube: Piccadilly Circus

Bought and refurbished and opened in 2005 by one of London's most renowned chefs, Richard Corrigan, who also has his hands on the Michelin-starred Lindsay House in Soho, this acquisition is rightly famous for its oysters. The downstairs bar is also perfect for relaxing with a drink if dinner seems a bit much. This is one of London's classic fish restaurants: both in terms of ambience and in clientele.

Richard Corrigan gehört zu den renommiertesten Küchenchefs Londons – ihm gehört auch das mit einem Michelin-Stern ausgezeichnete Lindsay House in Soho. 2005 hat er dieses Restaurant gekauft, umgebaut und sich gleich einen Namen mit dem Austernangebot gemacht. Für Gäste ohne Hunger gibt's im Untergeschoss eine Bar, an der man sich bei einem Drink entspannen kann. Bentley's ist eines der klassischen Londoner Fischrestaurants – mit entsprechendem Ambiente.

Racheté et restauré en 2005 par l'un des chefs les plus réputés de Londres, Richard Corrigan (également à l'œuvre à la Lindsay House à Soho, distinguée par Michelin), l'établissement est célèbre à juste titre pour ses huîtres. Si vous ne voulez pas dîner, le bar au sous-sol est très agréable. Ambiance et clientèle distinguées, un classique en matière de restaurants de poissons.

10 Gallery/Galerie/Galerie

Sadie Coles HQ
35 Heddon Street
London W1B 4BP
Tel: +44 20 7434 2227
www.sadiecoles.com
Tube: Piccadilly Circus

Sadie Coles runs a contemporary art empire from an unassuming gallery on a side street just off Regent Street. She started her career by working for Anthony D'Offay, who was one of the world's leading gallerists in the 1980s. She struck out on her own in 1997 and has since made stars (expensive ones, at that) of, among others, Richard Prince, Sarah Lucas, Elizabeth Peyton and Ugo Rondinone.

Ihre Galerie in der Nähe der Regent Street wirkt zwar bescheiden, doch davon darf man sich nicht täuschen lassen. Sadie Coles gehört zu den bedeutenden Namen der zeitgenössischen Kunstszene. Ihre Karriere begann sie bei Anthony O'Offay, einem der führenden Galeristen der 1980er. Coles machte sich dann 1997 selbstständig und vertritt seither (hoch-bezahlte) Stars wie Richard Prince, Sarah Lucas, Elizabeth Peyton und Ugo Rondinone.

10

11

12

Depuis sa galerie discrète dans une petite rue donnant sur Regent Street, Sadie Coles dirige un empire d'art contemporain. Après avoir fait ses classes chez Anthony D'Offay, un des plus grands galeristes des années 80, elle vole de ses propres ailes depuis 1997. Elle a lancé, entre autres, des stars (très chères) : Richard Prince, Sarah Lucas, Elizabeth Peyton et Ugo Rondinone.

11 Tailor/Couturier/Tailleur

Ozwald Boateng
9 Vigo Street
London W1X 1AL
Tel: +44 20 7437 0620
www.ozwaldboateng.co.uk
Tube: Piccadilly Circus

Bold, flashy and chic all at the same time, charismatic Ozwald Boateng is one of the new generation of tailors on Savile Row who are redefining how the English dandy will dress. The store opened in 2002 and his suits are beautifully cut with tasteful, bright coloured linings; the accessories are sharp and his store is like a boudoir for men, replete with hunky sales associates.

Der charismatische Ozwald Boateng ge hört zu einer neuen Generation von Savile Row-Schneidern: Seine Kreationen sind nicht nur schick, sondern auch gewagt. Damit definiert er den Look des englischen Dandys neu. Boateng eröffnete sein Geschäft 2002 im Stil eines Boudoirs für Männer. Die Anzüge, die er anbietet, sind fantastisch geschnitten und geschmackvoll mit satt-bunten Stoffen gefüttert. Dazu gibt's todschicke Accessoires. Sogar die Verkäufer sehen blendend aus.

Le charismatique Ozwald Boateng appartient à cette nouvelle génération de tailleurs de Savile Row qui redéfinissent le dandy anglais : audacieux, tapageur et chic tout à la fois. Ouverte en 2002, sa boutique, un boudoir pour hommes peuplé de vendeurs sexy, propose des costumes superbement taillés aux doublures vivement colorées. Les accessoires sont à la hauteur.

12 Gallery/Galerie/Galerie

Alison Jacques
4 Clifford Street
London W1X 1RB
Tel: +44 20 7287 7675
www.alisonjacquesgallery.com
Tube: Piccadilly Circus

This three-floor gallery is big in stature and not as small in size as it seems. Go down this little side street and enter the house to see what's in store: it could be Jack Pierson, Liz Craft, Uta Barth, Robert Mapplethorpe, the list of contemporary art luminaries goes on and on. It opened as Asprey Jacques in 1998 but since 2004 it has been solely run by Alison Jacques herself.

Die dreistöckige Galerie an einer kleinen Seitenstraße, in einem kleinen Haus hat durchaus Format und ist nicht so winzig, wie sie zunächst wirkt. Innen wird man jedenfalls von großer Kunst überrascht: Jack Pierson, Liz Craft, Uta Barth, Robert Mapplethorpe sind einige der bekannten zeitgenössischen Künstler, die hier gezeigt werden. Die 1998 gegründete Galerie hieß bis 2004 Asprey Jacques. Seither wird sie von Alison Jacques alleine geführt.

Une grande galerie dans tous les sens du terme. La maisonnette de trois étages située dans une ruelle vaut le détour : vous y verrez des œuvres de Jack Pierson, Liz Craft, Uta Barth, Robert Mapplethorpe, la liste des sommités de l'art contemporain n'en finit plus. Ouverte sous le nom d'Asprey Jacques en 1998, elle est entièrement dirigée par Alison Jacques depuis 2004.

Personal Finds/Eigene Entdeckungen/
Découvertes personnelles:

_____

_____

_____

_____

Dukes Hotel

35 St James Place, London SW1A 1NY
☎ +44 20 7491 4840   📠 + 44 20 7493 1264
bookings@dukeshotel.com
www.dukeshotel.com
Tube: Green Park
Booking: www.great-escapes-hotels.com

Dukes Hotel

Tucked away in a quiet courtyard between Mayfair and Green Park, Dukes is an oasis in one of the busiest parts of town. The rooms are comfortable, traditionally English with plenty of subtle floral fabrics. However, the common areas far overshadow the chambers here. Dukes Bar – decorated like a private gentlemen's club with a collection of framed political cartoons on the walls and cosy leather chairs – is a secret little hideaway and famous in London for its dry Martini. Winston Churchill and Ian Fleming have both been patrons. These days, high-powered judges might confer here after an afternoon's shopping for tailored shirts and hand-made shoes; or somewhere that a politician can conduct an affair away from the public eye. If it's the wagon you're on, then head to the drawing room, flop on an oversized sofa, order tea and enjoy pouring it from fine silverware and drinking it from dainty porcelain while chewing on a lovely biscuit. A visit to London does not get much more English than that.

Das Dukes ist eine Oase mitten im Stadtchaos zwischen Mayfair und Green Park und liegt versteckt an einem ruhigen Hinterhof. Die Zimmer, behaglich in traditionell englischem Blumenmuster-Dekor, überlassen den großen Auftritt den anderen Räumlichkeiten. Die Dukes Bar etwa, mit bequemen Ledersesseln und Polit-Karikaturen an den Wänden, erinnert an einen Gentlemen's Club. Bekannt wurde sie als diskretes Refugium für Gäste wie Winston Churchill und Ian Fleming – und nicht zuletzt für die Dry Martinis. Auch heute tummeln sich in der Dukes Bar wichtige Persönlichkeiten: Richter, die sich hier nach dem Einkauf von maßgeschneiderten Hemden und maßgefertigen Schuhen treffen, Politiker, die von der Öffentlichkeit abgeschirmt, ihren Geschäften nachgehen. Wer aufs Naschen aus ist, nimmt auf einem der üppigen Sofas im Salon platz, bestellt Tee, der aus feinstem Tafelsilber in zierliche Tassen gegossen wird, und genießt dazu ein köstliches Biscuit. Viel englischer kann es nicht werden.

Niché dans une cour tranquille entre Mayfair et Green Park, le Dukes est une oasis dans un des quartiers les plus animés de la ville. Les chambres, dans un style traditionnel anglais où abondent les imprimés subtilement fleuris, sont confortables. Mais ce sont surtout les parties communes qui épatent. Le bar, douillet et décoré comme un club privé pour gentlemen avec des dessins satiriques politiques aux murs et d'épais fauteuils en cuir, est célèbre pour ses Martinis dry. Winston Churchill et Ian Fleming en raffolaient. Aujourd'hui, de hauts magistrats s'y réfugient pour souffler un peu en sortant de chez leur tailleur ou leur bottier, ou des hommes politiques y amènent leurs maîtresses loin des regards indiscrets. Vautrez-vous dans un des sofas géants du salon et commandez du thé qui vous sera servi dans de l'argenterie et de la porcelaine délicate accompagné de délicieux petits biscuits. On ne peut pas faire plus british.

Rates: From 365 € (250 GBP) excl. VAT.
Rooms: 90 (6 suites).
Restaurants: Dukes Dining Room.
History: The historical courtyard at Dukes Hotel has been traced back to 1532. The building was erected in 1885 and has functioned as Dukes Hotel since 1908.
X-Factor: The Martinis. Don't leave this hotel without trying one.
Internet: WiFi at 18 GBP per day.

Preise: Ab 365 € (250 GBP) exkl. VAT.
Zimmer: 90 (6 Suiten).
Restaurants: Dukes Dining Room.
Geschichte: Der historische Hinterhof des Dukes wurde 1532 erstmals erwähnt. Erst 1885 wurde auf dem Gelände ein Haus gebaut. Seit 1908 ist es als Dukes Hotel in Betrieb.
X-Faktor: Die köstlichen Martinis. Das Hotel kann man nicht verlassen, ohne vorher einen ausprobiert zu haben.
Internet: WiFi für 18 GBP pro Tag.

Prix : À partir de 365 € (250 GBP), TVA non comprise.
Chambres : 90 (6 suites).
Restauration : Dukes Dining Room.
Histoire : La cour historique du Dukes remonte à 1532. Le bâtiment a été construit 1885 et transformé en hôtel en 1908.
Le « petit plus » : Les Martinis. Ne quittez pas l'hôtel sans y avoir goûté.
Internet : WiFi pour 18 GBP par jour.

1

2

1 Chemists & Perfumers/Apotheke & Parfumerie/Pharmacie & Parfumerie

D.R. Harris & Co.
29 St James's Street
London SW1A 1HB
Tel: +44 20 7930 3915/8753
www.drharris.co.uk
Tube: Green Park

D.R. Harris has been established in St James since 1790, when the area was known as Clubland because of the many gentlemen's clubs located there. This traditional pharmacy holds a royal warrant as chemist for HRH the Prince of Wales. Customers come in for the all-natural skincare products – some made from recipes that are 125 years old – and for badger-hair brushes.

Als D.R. Harris 1790 in St James gegründet wurde, nannte man diese Gegend wegen der vielen ansässigen Herrenklubs „Clubland". Die traditionelle Apotheke ist königlicher Hoflieferant der Prinzen von Wales und hat sich vor allem mit natürlichen Hautpflegeprodukten, die heute noch aus zum Teil 125 Jahre alten Rezepten hergestellt werden, einen Namen gemacht. Bei D.R. Harris findet man auch Bürsten aus echtem Dachshaar.

D.R. Harris est établi à St James depuis 1790 quand le quartier était surnommé Clubland en raison des nombreux clubs de gentlemen. Cette pharmacie traditionnelle est le fournisseur attitré de SAR le prince de Galles. On vient y chercher ses cosmétiques 100% naturels (certains confectionnés à partir de recettes vieilles de 125 ans) et ses blaireaux de barbier.

2 Shoes/Schuhe/Chaussures

John Lobb
88 Jermyn Street
London SW1Y 6JD
Tel: +44 20 7930 8089
www.johnlobb.com
Tube: Green Park/Piccadilly Circus

The newly refurbished John Lobb store effortlessly combines the hand-finished footwear and accessories for the discerning gentleman, with the contemporary backdrop of its interior. Their shoes have been sought after since Victorian times, and with a new generation of clientele to cater for, John Lobb brings innovation to the traditional shoe. As well as ready-to-wear, John Lobb also offers a "made-to-order" service, where clients are able to choose a style of shoe, and combine it with the range of leathers that are available in different colours.

Im neu gestylten Geschäft von John Lobb gehen traditionell handgefertigte Schuhe und Accessoires mit einem modernen Interiordesign aufs Schönste zusammen. Bereits seit viktorianischen Zeiten gehören die Schuhe von Lobb zu den Must-Haves für den anspruchsvollen Herrn. Heute weiss John Lobb eine neue Generation von Kunden mit der Verbindung von Tradition und Innovation zu begeistern. Neben einer Ready-To-Wear-Kollektion stellt Lobb auch Einzelanfertigungen her. Die Kunden können dabei Form, Leder und Farbe ganz nach ihrem persönlich Geschmack auswählen.

Récemment réaménagée, la boutique John Lobb propose ses chaussures cousues main et ses accessoires pour le gentleman avisé dans un décor contemporain. Ce bottier déjà prisé des Victoriens ravi aujourd'hui une nouvelle génération de clients en apportant de l'innovation au soulier traditionnel. Outre sa collection de prêt-à-porter, John Lobb propose aussi du sur-mesure, le client choisissant un modèle puis son cuir dans la vaste gamme de différentes couleurs.

3 Scents/Düfte/Scenteurs

Floris
89 Jermyn Street
London SW1Y 6JH
Tel: +44 20 7930 2885
www.florislondon.com
Tube: Green Park/Piccadilly Circus

Though the staff at Floris, founded in 1730, will no longer iron the bank notes before handing you your change, as they did in the 19th century, they will present it to you on a velvet-covered tray. Floris fragrances have been worn by British monarchs since 1820, as well as by such luminaries as Noel Coward and Eva Perón. The Sandalwood scent is particularly lovely.

Im 18. Jahrhundert pflegte das Personal beim 1730 gegründeten Parfumeur Floris die Banknoten, bevor sie den Kunden überreicht wurden, zu bügeln. Diese Zeiten sind zwar vorbei, doch das Wechselgeld wird heute – immer noch stilvoll – auf einem samtbezogenen Tablett übergeben Seit 1820 haben britische Monarchen und auch illustre Namen wie Noel Coward und Eva Perón die Düfte von Floris getragen. Besonders fein riecht der Sandelholz-Duft.

On n'y repasse plus les billets avant de vous rendre la monnaie comme au XIXle siècle mais elle vous est quand même tendue sur un plateau en velours. Fondé en 1730, Floris parfume les monarques britanniques depuis 1820 et a compté parmi ses clients des célébrités telles que Noel Coward et Eva Perón. Son santal est particulièrement divin.

4 Cheese/Käse/Fromagerie

Paxton and Whitfield
93 Jermyn Street
London SW1Y 6JE
Tel: +44 20 7930 0259
www.paxtonandwhitfield.co.uk
Tube: Piccadilly Circus

Paxton and Whitfield was famously Winston Churchill's favourite cheesemonger and it has been a London favourite since it opened in 1797. This is an excellent place to try traditional English cheeses, such as a crumbly Wensleydale or a mature Cheddar The knowledgeable staff will be happy to suggest appropriate wines to go with your choices.

Paxton and Whitfield war nicht nur Winston Churchills liebster Käsehändler, sondern ist seit 1797 auch einer der Fixsterne in London. Das Geschäft präsentiert eine ausgezeichnete Auswahl an

4

5

6

raditionellen englischen Käsen, wie den
mürben Wensleydale oder einen reifen
Cheddar. Auf Wunsch geben die sachkun-
digen Verkäufer eine zum Käse passende
Wein-Empfehlung.

Le fromager préféré de Winston Churchill
est un chouchou des Londoniens depuis
son ouverture en 1797. C'est l'endroit rêvé
où goûter des fromages traditionnels anglais, comme le friable Wensleydale ou un
vieux cheddar. Le personnel s'y connaît et
vous conseillera volontiers de bons crus
pour accompagner vos choix.

---

5 Hatter/Hutmacher/Chapelier

Bates
21a Jermyn Street
London SW1Y 6HP
Tel: +44 20 7734 2722
www.bates-hats.co.uk
Tube: Piccadilly Circus

London's world-renowned black cabs are
still designed to accommodate a man wear-
ing a top hat. So why not stop by Bates
and have one made to measure? This famous milliner, which has been outfitting
gentlemen since the turn of the last century,
can also supply such quintessentially British
styles as the bowler and the deerstalker.

Die weltberühmten schwarzen Londoner
Taxis sind so gebaut, dass man auch mit
einem Hut auf dem Kopf Platz hat. Ein
guter Grund, bei Bates vorbeizuschauen,
um sich einen maßgefertigten Hut anferti-
gen zu lassen. Der legendäre Hutmacher
stattet seit der vorletzten Jahrhundert-
wende die eleganten Herren der Stadt
aus, und hier findet man so typisch Briti-
sches wie Melonen und Sherlock-Holmes-
Kopfbedeckungen.

Les célèbres cabs noirs de Londres sont
conçus pour accueillir un gentleman en
haut-de-forme. Alors pourquoi ne pas
commander le vôtre sur-mesure chez
Bates? Ce célèbre chapelier qui coiffe
ces messieurs depuis un siècle peut aussi
vous proposer d'autres classiques anglais
comme le chapeau melon et la casquette
à la Sherlock Holmes.

---

6 Restaurant/Restaurant/Restaurant

Rowley's Restaurant
113 Jermyn Street
London SW1Y 6HJ
Tel: +44 20 7930 2707
www.rowleys.co.uk
Tube: Piccadilly Circus

Though the restaurant has only been in
operation since 1977, Rowley's occupies
the premises of what was once Walls
Butcher Shop, which in the 19th and early
20th centuries catered to the royal family.
The owners have preserved the original
tiled walls and ceilings and the stained-
glass windows. The house specialty at
Rowley's is the entrecote steak drizzled
with the signature secret herb butter sauce.

Das Rowley's befindet sich seit 1977 in
den Räumlichkeiten der „Walls Butcher
Shops", einer ehemaligen Metzgerei, die im
19. und frühen 20. Jahrhundert die königli-
che Familie belieferte. Die Restaurant-Be-
sitzer haben Kachelwände und -decken
und auch die Buntglasfenster im Original-
zustand gelassen. Hausspezialität ist das
Entrecôte mit einer Kräuterbutter-Soße, die
nach einem Geheimrezept zubereitet wird.

Bien qu'il n'ait ouvert qu'en 1977, Rowley's
occupe ce qui était autrefois la boucherie
Walls qui fournissait la famille royale au
XIXe et au début du XXe siècle. Les murs
et les plafonds carrelés ainsi que les vitraux d'origine ont été conservés. La spécialité maison est l'entrecôte arrosée d'un
beurre aux herbes dont la recette est ja-
lousement gardée.

Personal Finds/Eigene Entdeckungen/
Découvertes personnelles:

The Trafalgar

2 Spring Gardens, Trafalgar Square, London SW1A 2TS
☎ +44 20 7870 2900   ⌐ +44 20 7870 2911
www.thetrafalgar.com
Tube: Charing Cross
Booking: www.great-escapes-hotels.com

The Trafalgar

The Trafalgar sits right on London's famous and hectic Trafalgar Square and although it is a Hilton hotel, it is far from faceless. Decorated in dark woods and simple Scandinavian colour schemes, its bustling Rockwell bar and lobby area is a testament to the kind of young and energetic crowd it attracts. The hotel's location is super central: close to the Thames, to the Mall and St James's Park, to Covent Garden and its numerous galleries, theatres and restaurants. Also, shopping is very close by with a jaunt to Jermyn Street or Regent Street. The Trafalgar's rooms are modern and comfortable but the best thing about this hotel is the views. Some rooms overlook the heaving crowds, thousands of pigeons and Nelson's Column in Trafalgar Square, but take the lift to the bar on the roof garden. On a good summer's day there will be a light warm breeze, you will have a glass of Champagne in your hand and you can gaze down at this beautiful city working its magic beneath your feet.

Das Trafalgar Hotel, direkt am genau so bekannten wie hektischen Trafalgar Square, gehört zur Hilton-Gruppe. Gesichtslos ist es trotzdem nicht. Die Rockwell Bar (dunkles Holz, skandinavische Farbtöne) ist genau so angesagt und energiegeladen wie seine Gäste. Das Hotel ist super zentral gelegen: gleich in der Nähe der Themse, der Mall, des St James's Parks und ein Katzensprung von Covent Garden mit seinen unzähligen Galerien, Theatern und Restaurants. Auch die Shopping-nirvanas Jermyn Street oder Regent Street liegen ganz in der Nähe. Die Gästezimmer sind modern-schick und komfortabel, dennoch ist das schönste die Aussicht. Zum Beispiel auf den Trafalgar Square mit einer emsig herumschwirrenden Menge, tausenden von Tauben und der Nelson-Statue. Doch es wird noch besser: im Fahrstuhl auf den Dachgarten hochfahren, ein Glas Champagner bestellen und die Magie dieser tollen Stadt auf sich einwirken lassen. Am schönsten ist das an lauen Sommerabenden.

Bien qu'appartenant à la chaîne Hilton, l'hôtel Trafalgar situé directement sur la célèbre et trépidante place du même nom n'a rien d'anonyme. Décoré de boiseries sombres dans des tons scandinaves simples, son bar Rockwell et son hall très animés rendent hommage à sa clientèle jeune et énergique. L'emplacement ne peut être plus central : à deux pas de la Tamise, du Mall, de St James's Park, des galeries, théâ-tres et restaurants de Covent Garden, des boutiques de Jermyn et Regent Street. Les chambres sont modernes et confortables mais la cerise sur le gâteau, ce sont les vues. Certaines chambres donnent sur la foule bigarrée, les pigeons frénétiques et la colonne de Nelson. Prenez l'ascenseur jusqu'au bar en terrasse sur le toit. Par une belle journée d'été, dans une légère brise chaude, une coupe de champagne à la main, vous verrez la ville déployer sa beauté magique à vos pieds.

Rates: From 205 € (140 GBP) excl. VAT.
Rooms: 126 (1 rooftop studio).
Restaurant: Rockwell.
History: The Trafalgar Hotel's building was originally the headquarters of the Cunard Shipping Line, the company that built and ran the Titanic.
X-Factor: The rooftop views.
Internet: WiFi in the rooms at 15 GBP per day.

Preise: ab 205 € (140 GBP) exkl. VAT.
Zimmer: 126 (1 Dachterrassen-Studio).
Restaurant: Rockwell.
Geschichte: Das Trafalgar Hotel war ursprünglich der Hauptsitz der Cunard Schifffahrtsgesellschaft, der Besitzerin der legendären Titanic.
X-Faktor: Die Aussicht von der Dachterrasse.
Internet: WiFi in allen Zimmern für 15 GBP pro Tag.

Prix : À partir de 205 € (140 GBP), TVA non comprise.
Chambres : 126 (1 studio sur le toit).
Restauration : Rockwell.
Histoire : Le bâtiment était autrefois le siège de la compagnie de navigation Cunard, qui a construit le Titanic.
Le « petit plus » : Les vues depuis la terrasse sur le toit.
Internet : WiFi dans les chambres pour 15 GBP par jour.

1

2

3

1　Museum/Museum/Musée

ICA (Institute of Contemporary Arts)
The Mall
London SW1Y 5AH
Tel: +44 20 7930 3647
www.ica.org.uk
Tube: Charing Cross

This bastion of contemporary culture includes a gallery, cinema, bookshop, theatre, bar and café. If you like, you can make a day of it here, taking in an exhibit in the morning, lunch at the café, a film in the afternoon, then drinks and snacks at the bar followed by one of the ICA's club nights. In the spring, the ICA hosts the Becks Futures Award, which is given to a promising young British artist.

Galerie, Buchhandlung, Kino, Theater, Bar und Café – in dieser Bastion zeitgenössischer Kunst kann man den ganzen Tag verbringen: Ausstellungsbesuch am Morgen, Mittagessen im Café, nachmittags ein Kinobesuch, abends Drinks und Häppchen an der Bar und die Nacht kann man sich im ICA Club um die Ohren schlagen. Jedes Frühjahr wird hier der Becks Futures Award an einen jungen, vielversprechenden britischen Künstler verliehen.

Ce bastion de la culture contemporaine comprend une galerie, un cinéma, une librairie, un théâtre, un bar et un café; de quoi y passer la journée avec une expo le matin, déjeuner au café, un film l'après-midi, puis un verre au bar avant d'aller danser dans une des soirées de l'ICA. Au printemps, le centre accueille le Becks Futures Award qui récompense un jeune artiste britannique prometteur.

2　Restaurant/Restaurant/Restaurant

Inn The Park
St James's Park
Lakeside
London SW1A 2BJ
Tel: +44 20 7451 9999
www.innthepark.com
Tube: St James's Park/Charing Cross

The lakeside Inn the Park (owned by Oliver Peyton) offers the experience of dining in one of the loveliest parks in London without ever having to leave the comfort of the Tom Dixon-designed restaurant (though if you're bound and determined to be rustic, they will happily pack you a picnic hamper). The restaurant is open for breakfast, lunch, tea and dinner and the focus is on British cuisine.

Das Inn The Park von Oliver Peyton liegt direkt am See. Hier kann man mitten in einem der schönsten Parks Londons essen gehen, und trotz Nähe zur Natur muss man im von Designer Tom Dixon entworfenen Restaurant auf Komfort nicht verzichten. Wer's allerdings lieber naturnah mag, kann sich auch ein Picknick einpacken lassen. Für Frühstück, Mittagessen, Tee und Abendessen geöffnet. Die Küche ist hauptsächlich britisch.

Appartenant à Oliver Peyton, ce restaurant au bord du lac vous permet de dîner dans un des plus beaux parcs de Londres sans quitter le confort d'un décor signé Tom Dixon (mais si vous tenez à la jouer rustique, le restaurant prépare aussi des paniers pique-nique). Ouvert pour le petit déjeuner, le déjeuner, le goûter et le dîner, avec une cuisine typiquement british.

3　Restaurant/Restaurant/Restaurant

J. Sheekey
28-32 St Martin's Court
London WC2N 4AL
Tel: +44 20 7240 2565
www.j-sheekey.co.uk
Tube: Leicester Square

The 110-year-old, classic and classy J. Sheekey has been a favourite of generations of Londoners. The speciality of the house is seafood and this it does impeccably. The menu leans heavily toward shellfish and crustacea (including three kinds of oysters), but you can also sample the classic Cockney dish of jellied eels.

Das 110 Jahre alte Restaurant setzt ganz auf Tradition. Seit Generationen ist das J. Sheekey eines der Lieblingsrestaurants der Londoner. Die Spezialität des Hauses ist stets perfekt zubereitetes Seafood wie Muscheln und Krustentiere (es gibt drei Sorten Austern). Es es gibt aber auch einfache, traditionelle Cockney-Gerichte wie „Jellied Eels".

Cette élégante maison qui existe depuis 110 ans fait le bonheur des Londoniens depuis des générations. Spécialisée dans les fruits de mer délicieusement préparés (la carte inclut trois types d'huîtres), vous pouvez aussi y goûter un classique de la cuisine Cockney, les anguilles en gelée.

4　Restaurant/Restaurant/Restaurant

Rules
35 Maiden Lane
London WC2E 7LB
Tel: +44 20 7836 5314
www.rules.co.uk
Tube: Leicester Square/Covent Garden

Established in 1798, Rules is London's oldest restaurant and it specialises in British cookery, with game from the restaurant's own estate in the Pennines. The decor is English country house, making it the ideal setting in which to try the tasty fish'n chips, which come wrapped in the day's newspaper and served with silver cutlery. The service is polished and discreet.

Londons ältestes Restaurant, das es seit 1798 gibt, konzentriert sich auf britische Küche und Wild vom eigenen Gutshof in den Pennines. Das Dekor im englischen Landhausstil macht Lust auf die leckeren „Fish'n Chips", die hier in Zeitungspapier eingewickelt und mit Silberbesteck serviert werden. Der Service ist gepflegt und diskret.

Établi en 1798, Rules est le plus vieux restaurant de Londres. Il est spécialisé dans la cuisine britannique et son gibier provient de son domaine privé dans les Pennines. Le décor très maison de campagne anglaise en fait le lieu idéal où goûter le délicieux et léger fish'n chips présenté dans le quotidien du jour. Service courtois et discret.

4

5

6

5 Scents/Düfte/Fragrances

Penhaligon's
41 Wellington Street
London WC2E 7BN
Tel: +44 20 7836 2150
www.penhaligons.co.uk
Tube: Covent Garden

Classic scents in beautiful packaging is the essence of what this shop is about. The company was founded by William Henry Penhaligon in 1870, who came to London from Penzance to become a barber, but found himself selling perfumed waters and pomades to the aristocracy. Treat yourself to the citrus-y Blenheim Bouquet scent, created in 1902, in the beautiful glass bottle.

Penhaligon's, das sind klassische Düfte in wunderschöner Verpackung. Das Geschäft wurde 1870 von William Henry Penhaligon gegründet, der, weil er Frisör werden wollte, von Penzance, Cornwall, nach London zog. Frisör wurde er dann doch nicht. Stattdessen verkaufte er der Aristokratie parfümierte Wasser und Pomaden, und 1902 schuf er den Zitrusduft „Blenheim Bouquet". Der Lieblingsduft von Kate Moss ist Bluebell. Wer sich verwöhnen will, sollte eines der traumhaft schönen Glasflakons erstehen.

Des fragrances classiques superbement présentées. La maison a été fondée par William Henry Penhaligon en 1870, venu de Penzance pour devenir barbier mais s'étant retrouvé vendant des eaux parfumées et des pommades à l'aristocratie de Londres. Faites-vous plaisir avec le Blenheim Bouquet, aux senteurs citriques, créé en 1902 et vendu dans un magnifique flacon en verre.

6 Museum/Museum/Musée

Turner room at the Tate Britain
Millbank
London SW1P 4RG
Tel: +44 20 7887 8888
www.tate.org.uk
Tube: Pimlico

Tate Britain focuses on British art from the 16th century to the present while at Tate Modern, located in a former power station, the emphasis is on contemporary works from around the world. Visit at Tate Britain the Turner room: upon his death in 1851, J. M. W. Turner's collection of 30.000 watercolours and sketches and 300 paintings were left to the British people and a good selection sits here in a room with windows on the Thames which he loved to paint.

Tate Britain ist Ausstellungsort für britische Kunst zwischen dem 16. und 21. Jahrhundert, während Tate Modern (in einem ehemaligen Kraftwerk) internationale, zeitgenössische Kunst zeigt. Unbedingt den „Turner Room" in der Tate Britain besichtigen: der eine schöne Auswahl aus 30.000 Aquarellen, Zeichnungen und 300 Gemälden zeigt, die J. M. W. Turner nach seinem Tod 1851 dem britischen Königreich vermachte. Von einem der Räume sieht man auf die Themse, eines der Lieblingssujets Turners.

Tate Britain se concentre sur l'art britannique du XVIe siècle à nos jours tandis que Tate Modern, située dans une ancienne centrale électrique, présente l'art contemporain international. Dans la première, ne manquez pas la salle des Turner. À sa mort en 1851, le peintre a légué à ses compatriotes 30 000 aquarelles, dessins et 300 huiles dont un beau choix est présenté dans une salle aux fenêtres donnant sur la Tamise qu'il aimait tant peindre.

Personal Finds/Eigene Entdeckungen/ Découvertes personnelles:

1 Vegan Restaurant/Veganes-Restaurant/Restaurant végétalien
VitaOrganic

2 Lingerie/Dessous/Lingerie
Agent Provocateur

3 Department Store/Kaufhaus/Grand magasin
Liberty

4 Fashion/Mode/Mode
Topshop

5 Restaurant/Restaurant/Restaurant
Soba Noodle Bar

6 Restaurant/Restaurant/Restaurant
Andrew Edmunds

1 Coffee Shop/Café/Café
Bar Italia

2 Coffee Shop/Café/Café
Patisserie Valerie

3 Tea Room/Teehaus/Salon de thé
Maison Bertaux

4 Pub/Pub/Pub
Coach & Horses

5 Restaurant/Restaurant/Restaurant
Refuel at The Soho Hotel

6 Chinese Herbal Remedies/Chinesische Kräutermedizin/Médecine chinoise
Beijing Tong Ren Tang

1 Remedies/Heilmittel/Remèdes
Neal's Yard Remedies

2 British Cheese/Britischer Käse/Fromagerie britannique
Neal's Yard Dairy

3 Restaurant/Restaurant/Restaurant
The Ivy

4 Ballet/Ballett/Ballet
Royal Opera House

5 Museum/Museum/Musée
Sir John Soane's Museum

6 Silver/Silberwaren/Argenterie
London Silver Vaults

1 Umbrellas/Schirmgeschäft/Parapluies
James Smith & Sons

2 Asian Restaurant/Asiatisches Restaurant/Restaurant asiatique
Hakkasan

3 Japanese Restaurant/Japanisches Restaurant/Restaurant japonais
Roka

4 Spanish Restaurant/Spanisches Restaurant/Restaurant espagnol
Navarro's

5 Picnic/Picknick/Pique-nique
Mahatma Gandhi Statue in Tavistock Square

6 Museum/Museum/Musée
The Charles Dickens Museum

W1

& WC2
Soho
Covent Garden
Fritzrovia

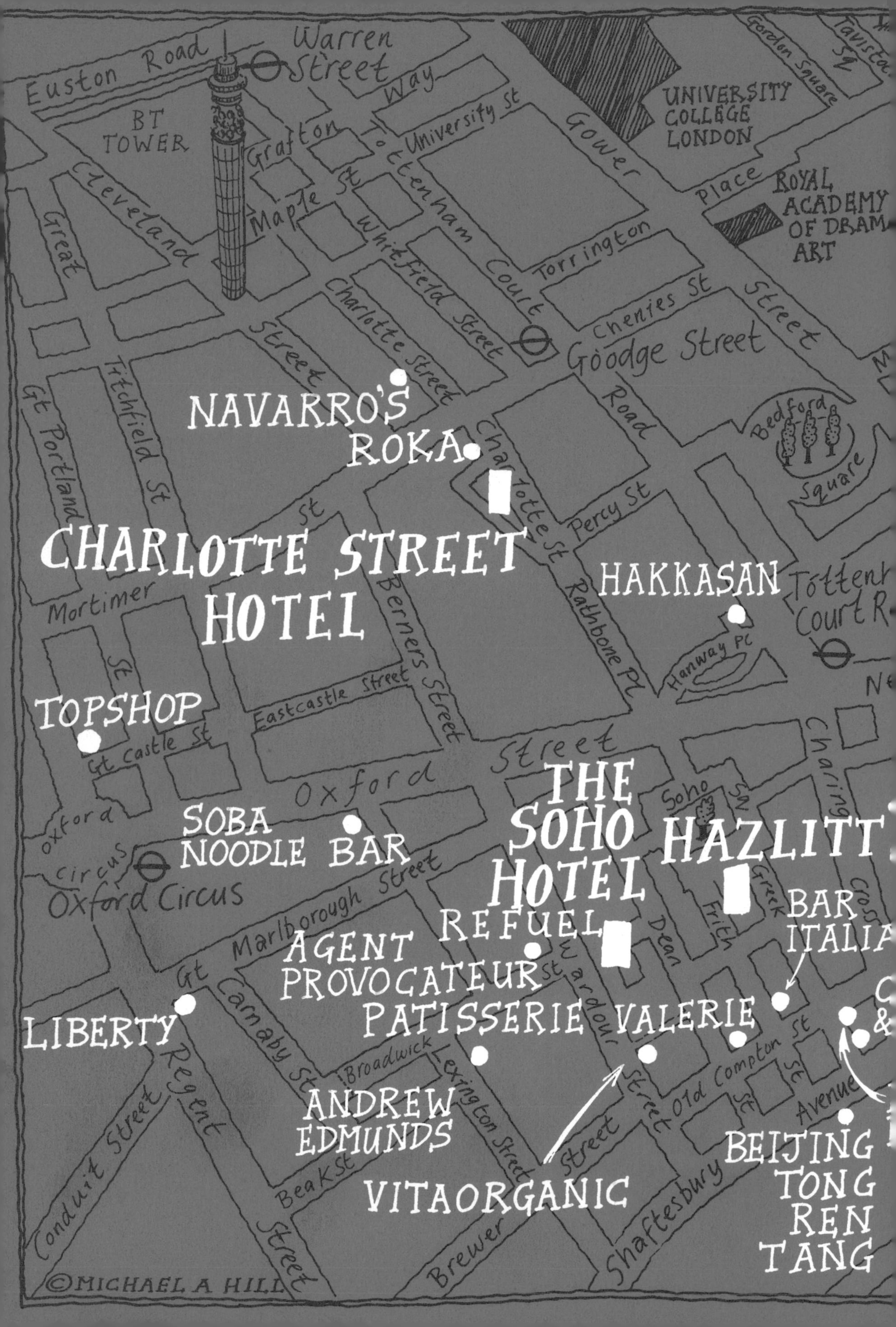

Euston Road
Warren Street
Way
University St
Gower
Grafton
BT TOWER
Maple St
Tottenham Court
Torrington
UNIVERSITY COLLEGE LONDON
Gordon Square
Tavista St
Place
ROYAL ACADEMY OF DRAM ART
Cleveland
Great
Gt Portland
Titchfield St
Street
Whitfield Street
Charlotte Street
Street
Chenies St
Goodge Street
Bedford Square
St

NAVARRO'S
ROKA
Charlotte St.
Percy St
HAKKASAN
Tottenh Court R
Mortimer
St
Berners Street
Rathbone Pl.
Hanway PC
Hanway PC

CHARLOTTE STREET HOTEL

TOPSHOP
Gt Castle St.
Eastcastle street
Street
Oxford
THE SOHO HOTEL
HAZLITT
Charing Cross

Oxford
Circus
SOBA NOODLE BAR
Oxford Circus
Marlborough Street
REFUEL
Soho Sq
Greek
Frith
Dean
Wardour St
BAR ITALIA

Gt Marlborough Street
AGENT PROVOCATEUR
PATISSERIE VALERIE
Old Compton St.
St.

LIBERTY
Gt
Carnaby St
Regent
Broadwick
Lexington Street
Street
Street
Avenue
C &

Conduit Street
Regent
Street
Beak St
ANDREW EDMUNDS
Brewer
Shaftesbury
BEIJING TONG REN TANG

VITAORGANIC

©MICHAEL A HILL

VISTOCK SQUARE

CORAM'S FIELDS

THE CHARLES DICKENS MUSEUM

Holburn Place

Russell

Bernard Street

Russell Square

Guilford Street

Gray's

Doughty St

Rosebery Ave

Gt Ormond St

Lamb's Conduit St

Northington St

Place

Square

THE BRITISH MUSEUM

Southampton Row

Old Gloucester Street

Boswell St

Theobald's

Road

Red Lion

Bedford Row

Jockey's Fields

Inn Road

Great Russell Street

Bloomsbury Way

Procter Street

Street

High Holborn

Chancery Lane

LONDON SILVER VAULTS

High Holborn

High Holborn

Holborn

SIR JOHN SOANE'S MUSEUM

Chancery Lane

ord Street

Ave

MES SMITH & SONS

Macklin St

Parker St

Gt Queen St

Kingsway

Lincoln's Inn Field

OVENT ARDEN HOTEL

Endell

NEAL'S YARD REMEDIES

NEAL'S YARD DAIRY

Portugal Street

terbury

Neal

Street

Acre

Drury Lane

ST MARY LE-STRAND

ES

ON AUX

THE IVY

Garden

Monmouth

Long

Floral

King St

Bow Street

ROYAL OPERA HOUSE

A l d w y c h

Strand

COURTAULD INSTITUTE OF ART

Temple

Garrick St

COVENT GARDEN MARKET

cester are

The Soho Hotel

4 Richmond Mews (off Dean Street), London W1D 3DH
☎ + 44 20 7559 3000   📠 + 44 20 7559 3003
soho@firmdale.com
www.sohohotel.com
Tube: Tottenham Court Road
Booking: www.great-escapes-hotels.com

Our desires do not age. The sudden leaping up of feeling, as a flame leaps up, or the s

The Soho Hotel

The Soho Hotel is the embodiment of all that is cool and colourful about London's Soho district. It is the Firmdale group's largest and edgiest property yet retains the cosy refinement for which its hotels are so well known. Just off busy Dean Street, the building used to function as a multi-storey car park and was completely redesigned to create the hotel's spacious rooms and suites. The enormous Fernando Botero cat statue in the lobby is the first clue that this is not like any other hotel. Designer Kit Kemp has gone all out with the use of colourful, graphic fabrics, oversized paintings and flower arrangements as well as larger-than-life furniture to fill this cavernous space. Luxury doubles are very roomy but, if you possibly can, spring for the terrace suite. It has a kitchenette, a butler, an enormous bathroom with freestanding bath and a balcony that wraps around the building.

Das Soho Hotel verkörpert die coole und farbige Seite Sohos. Es ist das größte und ausgefallenste Objekt von Firmdale – allerdings mit derselben komfortablen Eleganz, für die die Hotelgruppe bekannt ist. Das Hotel liegt in der Nähe der belebten Dean Street und war zuvor ein mehrstöckiges Parkhaus. Nach dem Umbau entstand daraus ein Hotel mit großzügigen Gästezimmern und Suiten. Ein erster Hinweis darauf, dass dies kein gewöhnliches Hotel ist, gibt die riesige Katzenplastik von Fernando Botero in der Lobby. Designerin Kit Kemp hat hier mit bunten, grafischen Stoffen, übergroßen Bildern, Möbeln und Blumenarrangements ihre Akzente gesetzt. Obschon die Luxury Doppelzimmer sehr geräumig sind, empfiehlt es sich (sofern es das Budget erlaubt), die Terrace Suite zu buchen. Neben einer kleinen Küche steht ein Butler zu Diensten. Das riesige Badezimmer verfügt zudem über eine frei stehende Badewanne und einen rund ums Gebäude gehenden Balkon.

Le Soho est à l'image de son quartier coloré et nonchalant. Hôtel le plus branché et le plus grand du groupe Firmdale, il n'a rien sacrifié au raffinement cosy qui fait la réputation de la chaîne. À deux pas de la grouillante Dean Street, le bâtiment abritait autrefois un parking sur plusieurs étages entièrement remodelé pour créer des chambres et des suites spacieuses. Dès le chat monumental de Fernando Botero qui orne le lobby, on sait qu'on ne se trouve pas dans un hôtel ordinaire. Pour décorer cet espace immense, Kit Kemp n'a pas lésiné sur les couleurs, les tissus graphiques, les tableaux démesurés, les arrangements floraux et le mobilier plus grand que nature. Les doubles de luxe sont agréables mais, tant qu'à faire, optez pour la suite avec terrasse. Elle possède une kitchenette, un major dome, une immense salle de bains avec baignoire sur pied et un balcon panoramique.

Rates: From 350 € (240 GBP) excl. VAT.
Rooms: 85 (+ 6 apartments).
Restaurant: Refuel.
History: The car park that used to occupy the hotel's land was knocked down and the Soho Hotel erected by architect Peter French.
X-Factor: The staff uniforms – charcoal-grey suits – are by Soho-based bespoke tailor Mark Powell, ties by Paul Smith and pink knits by John Smedley.
Internet: WiFi in all rooms for 20 GBP per day.

Preise: ab 350 € (240 GBP), exkl. VAT.
Zimmer: 85 (+ 6 Apartments).
Restaurant: Refuel.
Geschichte: Das Soho Hotel wurde vom Architekten Peter French entworfen – dafür musste ein Parkhaus demoliert werden.
X-Faktor: Die anthrazitgrauen Anzüge der Angestellten wurden vom Atelier von Mark Powell maßgeschneidert, die Krawatten sind von Paul Smith und der rosa Strick von John Smedley.
Internet: WiFi in allen Zimmern für 20 GBP pro Tag.

Prix : À partir de 350 € (240 GBP), TVA non comprise.
Chambres : 85 (+ 6 appartements).
Restauration : Refuel.
Histoire : L'hôtel a été construit par l'architecte Peter French à la place d'un ancien parking.
Le « petit plus » : Les uniformes du personnel – costumes gris anthracite faits sur mesure par le tailleur Mark Powell, basé à Soho, cravates de Paul Smith et petits pulls roses de John Smedley.
Internet : WiFi dans toutes les chambres pour 20 GBP par jour.

1   Vegan Restaurant/Veganes-Restaurant/Restaurant végétalien

VitaOrganic
74 Wardour Street
London W1F 0TE
Tel: +44 20 7734 8986
www.vitaorganic.co.uk
Tube: Tottenham Court Road/Leicester Square

If you're vegan or vegetarian, travelling can present difficulties. VitaOrganic is one of the more delicious solutions to a veggie's food search. A light and airy café, it features communal tables and a self-serve buffet. Both vegans and vegetarians are catered to, with a wide selection of hot and cold dishes, a juice bar and a separate raw menu. VitaOrganic is open for lunch and dinner.

Veganer und Vegetarier haben es beim Reisen auf der Suche nach dem richtigen Essen nicht immer einfach. Bei VitaOrganic, einem hellen, offenen Café mit Gemeinschaftstischen und Selbstbedienungs-Büffet, finden sie eine köstliche Auswahl an warmen und kalten Gerichten, Rohkost und eine Saftbar. Das Lokal ist mittags und abends geöffnet.

Quand vous êtes végétalien ou végétarien, voyager n'est pas toujours facile. VitaOrganic offre la plus délicieuse des solutions à votre quête de nourriture. Ce café lumineux propose des tables communes et un buffet self-service avec une vaste sélection de plats chauds et froids ainsi qu'un menu cru séparé. VitaOrganic est ouvert midi et soir.

2   Lingerie/Dessous/Lingerie

Agent Provocateur
6 Broadwick Street
London W1V 1FH
Tel: +44 20 7439 0229
www.agentprovocateur.com
Tube: Tottenham Court Road/Oxford Circus

Soho has always had a risqué reputation, but it's seldom as stylishly executed as at Agent Provocateur, the lingerie shop opened by Joseph Corre and Serena Rees in 1994. The emphasis is on vintage styles and a saucy, touch-in-cheek eroticism, as evidenced in the pale pink nurses' uniforms worn by the sales girls and the naughty tableaux in the windows.

Gewagtes fand man in Soho schon immer. Doch so richtig stilvoll wird es erst beim Dessous-Geschäft Agent Provocateur, das von Joseph Corre und Serena Rees 1994 gegründet wurde. Vintage-Look wird hier mit frech-ironischer Erotik umgesetzt, kesse Verkäuferinnen tragen blassrosa Krankenschwester-Uniformen, und im Schaufenster hängen leicht anzügliche Bilder.

Soho a toujours eu une réputation de quartier chaud mais le libertinage a rarement été aussi chic que chez Agent Provocateur, la boutique de lingerie ouverte par Joseph Corre et Serena Rees en 1994. Le style rétro est à l'honneur ainsi que l'érotisme coquin et ironique comme en attestent les blouses d'infirmière rose pâle des vendeuses et les tableaux grivois en vitrine.

3   Department Store/Kaufhaus/Grand magasin

Liberty
210–220 Regent Street
London W1B 5AH
Tel: +44 20 7734 1234
www.liberty.co.uk
Tube: Oxford Circus

With its Tudor façade, signature floral prints and mellow wood interior, Liberty is one of the more old-fashioned of London's department stores. But don't let that fool you: the shopping here is second to none. It has an ever-changing selection of new and exciting labels, as well as a fantastic interiors section with vintage and classic designs mixed in with newer ones.

Mit einer Fassade im Tudor-Stil und behaglichem Blumenmuster- und Holz-Dekor gehört Liberty zu den Kaufhäusern der altmodischen Sorte. Doch von solchen Äußerlichkeiten sollte man sich nicht täuschen lassen. Hier gibt's die neuesten und aufregendsten Labels und eine fantastische Interior-Abteilung mit Vintage-Möbeln, Design-Klassikern zusammen mit ein paar neuen Entwürfen.

Avec sa façade Tudor, ses imprimés fleuris et ses boiseries patinées, Liberty a un charme désuet mais ne vous y trompez pas : c'est un paradis du shopping. Sa sélection de nouvelles marques intéressantes est constamment renouvelée et son formidable rayon décoration mêle le classique et le vintage aux dernières créations.

4   Fashion/Mode/Mode

Topshop
36–38 Great Castle Street
London W1W 8L6
Tel: +44 20 7636 7700
www.topshop.co.uk
Tube: Oxford Circus

No visit to London is complete without a stop at Topshop's flagship store. If it was on the runway, you'll find an affordable version of it here, along with a nail bar and a café. Expectant mothers can also keep up to date with Topshop's maternity range. If you're having trouble finding what you want, consult one of the resident Style Advisers, who'll be happy to scour the rails for you.

Ohne einen Abstecher in den Topshop-Flagship-Store gemacht zu haben, kann man London unmöglich verlassen. Hier findet man eine erschwingliche Version von Laufsteg-Mode, eine Nagelpflege-Bar und ein Café. Auch werdende Mütter müssen nicht auf die letzten Trends verzichten: Die Umstandsmode ist modisch auf dem neuesten Stand. Praktisch: die Topshop-Style-Berater, die für ihre Kunden nach den passenden Stücken herumrennen.

Une visite à Londres ne serait pas complète sans un passage par la boutique phare de Topshop. Vous y trouverez toutes les nouvelles tendances à des prix abordables, ainsi qu'un nail bar et un café. Les futures mamans ne seront pas en reste grâce à une section maternité branchée. Si vous êtes perdu, des conseillers en style vous aideront à parcourir les rayons.

4

5

6

5   Restaurant/Restaurant/Restaurant

Soba Noodle Bar

38 Poland Street
London W1F 7LY
Tel: +44 20 7734 6400
www.soba.co.uk
Tube: Oxford Circus

Poland Street needed Soba to complete
its transformation from cheap-and-cheer-
ful to "wow" destination. Soba's interior itself is worth a visit to the restaurant: David
Adjaye and William Russell, who used
corrugated plastic to face the walls, and
graphic elements by Rana Salam, who created the Japanese-flag motif. The noodle
menu is affordable and the food delicious.

Mit der Soba Noodle Bar wurde die Ver-
wandlung der Poland Street von billig-bunt
zu angesagt vollbracht. Es lohnt sich
schon, nur wegen dem Interieur herzu-
kommen. Die Architekten David Adjaye
und William Russell haben die Wände mit
gewelltem Plastik verkleiden lassen, und
die grafischen Elemente, darunter ein
japanisches Flaggen-Motiv, stammen von
der Künstlerin Rana Salam. Die Nudelge-
richte sind preiswert und köstlich.

Avec Soba, Poland Street a achevé sa tran-
sition du coin sympa et pas cher au lieu à
ne pas manquer. La décoration à elle seule
vaut le détour. David Adjaye et William
Russell ont tapissé les murs de polypropy-
ène ondulé tandis que les éléments graphiques et le drapeau nippon revisité sont
de Rana Salam. La carte de nouilles est
abordable et les plats délicieux.

6   Restaurant/Restaurant/Restaurant

Andrew Edmunds

46 Lexington Street
London W1F 0LP
Tel: +44 20 7437 5708
Tube: Piccadilly Circus/Oxford Circus

Unpretentious and reliable, this long-run-
ning bistro is many Londoners' favourite
restaurant. From the cream-coloured walls
and chalkboard menus to the pew seating
and small vases of wildflowers on the
tables, every detail is seen to. The menu
focuses on high-quality seasonal produce,
simply and expertly prepared. Leave room
for the traditional English desserts, such
as sticky toffee pudding.

Null Attitüde, gute Qualität: Dieses Bistro
ist das Lieblingslokal vieler Londoner. Mit
crèmefarbenen Wänden, Schiefertafeln,
auf denen die Menüs aufgelistet sind,
alten Kirchenbänken zum Sitzen und
kleinen Vasen mit Wildblumen auf den
Tischen zeigt es zudem viel Liebe zum
Detail. Hier kommen saisonale Qualitäts-
produkte auf den Tisch, einfach aber gekonnt umgesetzt. Unbedingt die traditionell
englischen Nachspeisen, wie den Kara-
mell-Pudding, kosten.

Sans prétention et fiable, ce bistrot est
depuis longtemps un chéri des Londoniens. Tous les détails sont soignés : murs
beiges, bancs d'église, menus sur ardoise,
petits bouquets de fleurs sauvages sur
les tables. La cuisine à base de produits
de saison de qualité est préparée avec art
et simplicité. Laissez de la place pour les
desserts traditionnels comme le pudding
au caramel mou.

Personal Finds/Eigene Entdeckungen/
Découvertes personnelles:

_____

_____

_____

_____

_____

_____

_____

_____

_____

WILLIAM HAZLITT
1778-1830
Essayist
Died Here

HAZLITT'S

BUILT
1718

6

City of Westminster

P
G

Resident
permit
holders
only

At any time

3

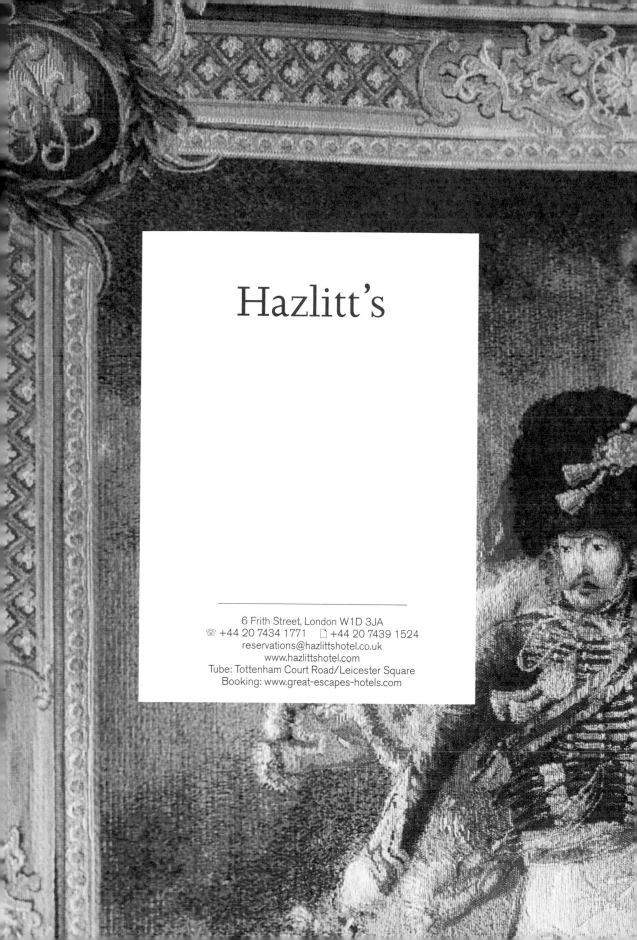

Hazlitt's

6 Frith Street, London W1D 3JA
☎ +44 20 7434 1771   📠 +44 20 7439 1524
reservations@hazlittshotel.co.uk
www.hazlittshotel.com
Tube: Tottenham Court Road/Leicester Square
Booking: www.great-escapes-hotels.com

Hazlitt's

Hazlitt's is a magical little nook in Soho where you can imagine yourself hiding away to write that novel you've been putting off, or a secret place in which to conduct les liaisons dangereuses. It is in the centre of the action – innocent or naughty (your choice) – that this part of town offers. Hazlitt's occupies three historic houses that date back to 1718 and, because the building is listed, crooked stairs and leaning walls are all part of the deal. The rooms are decorated with a mixture of English and French antiques; walls are painted rich, dark colours, such as raspberry and charcoal grey and four-poster beds are so plush and high that it's a wonder guests don't fall off in the middle of the night. Instead of room numbers, each chamber is named after 18th or 19th-century residents or visitors to the house. The Jonathan Swift room is the most luxurious, all mysterious and dark woods with an elegant chandelier making it look more like a salon than a bedroom.

Das Hazlitt's ist ein magischer kleiner Ort in Soho. Man kann sich gut vorstellen, hier den Roman zu schreiben, den man schon immer schreiben wollte. Oder unbemerkt irgendwelchen „Liaisons Dangereuses" nachzugehen. Was immer man tut, und sei's noch so harmlos, das Hotel bleibt das Zentrum des Geschehens. Das Hazlitt's liegt in drei historischen Häusern, die auf das Jahr 1718 zurückgehen. Weil das Gebäude unter Denkmalschutz steht, gehören schräge Treppen und Wände zum Erlebnis. Die Gästezimmer sind mit französischen und englischen Antiquitäten eingerichtet, die Wände in kräftigen, dunklen Farben gehalten – etwa Himbeerrot oder Anthrazit. Ein Wunder, dass noch niemand aus einem der Himmelbetten gefallen ist – sie sind riesig und sehr hoch! Die Zimmer haben keine Nummern, sie tragen die Namen von Bewohnern aus dem 18. und 19. Jahrhundert. Das Jonathan-Swift-Zimmer ist das luxuriöseste von allen. Mit dunklem Holz und elegantem Leuchter sieht es mehr aus wie ein Salon als ein Schlafzimmer.

Le Hazlitt's est le petit nid magique au cœur de Soho où écrire ce roman que vous repoussez depuis si longtemps ou ourdir en secret vos Liaisons Dangereuses. Dans ce quartier, c'est ici que tout se passe, innocent ou coquin (à vous de choisir). Occupant trois maisons classées datant de 1718, les escaliers sont tordus et les murs penchent. Les chambres peintes de couleurs riches et sombres comme framboise ou gris anthracite sont meublées avec des antiquités anglaises et françaises, et les somptueux lits à baldaquins sont si hauts que c'est un miracle que les clients n'en tombent pas au milieu de la nuit. À la place de numéros, les chambres portent le nom d'anciens visiteurs célèbres du XVIIIe et XIXe siècle. La Jonathan Swift est la plus luxueuse. Mystérieuse avec ses boiseries sombres et son lustre élégant, on se croirait dans un salon.

Rates: From 300 € (205 GBP) excl. VAT.
Rooms: 23 (1 suite).
Restaurants: None although there is 24-hour room service and breakfast is served in your room.
History: Author William Hazlitt, after whom the hotel is named, was the son of a clergyman who had founded the Unitarian Church in Boston.
X-Factor: Writers who stay here (notable names include JK Rowling and Terry Pratchett) leave signed copies of their latest books for others to read.
Internet: Broadband at 5 GBP per day.

Preise: ab 300 € (205 GBP) exkl. VAT.
Zimmer: 23 (1 Suite).
Restaurants: Keines. 24-Stunden-Zimmerservice, das Frühstück wird aufs Zimmer gebracht.
Geschichte: Das Hotel ist nach dem Autor William Hazlitt benannt, dem Sohn des Gründers der Unitarian Church in Boston.
X-Faktor: Schriftsteller wie JK Rowling und Terry Pratchett, die hier abgestiegen sind, haben für andere Gäste signierte Bücher hinterlassen.
Internet: Breitbandanschluss für 5 GBP pro Tag.

Prix : À partir de 300 € (205 GBP), TVA non comprise.
Chambres : 23 (1 suite).
Restauration : Service assuré 24h/24 et petit-déjeuner servi dans les chambres.
Histoire : L'auteur William Hazlitt était le fils du fondateur de l'église protestante unitaire de Boston.
Le « petit plus » : Les écrivains qui y ont séjourné (notamment JK Rowling et Terry Pratchett) ont laissé des exemplaires dédicacés de leurs œuvres pour les autres clients.
Internet : Accès haut débit pour 5 GBP par jour.

Through door to....

THOMAS ARCHER   Bsmt
GREGORY KING   Bsmt
BARON WILLOUGHBY   Grd
MADAME KENNEDY   1st
WILLIAM BENTINCK   1st
MRS MILLET   2nd
WILLIAM BATEMAN   2nd
MRS NEWDIGATE   3rd
WILLIAM DUNCOMBE   3rd

1

2

1   Coffee Shop/Café/Café

Bar Italia
22 Frith Street
London W1D 4RP
Tel: +44 20 7437 4520
Tube: Leicester Square

Crowded at all hours of the day and night, this quintessential Italian coffee shop – black-and-white photos crowd the mirrored walls, the TV is always on, and the clatter of espresso cups is the background white noise – is Soho at its best. Come for the coffee and stay for the people watching: everyone from bikers to drag queens congregates here.

In diesem Café fühlt man sich wie in Italien: Es ist tagsüber genau so wie nachts, stets rappelvoll, die verspiegelten Wände sind mit schwarz-weißen Fotos zugepflastert, Espressotassen klirren und der Fernseher läuft ohne Unterbrechung. Diese Italianità passt perfekt zu Soho. Beim Kaffeetrinken kann man gut Leute beobachten: Vom Motorradfahrer bis zur Drag Queen sieht man hier alles.

Bondé à toute heure de la journée et de la nuit, ce café typiquement italien (des photos noir et blanc qui tapissent les murs en miroir à la télé toujours allumée et au bruit de fond des tasses à expresso) est l'âme de Soho. Venez prendre un café et restez pour admirer la foule bigarrée, des motards aux drag-queens.

2   Coffee Shop/Café/Café

Patisserie Valerie
44 Old Compton Street
London W1D 5JX
Tel: +44 20 7437 3466
www.patisserie-valerie.co.uk
Tube: Leicester Square

Though this mini-chain now has branches all over the city, the original opened in nearby Frith Street in 1926 and moved to Old Compton Street during the Second World War. The decor is pure 1950s Soho, and the café is still popular with art stu-dents from nearby Central St Martins. Along with the luscious pastries and cof-fees, Patisserie Valerie is considered the best place in Soho to get breakfast.

Patisserie Valerie gibt's bereits seit 1926. Heute sind die Patisserien über ganz London verstreut. Das erste Geschäft eröffnete an der nahe gelegenen Frith Street, doch nachdem es im Zweiten Weltkrieg ausgebombt wurde, zog Valerie an die Old Compton Street. Im 1950er Dekor des Cafés tummeln sich viele Kunst-studenten des nahe gelegenen Central St Martins College. Die Patisserien sind deliziös, der Kaffee köstlich, und hier gibt's das beste Frühstück in Soho.

Cette chaîne qui possède des enseignes dans toute la ville a vu le jour sur Frith Street en 1926 avant de déménager sur Old Compton Street pendant la Seconde Guerre mondiale. Avec son décor pur Soho années 50, c'est la cantine des étu-diants de l'école d'art voisine, Central St Martins. Outre ses délicieuses pâtisseries, le café est réputé pour servir les meilleurs petits-déjeuners de Soho.

3   Tea Room/Teesalon/Salon de thé

Maison Bertaux
28 Greek Street
London W1D 5DQ
Tel: +44 20 7437 6007
Tube: Leicester Square

In the age of Starbucks and other homo-genized coffee-and-muffin chains, this 130-year-old patisserie, sandwiched between a strip club and a pub, is a Soho treasure. The window is filled with au-thentically French, lovingly made gateaux, flans, mille-feuilles, éclairs and cream cakes, and the decor, which runs to dark wood tables and chairs, hasn't changed in 50 years.

Diese 130 Jahre alte Patisserie, einge-klemmt zwischen einem Strip-Club und einem Pub, ist ein Juwel, das man im Zeit-alter von Starbucks besonders zu schätzen weiß. Im Schaufenster türmen sich Kuchen, Flans, Mille-Feuilles und Eclairs nach origi-nal französischen Rezepten. Innen hat sich seit fünfzig Jahren nichts verändert – die dunklen Holztische und -stühle sind imme noch dieselben.

À l'ère des Starbucks et autres chaînes homogénéisées, cette pâtisserie vieille de 130 ans coincée entre une boîte de strip-tease et un pub est un véritable trésor. Sa vitrine regorge de flans, mille-feuilles, éclairs, choux à la crème et autres pâtisseries françaises confectionnées avec amour. Le décor, avec son mobilier en bois sombre, n'a pas changé depuis 50 ans.

4   Pub/Pub/Pub

Coach & Horses
29 Greek Street
London W1D 5DH
Tel: +44 20 7437 5920
Tube: Leicester Square

The Coach and Horses is a proper Soho boozer, and that's just how the patrons like it. Because of its association with journal-ists – the staff of Private Eye and the late columnist Jeffrey Bernard were amongst the regulars – it's something of a local legend. Its former owner Norman Balon (he retired in May 2006), was the self-proclaimed "rudest landlord in London."

So stellt man sich eine typische Kneipe vor Im Coach & Horses verkehren vor allem Journalisten, etwa die Macher des Satire-magazins „Private Eye". Auch der verstor-bene Kolumnist Jeffrey Bernard gehörte z den Stammgästen. Coach & Horses ist ein lokale Legende, zu der auch der ehemalige Besitzer Norman Balon, der sich im Mai 2006 zur Ruhe setzte, beigetragen hat. Er bezeichnete sich als den ruppigsten Gastgeber Londons.

Le Coach & Horses est un troquet de Soho pur jus et ses clients tiennent à ce qu'il le reste. Fréquenté par des journalis-tes (notamment ceux du Private Eye et feu le chroniqueur Jeffrey Bernard), c'est une légende locale. Son ancien propriétaire Norman Balon (à la retraite depuis mai 2006), se vantait d'être « le bistrotier le plus grossier de Londres ».

4

5

6

5   Restaurant/Restaurant/Restaurant

Refuel at The Soho Hotel
4 Richmond Mews (off Dean Street)
London W1D 3DH
Tel: +44 20 7559 3000
www.firmdale.com/shrefuel.html
Tube: Tottenham Court Road

The only thing at Refuel that reflects this restaurant and bar's former incarnation as a multi-level car park is the mural behind the bar. With its spacious interior and comfortable chairs, Refuel is the perfect spot to do just that. The wine list is short but thoughtful, and the menu changes frequently to reflect executive chef Robin Read's use of seasonal organic produce.

Das Refuel war einmal ein Parkhaus – doch das sieht man aber nur noch der Wand hinter der Bar an. Mit bequemen Sessel bestückt, lädt der großzügige Raum zum Verweilen ein. Die Weinkarte ist zwar klein, doch sehr durchdacht, und die von Küchenchef Robin Read kreierten Bio-Menüs passen sich der jeweiligen Saison an.

La fresque derrière le bar est le seul détail qui trahit l'ancienne vie de ce restaurant/bar, à savoir un parking sur plusieurs étages. Spacieux et confortable, Refuel est l'endroit idéal pour recharger ses batteries. La carte des vins est courte mais bien pensée et le chef Robin Read change son menu au fil des saisons afin de n'utiliser que des produits bios.

6   Chinese Herbal Remedies/Chinesische Kräutermedizin/Médecine chinoise

Beijing Tong Ren Tang
124 Shaftesbury Avenue
London W1D 5ES
Tel: +44 20 7287 0098
Tube: Leicester Square

Chinese medicine is about preventing a malaise rather than curing it and no better place to do this in London than here, in the heart of Soho, in Chinatown. Tong Ren Tang has a classic wood-pannelled interior and its displays of medicines and herbal teas are beautiful and even smell therapeutic and exotic. Customers can walk in and get a doctor's recommendation through pulse and tongue diagnosis.

Die chinesische Medizin setzt das Schwergewicht auf Prävention. Und dafür gibt es keinen besseren Ort als in Chinatown mitten in Soho. Im Tong Ren Tang mit traditioneller Holzvertäfelung sind die Heilmittel und Kräutertees auf den Regalen eine Augenweide. Zudem riechen sie schön therapeutisch und exotisch. Nach einer Pulsdiagnose und dem Prüfen der Zunge vor Ort verschreibt ein Arzt die chinesischen Heilmittel.

Selon la médecine chinoise, « mieux vaut prévenir que guérir », or le meilleur endroit à Londres pour cela, c'est Chinatown, au cœur de Soho. La pharmacie de Tong Ren Tang, avec ses boiseries et ses rayons de remèdes et d'infusions, est aussi belle qu'odorante et exotique. À votre demande, un médecin établira votre diagnostic en examinant votre pouls et votre langue.

Personal Finds/Eigene Entdeckungen/
Découvertes personnelles:

Covent Garden Hotel

10 Monmouth Street, London WC2H 9HB
☎ + 44 20 7806 1000   📠 + 44 20 7806 1100
covent@firmdale.com
www.coventgardenhotel.co.uk
Tube: Covent Garden
Booking: www.great-escapes-hotels.com

Covent Garden Hotel

ovent Garden is one of the most onderful and diverse neighbour-oods in London. It's a mix of flats, ool shops, fabulous restaurants and heatres. It goes without saying, hen, that one expects a bit of drama om the Covent Garden Hotel. The obby resembles a stage set; the narvellous stone staircase swoops o one side and leads up to the rawing room and bedrooms where he drama continues. Designed by wner Kit Kemp, the hotel is a nodern update on traditional nglish design. Florals are done ith flair and in abundance, and her ignature is a mannequin in each hamber covered in the dominant bric used in the room's decora-on. The hotel's Brasserie Max is a rilliant little restaurant in which o spy on the theatre actors, Holly ood producers and local media ros gathered over drinks and din-er. Try the chips (French fries): hey are delicious with a glass of d wine after a hard day's stomp-g around the greatest city in the orld.

Covent Garden gehört zu den inter-essantesten Stadtteilen Londons – ein Mix aus Wohnungen, coolen Shops, ausgezeichneten Restaurants und Theatern. Das Covent Garden Hotel reflektiert diese außergewöhnliche Mélange perfekt. Bereits die Lobby überrascht mit einer bühnenreifen Szenerie und prächtiger Steintreppe, die sich auf eine Seite hochschwingt und nach oben in den Salon und zu den Gästezimmern führt. Das Interi-eur wurde von Besitzerin Kit Kemp entworfen: tradtionell englisches Design neu interpretiert – natürlich mit vielen üppigen, floralen Mus-tern. Sogar die Schaufensterpuppen, die als Dekor-Element in jedem der Gästezimmer stehen, sind mit dem Blümchenstoff des jeweiligen Zim-mers bezogen. Hervorragend ist die Brasserie Max. Hier verkehren Thea terschauspieler, Hollywood-Produ-zenten und die Medien-Prominenz. Besonders gut schmecken die Pommes Frites. Zusammen mit einem guten Glas Rotwein sind sie eine Wohltat nach einem langen Tag in einer der aufregendsten Städte der Welt.

Covent Garden est l'un des quartiers les plus fascinants et variés de Londres, mélange d'appartements, de boutiques branchées, d'excel-lents restaurants et de théâtres. Le Covent Garden Hotel se devait donc d'êtreà la hauteur. Son hall rappelle un décor de théâtre avec son mer-veilleux escalier en pierre qui mène au salon et aux chambres où le spectacle continue. Sa propriétaire Kit Kemp l'a décoré dans une ver-sion moderne du style traditionnel anglais, agrémenté de merveilleux et nombreux bouquets de bon goût. Chaque chambre contient un man-nequin de couture tapissé du même tissu que les murs. Max, la brasserie de l'hôtel, est un délicieux petit restaurant où espionner les acteurs, les producteurs hollywoodiens et les professionnels des médias. Essayez les frites, délicieuses avec un verre de vin rouge après avoir arpenté toute la journée la ville la plus exci-tante du monde.

---

ates: From 320 € (220 GBP) excl. VAT. ooms: 58. estaurant: Brasserie Max. istory: The building that the hotel now ccupies was once a French hospital. Factor: The bathroom products by ondon perfumer Miller Harris. ternet: Broadband access at 20 GBP er day.

Preise: ab 320 € (220 GBP) exkl. VAT. **Zimmer:** 58. **Restaurant:** Brasserie Max. **Geschichte:** Das Hotelgebäude war früher ein französisches Krankenhaus. **X-Faktor:** Im Badezimmer stehen Produkte des Londoner Parfumeurs Miller Harris. **Internet:** Breitbandanschluss für 20 GBP pro Tag.

Prix : À partir de 320 € (220 GBP), TVA non comprise. **Chambres :** 58. **Restauration :** Brasserie Max. **Histoire :** Le bâtiment abritait autrefois un hôpital français. **Le « petit plus » :** Les salles de bains sont équipées de produits du parfumeur londonien Miller Harris. **Internet :** Accès haut débit pour 20 GBP par jour.

1

2

3

1   Remedies/Heilmittel/Remèdes

Neal's Yard Remedies
15 Neal's Yard
London WC2H 9DH
Tel: +44 20 7379 7222
www.nealsyardremedies.com
Tube: Covent Garden

Neal's Yard Remedies opened this charming little shop in a hippy dippy courtyard 25 years ago. Surrounded by groovy hair salons, tattoo parlours and vegetarian restaurants, the company has stuck to its philosophy of providing natural, organic, handmade products using its own herbs grown in Dorset. The signature blue bottles are as practical as they are pretty: they cut down 97% of UV light and protect the sensitive herbal extracts.

Neal's Yard Remedies wurde vor 25 Jahren in diesem alternativen Hinterhof gegründet und ist heute von coolen Hairsalons, Tattoo Shops und vegetarischen Restaurants umgeben. Das Unternehmen stellt natürliche, handgemachte Bio-Heilmittel und -pflegeprodukte aus eigens dafür angebauten Kräutern in Dorset her. Die dunkelblauen Fläschchen sind praktisch – sie schützen die empfindlichen Kräuterextrakte vor UV-Strahlung – und schön anzuschauen.

Voilà 25 ans que Neal's Yard a ouvert sa charmante boutique dans cette cour aux accents baba cool. Entourée de salons de coiffure branchés, d'échoppes de tatoueurs et de restaurants végétariens, elle est restée fidèle à sa philosophie : proposer des produits naturels, bios et artisanaux à base de ses propres herbes cultivées dans le Dorset. Aussi jolis que pratiques, ses flacons bleus protègent les extraits végétaux des UV.

2   British Cheese/Britischer Käse/
     Fromagerie britannique

Neal's Yard Dairy
17 Shorts Gardens
London WC2H 9UP
Tel: +44 20 7240 5700

www.nealsyarddairy.co.uk
Tube: Covent Garden

If you love cheese, you'll love Neal's Yard Dairy. Since opening in 1979, it's been providing Londoners with all-natural, hand-crafted cheeses and yoghurts. You can get everything here from Italian-style Mozzarella di Bufalo to a Gloucestershire favourite known as Stinking Bishop. All the Dairy's cheeses are seasonal, so you may not find what you came in for – but you'll no doubt find something just as good.

Die Neal's Yard Dairy ist ein Schlaraffenland für Liebhaber britischer Käsesorten. Seit 1979 werden hier Londoner mit handgemachtem Käse und Joghurt aus natürlichen Zutaten verwöhnt. Ob ein Mozzarella di Bufala oder ein Stinking Bishop aus Gloucestershire –man findet so ziemlich alles. Die Käse werden saisonal hergestellt, deshalb findet man nicht immer, was man sucht. Ein Ersatz wird aber garantiert genau so gut schmecken.

Amateurs de fromages, Neal's Yard Dairy est faite pour vous. Depuis 1979, cette boutique approvisionne les Londoniens en fromages et yaourts naturels et artisanaux, de la mozzarella de buffle à « l'évêque puant », une spécialité du Gloucestershire. Les produits étant saisonniers, vous n'y trouverez peut-être pas ce que vous cherchez mais vous ressortirez certainement avec autre chose d'aussi bon.

3   Restaurant/Restaurant/Restaurant

The Ivy
1–5 West Street
London WC2H 9NQ
Tel: +44 20 7836 4751
www.the-ivy.co.uk
Tube: Covent Garden/Leicester Square

If celebrity spotting is your game, this is the place to do it; everyone from David Beckham to Madonna has dined here. The staff has seen them all, and is suitably blasé about the bold-faced names dotted around the room. The food's really quite good, with an emphasis on British stal-

warts such as steak-and-kidney pie and kedgeree, and for dessert, nursery classics like rice pudding.

David Beckham, Madonna, so ziemlich jeder prominente Namen hat hier im klassischen Ambiente diniert. Die hochkarätige Prominenz kann dem Personal leider manchmal etwas zu Kopf steigen. Doch dafür ist das Essen wirklich gut. Auf der Karte findet man vor allem britische Spezialiäten wie Steaks, Kidney Pie und Kedgeree. Und zum Nachtisch werden Köstlichkeiten aus Kindertagen wie Reispudding aufgetragen.

Si la chasse aux célébrités est votre sport favori, foncez-y. Tout le monde y a dîné, de David Beckham à Madonna. Par conséquent, le personnel est blasé à souhait. Très bonne, la cuisine met l'accent sur les classiques anglais tels que la steak-and-kidney pie et le kedgeree, avec de délicieux desserts de notre enfance comme le riz au lait.

4   Ballet/Ballett/Ballet

Royal Opera House
Bow Street
London WC2E 9DD
Tel: +44 20 7304 4000
www.royaloperahouse.org
Tube: Covent Garden

The ROH is the third theatre to be constructed on this site. Since its opening night on 7 December, 1732 it's had an eventful history: it was twice destroyed by fire (in 1808 and 1856) and was used as a dance hall during the Second World War. Following a 200 GBP million facelift in 1999, it is once again a London showpiece. In the 1960s and 1970s the partnership of Margot Fonteyn and Rudolf Nureyev made the company famous and the classical pieces (Giselle, Romeo & Juliet) are still performed today with the same choreographies and an excellent ensemble.

Es ist bereits das dritte Gebäude, in dem das ROH untergebracht ist. Es feierte am 7. Dezember 1732 seine allererste Pre-

© Martin Charles

4

5

6

iere und brannte dann zweimal, 1808
nd 1856, ab. Im Zweiten Weltkrieg diente
s sogar als kommunaler Tanzsaal. Zu
inem der Vorzeigestücke Londons wurde
s 1999 nach einer 200 Millionen GBP
euren Renovierung. Unvergessen sind die
960er und 1970er, als Margot Fonteyn
nd Rudolf Nureyev das Haus zu Welt-
uhm führten. Giselle und Romeo und Julia
erden auch heute auf gleich hohem
iveau aufgeführt.

roisième théâtre érigé sur ce site, le ROH
connu une histoire mouvementée depuis
on inauguration le 7 décembre 1732.
étruit à deux reprises par le feu (en
808 et 1856), il fut converti en dancing
endant la Seconde Guerre mondiale.
près un lifting de 200 millions GBP en
999, c'est de nouveau un joyau londo-
en. Dans les années 60 et 70, Margot
onteyn et Rudolf Noureïev ont rendu sa
ompagnie célèbre et on y donne encore
s grands classiques (Giselle, Roméo et
uliette) dans les mêmes chorégraphies.
orchestre est excellent.

Museum/Museum/Musée

ir John Soane's Museum
3 Lincoln's Inn Fields
ondon WC2A 3BP
el: +44 20 7405 2107
ww.soane.org
ube: Holborn

his delightful townhouse museum was
nce the home of Sir John Soane (1753-
837), an architect and member of the
oyal Academy. Sir John was a collector of
ntiquities, stained glass, paintings (among
hers by Canaletto and Turner), drawings
y t.e. Christopher Wren and Piranesi) and
rnishings. Sir John and his family lived in
e house though it's hard to believe there
as any room for them.

eses entzückende Stadthaus, das heute
n Museum ist, gehörte dem Architekten
nd Mitglied der Royal Academy, Sir John
oane (1753–1837). Sir John war passio-
erter Sammler von Antiquitäten, Bunt-
as, Gemälden (z. B. von Canaletto und
rner), Zeichnungen (beispielsweise von

Christopher Wren und Piranesi) und Ein-
richtungsstücken. Sir John lebte hier mit
seiner Familie – es ist heute schwer vor-
stellbar, wie alle darin Platz fanden.

Cette merveilleuse maison musée était
autrefois la demeure de sir John Soane
(1753-1837), architecte, membre de la
Royal Academy, collectionneur d'antiquités,
de vitraux, de tableaux (dont des Canaletto
et des Turner), de dessins (Christopher
Wren, Piranèse…) et de mobilier. Il y en a
tellement qu'on se demande où vivaient sir
John et sa famille!

6   Silver/Silberwaren/Argenterie

London Silver Vaults
Chancery House
53–64 Chancery Lane
London WC2A 1QS
Tel: +44 20 7242 3844
www.thesilvervaults.com
Tube: Chancery Lane

With more than 25 dealers hawking everything from thimbles to elaborate cande-
labra, you can bet that if it's made of silver,
you'll find it here. This is the place em-
bassies go to replace missing teapots and
decorators go to find objets d'art for their
celebrity clients. The emphasis is on
household goods, but some dealers also
sell jewellery.

Wer irgendetwas aus Silber sucht, wird
hier fündig. Mehr als 25 Händler bieten
zwischen thimbles und elaborierten Kande-
labern die ganze Palette an. In den Silver
Vaults machen sich Botschaftsangestellte
auf die Suche nach einem Ersatz für die
verloren gegangene Teekanne, und Innen-
dekorateure finden Objets d'Art für ihre
prominenten Kunden. Die meisten Händler
haben sich auf Haushaltswaren spezialisiert, ein paar führen aber auch Schmuck.

Avec plus de 25 marchands vendant tout,
de la timbale au candélabre ouvragé, c'est
le paradis de l'argenterie. C'est ici que les
ambassades viennent remplacer les théiè-
res disparues et que les décorateurs déni-
chent des pièces rares pour leurs clients
célèbres. L'accent est sur les arts ména-

gers mais certains vendent également des
bijoux.

Personal Finds/Eigene Entdeckungen/
Découvertes personnelles:

_____

_____

_____

_____

_____

_____

_____

_____

_____

_____

_____

_____

_____

_____

_____

_____

_____

_____

_____

Charlotte Street Hotel

15 Charlotte Street, London W1T 1RJ
☎ +44 20 7806 2000   📠 +44 20 7806 2002
charlotte@firmdale.com
www.charlottestreethotel.com
Tube: Goodge Street
Booking: www.great-escapes-hotels.com

Charlotte Street Hotel

The Charlotte Street Hotel is a perfect reflection of the neighbourhood in which it sits. Fitzrovia, just north of groovy Soho and west of intellectual Bloomsbury, is a healthy mix of the cool and the clever. The hotel holds court on buzzing Charlotte Street among the small galleries, cute shops and eclectic restaurants frequented by advertising executives, film editors, students and artists. The hotel was inspired by the Bloomsbury Group, which included amongst its set the writer Virginia Woolf. There is a sense of calm that pervades this hotel, much like entering a fancy library. It's a beautiful mix of oak-pannelled walls with a cat statue by Botero guarding the premises. Oscar, the restaurant and bar, has an air of low-key glamour and has been so popular that it has been expanded. Whether it's for a business breakfast or the cocktail hour, it's a venue that is particularly great in summer when the big windows can be opened to the street and patrons can spill out onto the sidewalk.

Das Charlotte Street Hotel passt bestens in seine Umgebung. Fitzrovia, das nördlich an das unternehmenslustige Soho und westlich an das eher intellektuelle Bloomsbury grenzt, ist die perfekte Mischung aus beidem. Das Hotel liegt an der lebendigen Charlotte Street mit kleinen Galerien, entzückenden Läden und eklektischen Restaurants, die Werber, Filmemacher, Studenten und Künstler zu ihren Gästen zählen. Inspiriert wurde das Hotel von der Bloombury Gruppe, der unter anderem die Schriftstellerin Virginia Woolf angehörte. So wie in einer ehrwürdigen Bibliothek herrscht hier eine wunderbare Ruhe. Eichenpaneele zieren die Wände, der Eingang wird von einer Katzenplastik von Botero bewacht und Oscar Restaurant und Bar sind von schlichtem Glamour. Das Oscar ist so beliebt, dass es vergrößert werden musste. Hier ist es besonders schön im Sommer, wenn die großen Fenster geöffnet werden und die Gäste draußen auf dem Gehsteig sitzen.

Le Charlotte Street Hotel reflète parfaitement son quartier, Fitzrovia, situé entre le Soho branché au nord et Bloomsbury l'intellectuel à l'ouest. La rue animée accueille des petites galeries, des boutiques charmantes et des restaurants éclectiques fréquentés par des gens de la pub, du cinéma, des étudiants et des artistes. L'hôtel, décontracté et raffiné, a été inspiré par le groupe de Bloomsbury, dont Virginia Wolf faisait partie. Il y règne un calme serein, un peu comme dans une élégante bibliothèque. Ses belles boiseries en chêne sont gardées par un chat sculpté par Botero. Le chic discret d'Oscar, le restaurant-bar, a rencontré un tel succès que les lieux ont dû être agrandis. Pour un petit-déjeuner d'affaires ou un cocktail, c'est un endroit idéal en été quand les grandes fenêtres s'ouvrent pour faire terrasse sur le trottoir.

Rates: From 285 € (195 GBP) excl. VAT.
Rooms: 52.
Restaurant: Oscar.
History: The building the hotel now occupies used to be a dental warehouse.
X-Factor: The artworks by Vanessa Bell, Duncan Grant, Roger Fry and Henry Lamb, as well as Roger Cecil.
Internet: WiFi in all rooms at 20 GBP per day.

Preise: ab 285 € (195 GBP) exkl. VAT.
Zimmer: 52.
Restaurant: Oscar.
Geschichte: Das Hotelgebäude diente früher als Lager für Dentalprodukte.
X-Faktor: Kunstwerke von Vanessa Bell, Duncan Grant, Roger Fry, Henry Lamb und Roger Cecil.
Internet: WiFi in allen Zimmern für 20 GBP pro Tag.

Prix : À partir de 285 € (195 GBP), IVA non comprise.
Chambres : 52.
Restauration : Oscar.
Histoire : Le bâtiment abritait autrefois un entrepôt de dentisterie.
Le « petit plus » : Les œuvres originales de Vanessa Bell, Duncan Grant, Roger Fry, Henry Lamb et Roger Cecil.
Internet : WiFi dans toutes les chambres pour 20 GBP par jour.

1

2

3

---

1   Umbrellas/Schrimgeschäft/Parapluies

James Smith & Sons
Hazelwood House
53 New Oxford Street
London WC1A 1BL
Tel: +44 20 7836 4731
www.james-smith.co.uk
Tube: Tottenham Court Road

This is where to turn when the British weather does what it does best: pour with rain. Locals go to this legendary shop – and have done since 1857 – for the tried-and-tested brands of umbrellas, and some contemporary styles (the line by Paul Smith, for example). There are few London rituals so time-honoured as a visit to Smith's, rain or shine. And its classic walking sticks make great souvenirs.

Sollte sich das britische Wetter von seiner besten Seite zeigen und wieder mal Regen schicken, sollte man diesen Ort aufsuchen. In diesem legendären Geschäft decken sich die Londoner seit 1857 mit Schirmen ein. Neben altbewährten Modellen gibt es auch neue, etwa solche von Paul Smith. Es gibt wenige Rituale, die den Test der Zeit so überstehen wie der Besuch bei Smith & Sons. Zu den Klassikern gehören die Gehstöcke: Sie sind super Geschenke.

Quand le climat anglais est fidèle à sa réputation, à savoir qu'il pleut, c'est l'endroit où aller. Les Londoniens fréquentent cette boutique légendaire depuis 1857 pour s'équiper en parapluies solides ou en marques contemporaines (comme la ligne de Paul Smith). Même si le soleil est au rendez-vous, une visite chez Smith est un rituel londonien. Ses cannes classiques font de beaux cadeaux.

---

2   Asian Restaurant/Asiatisches Restaurant/Restaurant asiatique

Hakkasan
8 Hanway Place
London W1P 9HD
Tel: +44 20 7927 7000
Tube: Tottenham Court Road

Hakkasan benefits from its central location, just off Tottenham Court Road. It opened in 2001 and is owned by Alan Yau, who launched the successful budget chains Wagamama and Busaba Eathai, but it is decidedly swish, with dim sum to die for and cocktails from classic to exotic, such as the Lychee Martini. The atmosphere is dark and dreamy with Asian touches, and the food is excellent.

Hakkasan liegt zentral in der Nähe der Tottenham Court Road. Das Lokal wurde 2001 von Alan Yau eröffnet, dem auch die erfolgreichen (und preiswerten) Wagamama und Busaba Eathai Restaurants gehören. Die Dim Sums hier sind himmlisch und die Auswahl an Cocktails reicht von klassisch bis exotisch, wie zum Beispiel der Lychee Martini. Das Interieur mit asiatischen Akzenten ist dunkel und etwas verträumt.

Ouvert en 2001, ce restaurant central (à deux pas de Tottenham Court Road) appartient à Alan Yau, créateur des chaînes bon marché Wagamama et Busaba Eathai. Chic, à l'atmosphère tamisée et onirique saupoudrée de touches asiatiques, sa cuisine est exquise (le Dim Sum est à mourir !). Les cocktails vont du classique à l'exotique, comme le martini aux lychees.

---

3   Japanese Restaurant/Japanisches Restaurant/Restaurant japonais

Roka
37 Charlotte Street
London W1T 1RR
Tel: +44 20 7580 6464
www.rokarestaurant.com
Tube: Goodge Street

Roka first moved into its designer digs in 2004 and now it has a true blue loyal following. You can eat melt-in-your-mouth finger food while people outside gawk through the expansive glass façade. A traditional Japanese grill in the centre of the room provides a distraction when conversation isn't enough. Finish the night downstairs at the Shochu cocktail lounge.

Seit Roka 2004 in dieses Designer-Lokal gezogen ist, hat es eine treue Gefolgschaft. Das Finger-Food ist so köstlich, dass es im Mund schmilzt. Doch aufgepasst: Durch die riesige Fensterfront wird man beim Genießen von Passanten beobachtet. In der Mitte des Raums steht ein traditionell japanischer Grill. Geht der Gesprächsstoff aus, sorgt er für Unterhaltung. Ein Besuch der Shochu Cocktail Lounge im Untergeschoss schließt den Abend perfekt ab.

Depuis qu'il a emménagé dans ses locaux super branchés en 2004, Roka a développé une clientèle d'accros. Dégustez-y de succulents amuse-gueules pendant que les badauds vous observent ébahis devant la grande façade en verre. Un grill traditionnel japonais au centre de la salle vous divertira si la conversation tarit. Finissez la soirée au bar Shochu au sous-sol.

---

4   Spanish Restaurant/Spanisches Restaurant/Restaurant espagnol

Navarro's
67 Charlotte Street
London W1T 4PH
Tel: +44 20 7637 7713
www.navarros.co.uk
Tube: Goodge Street

Navarro's serves delicious no-nonsense Spanish-style tapas and is entirely without attitude. Its decor, like its atmosphere, is lively, with Moorish tiles on walls with archways leading from nook to nook. Tapas plates are filled with big, fat chunks of meat, sizzling prawns and potatoes, all light on the grease. While it may not sound glamorous, it is hugely popular and very hard to get a table.

Im Navarro's gibt's köstliche spanische Tapas ohne Firlefanz. Umso kitschiger allerdings das Dekor: maurische Kacheln und Torbögen, die den Raum in verschiedene Bereiche unterteilen. Auf den Tapas-Tellern türmen sich große Fleischstücke, brutzelnde Garnelen und Kartoffeln – alles mit wenig Fett zubereitet. Zugegeben, all dies klingt nicht besonders aufregend.

4

5

6

Doch das Lokal ist sehr beliebt: Es ist schwierig, einen Tisch zu ergattern.

Navarro's sert de délicieux tapas sans chichis dans un décor coloré et une ambiance animée. Les murs sont tapissés d'azulejos et des arches mènent de recoin en recoin. Les assiettes débordent de viandes, de crevettes croustillantes et de pommes de terre sans dégouliner de graisse. Cela ne paraît peut-être pas glamour mais il est pris d'assaut tous les soirs et il est difficile d'obtenir une table.

5　Picnic/Picknick/Pique-nique

Mahatma Gandhi Statue in Tavistock Square

Tavistock Square
London WC1 H
Tube: Russell Square/Euston Square

Tavistock Square is also known as "the peace park", largely because of its serene-looking 1968 monument to Gandhi by British sculptor Fredda Brilliant. Since the 1960s a cherry tree has been planted to memorialise the victims of Hiroshima; a maple grown to mark the International Year of Peace; and a granite monument raised in honour of conscientious objectors.

Der Tavistock Square wird auch „Friedenspark" genannt. Dies hauptsächlich wegen des Gandhi-Monuments der britischen Bildhauerin Fredda Brilliant von 1968. Zudem wurde hier in den 1960ern ein Kirschbaum im Gedenken an die Opfer von Hiroschima gepflanzt und ein Ahornbaum zum Internationalen Jahr des Friedens. Und zu Ehren der Wehrdienstverweigerer wurde ein Monument aus Granit erstellt.

Tavistock Square est surtout connu comme « le parc de la paix » en raison du monument à Gandhi de la sculptrice britannique Fredda Brilliant érigé en 1968. Depuis les années 60, un cerisier a été planté en souvenir des victimes d'Hiroshima, un érable célèbre l'année internationale de la paix et un monument en granit rend hommage aux objecteurs de conscience.

6　Museum/Museum/Musée

The Charles Dickens Museum

48 Doughty Street
London WC1N 2LX
Tel: +44 20 7405 2127
www.dickensmuseum.com
Tube: Chancery Lane/Russell Square

This house in Bloomsbury where Charles Dickens lived from 1837 to 1839 is a slice of British history all its own – and a very digestible one. This is the only one of the author's many London homes that wasn't demolished, the place where he holed up while writing Nicholas Nickleby and Oliver Twist. To celebrate those years, the curators have converted it into a museum of Dickens-abilia.

In diesem Haus in Bloomsbury lebte Charles Dickens zwischen 1837 und 1839 – es ist ein Stück britische Geschichte. Von allen Londoner Häusern, in denen der Schriftsteller lebte, ist es das einzige, das nicht abgerissen wurde, und hier hat er Nicholas Nickleby und Oliver Twist geschrieben. Heute ist das Haus ein Museum, das mit vielen Dickens Erinnerungsstücken Leben und Werk des großen Schriftstellers ehrt.

Située à Bloomsbury, c'est la seule des nombreuses maisons londoniennes de Charles Dickens encore debout (il y a vécu de 1837 à 1839). Il s'y est cloîtré pour écrire Nicholas Nickleby et Oliver Twist. Les conservateurs y ont rassemblé des objets personnels de l'écrivain, ses manuscrits et des éditions rares de ses œuvres.

Personal Finds/Eigene Entdeckungen/
Découvertes personnelles:

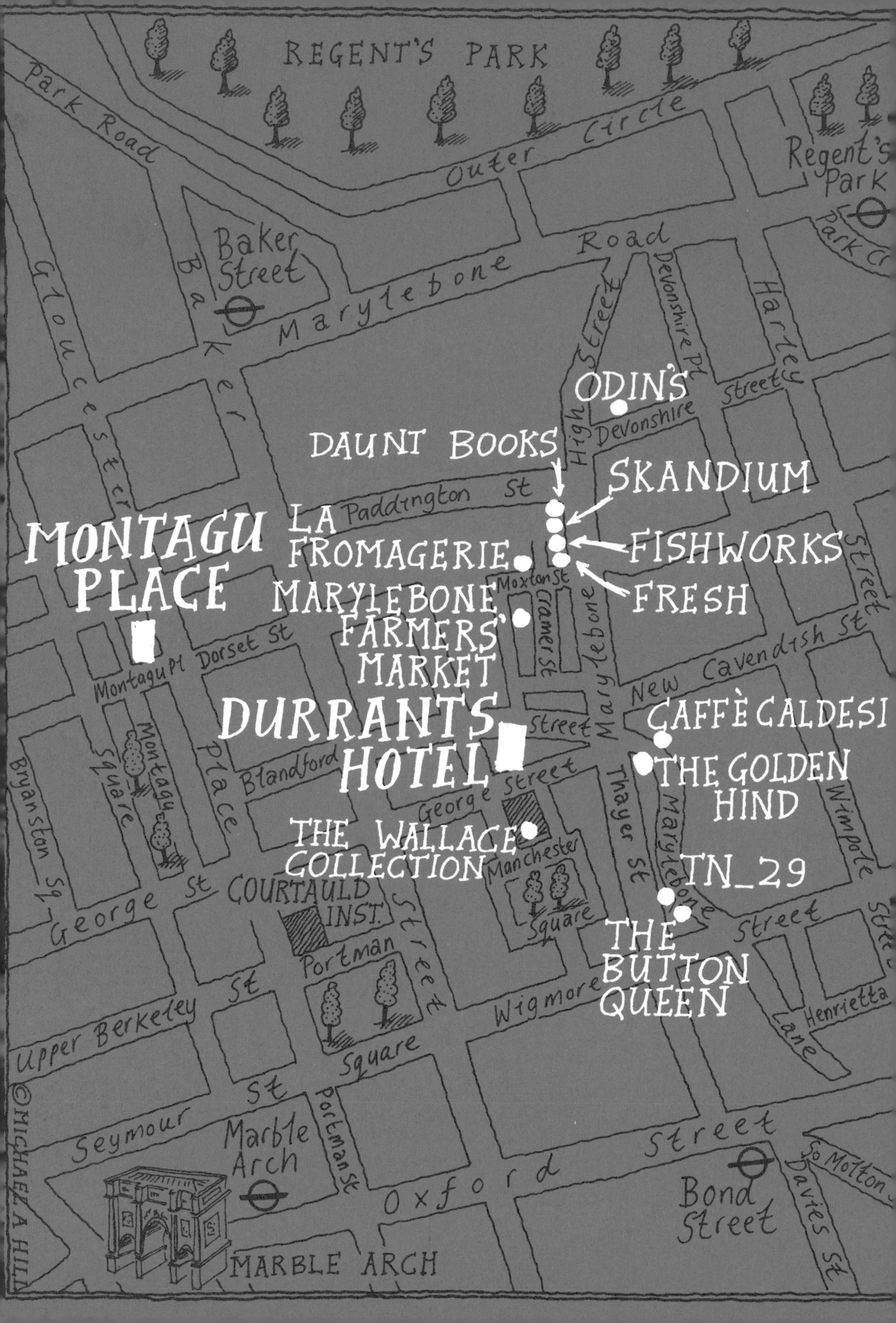

REGENT'S PARK

Park Road

Baker Street

Outer Circle

Regent's Park

Marylebone Road

Gloucester

Baker Street

Harley Street

High Street

Devonshire Pl

Devonshire Street

ODIN'S

DAUNT BOOKS

Paddington St

SKANDIUM

MONTAGU PLACE

LA FROMAGERIE

Moxton St

Cramer St

FISHWORKS

FRESH

MARYLEBONE FARMERS' MARKET

Montagu Pl

Dorset St

Marylebone Street

New Cavendish St

Wimpole St

DURRANTS HOTEL

CAFFÈ CALDESI

THE GOLDEN HIND

Bryanston Sq

Montagu Square

Blandford Street

George Street

Thayer St

Marylebone

TN_29

George St

THE WALLACE COLLECTION

Manchester Square

Street

THE BUTTON QUEEN

COURTAULD INST.

Portman

Wigmore

Henrietta

Upper Berkeley

St

Street

Square

Portman St

Seymour

Marble Arch

Oxford Street

Bond Street

So Molton

Davies St

©MICHAELA HILL

MARBLE ARCH

W1H

Marylebone

1 Museum/Museum/Musée
The Wallace Collection

2 Books/Bücher/Librairie
Daunt Books

3 Fishmonger & Restaurant/Fischhändler & Restaurant/
Poissonnerie & Restaurant
FishWorks

4 Restaurant/Restaurant/Restaurant
Odin's

5 Shoes/Schuhe/Chaussures
TN_29

6 Buttons/Knöpfe/Boutons
The Button Queen

---

1 Market/Markt/Marché
Marylebone Farmers' Market

2 Food & Café/Feinkost & Café/Épicerie fine et café
La Fromagerie

3 Beauty Products/Kosmetik/Produits de beauté
Fresh

4 Scandinavian Design/Skandinavisches Design/Design scandinave
Skandium

5 Fish'n'Chips/Fish'n'Chips/Fish'n'Chips
The Golden Hind

6 Italian Restaurant/Italienisches Restaurant/Restaurant italien
Caffè Caldesi

110 **Durrants Hotel**
120 **Montagu Place**

Durrants Hotel

George Street, London W1H 5BJ
☎ +44 20 7935 8131   📠 +44 20 7487 3510
enquiries@durrantshotel.co.uk
www.durrantshotel.co.uk
Tube: Bond Street
Booking: www.great-escapes-hotels.com

Durrants Hotel

Durrants Hotel has been owned by the Miller family since 1921 and is one of the last hotels in private hands in London. Charles Miller, the current owner's grandfather, brought together the three Georgian townhouses to create this 92-room inn just off Marylebone High Street in Mayfair. Its location is ideal for visiting places such as the Wallace Collection and for shopping in this very smart district. Largely a business hotel during the week, families and tourists descend on weekends and bring the place to life. With its oak-pannelled walls, wooden staircase and the traditional English textiles in all the rooms, Durrants is very much a slice of old world London in a historic neighbourhood. The Grill Room is a lovely place to have a traditional Sunday roast while the George Bar is a cozy little nook in which to have a cocktail before heading out for dinner. The various little lounges with their comfortable leather chairs are also a nice touch.

Seit 1921 gehört das Hotel der Familie Miller und ist damit eines der letzten Hotels in London im Privatbesitz. Charles Miller, der Großvater des heutigen Besitzers, kaufte in Mayfair drei nebeneinander liegende, im Georgian-Stil gebaute Stadthäuser in der Nähe der Marylebone Hight Street und machte daraus ein Hotel mit 92 Zimmern. Es liegt direkt hinter der wunderbaren Wallace Collection und nicht weit von Mayfair mit seinen eleganten Läden. Während unter der Woche vor allem Geschäftsleute absteigen, wird es hier an Wochenenden dank dem Einzug von Familien und Touristen etwas belebter. Mit den eichengetäfelten Wänden, den knarrenden Holztreppen und traditionellen englischen Textilien in den Zimmern ist das Durrants ein Stück altes London mitten in einem historischen Stadtviertel. Der Grill Room ist ein sehr intimes, typisch englisches Restaurant und die Bar ist klein und gemütlich, im Winter wird sie von einem Kamin beheizt und ist perfekt für ein Cocktail vor oder einem Nightcup nach dem Essen.

Dans la famille Miller depuis 1921, Le Durrants Hotel est l'un des derniers hôtels de Londres appartenant à des particuliers. Charles Miller, grand-père du propriétaire actuel, a réuni trois maisons du XVIIIe siècle pour créer ces 92 chambres à deux pas de Marylebone High Street à Mayfair, un emplacement idéal pour visiter la Wallace Collection ou faire du shopping dans ce coin très sélect. Accueillant principalement des hommes d'affaire pendant la semaine, il prend vie le week-end quand arrive les familles et les touristes. Avec ses boiseries en chêne, son escalier en bois et ses tissus traditionnels anglais dans toutes les chambres, c'est toute une tranche du vieux Londres dans un quartier historique. La Grill Room est parfaite pour la grillade traditionnelle du dimanche et le George Bar cos y à souhait pour prendre un verre avant de sortir dîner. Autre touche agréable : les petits salons avec leurs profonds fauteuils en cuir.

Rates: Prices from 150 € (105 GBP) excl. VAT.
Rooms: 92 (4 suites).
Restaurants: The Grill Room, George Bar.
History: The building has been around since 1790 and the hotel served as a coaching inn before it became a hotel in 1921.
X-Factor: The pretty wooden post boxes in the lobby hark back to a long-lost era.
Internet: Broadband access at 10 GBP per day.

Preise: Ab 150 € (105 GBP) exkl. VAT.
Zimmer: 92 (4 Suiten).
Restaurant: The Grill Room, George Bar.
Geschichte: Das Gebäude wurde 1790 erbaut. Bevor es 1921 in ein Hotel umgewandelt wurde, diente das Haus als Poststations-Herberge.
X-Faktor: Die hübschen Holz-Postfächer in der Lobby erinnern an die gute alte Zeit.
Internet: Breitbandanschluss für 10 GBP pro Tag.

Prix : À partir de 150 € (105 GBP), TVA non comprise.
Chambres : 92 (4 suites).
Restauration : The Grill Room, George Bar.
Histoire : Le bâtiment existe depuis 1790 et a été un relais/auberge avant de devenir un hôtel en 1921.
Le « petit plus » : Les jolies boîtes à lettres en bois dans le lobby évoquent une époque révolue.
Internet : Accès haut débit pour 10 GBP par jour.

1

2

1   Museum/Museum/Musée

The Wallace Collection

Hertford House
Manchester Square
London W1U 3BN
Tel: +44 20 7563 9500
www.wallacecollection.org
Tube: Bond Street

The Wallace Collection is truly a national treasure. One of the best private collections ever amassed by one family, it was given to the nation by Lady Wallace, widow of Sir Richard Wallace, in 1897. It includes the rococo painting The Swing by Fragonard, which is one of the most beautiful paintings in art history. Once you've seen everything, sit in the light beamed Café Bagatelle in the covered courtyard and discuss.

Die Wallace Collection gehört zu den Nationalschätzen Großbritanniens. Sie gilt als eine der besten Privatsammlungen überhaupt und wurde 1897 von Lady Wallace, der Witwe von Sir John Wallace, der Nation vermacht. Zur Sammlung gehört auch das Rokoko-Gemälde „Die Schaukel" von Fragonard, das als eines der schönsten Gemälde der ganzen Kunstgeschichte gilt. Nach der Besichtung kann man sich im lichtdurchfluteten Café „Bagatelle", das sich im überdachten Innenhof befindet, erfrischen.

Véritable trésor national, cette collection privée, une des plus belles jamais créées par une seule famille, fut donnée à la nation en 1897 par lady Wallace, veuve de sir Richard Wallace. Vous y verrez entre autres le fameux chef-d'œuvre rococo de Fragonard, « L'escarpolette ». Une fois que vous aurez tout vu, vous pourrez en discuter sous la verrière du café Café Bagatelle, dans la cour centrale.

2   Books/Bücher/Librairie

Daunt Books

83–84 Marylebone High Street
London W1U 4 QW
Tel: +44 20 7224 2295

www.dauntbooks.co.uk
Tube: Baker Street/Bond Street

This is easily one of the most beautiful bookshops in London, housed in an original Edwardian building with oak galleries and skylights that fill the store with natural light. It has a fabulous selection of children's books, fiction, non-fiction as well as an extensive travel section that has little competition in this city. Staff are friendly, knowledgeable and helpful. Get a novel by Jane Austen and read it in the beautiful garden on Manchester Square in front of the Wallace collection.

Ein Gebäude aus der Zeit Edwards VII., Eichengalerien, Oberlichter, die den Raum mit Licht durchfluten: Dies ist die schönste Buchhandlung ganz Londons. Kinderbücher, Romane, Sachbücher, die Auswahl ist fantastisch; das Angebot an Reisebüchern so groß wie nirgends. Das Personal steht mit großem Wissen hilfreich zur Seite. Tipp: einen Roman von Jane Austen erstehen und ihn im lauschigen Manchester Square, gleich vor der Wallace Collection, lesen.

Située dans un bâtiment de la Belle Époque, avec des galeries en chêne et une verrière qui l'inonde de lumière naturelle, c'est de loin la plus belle librairie de Londres. On y trouve un merveilleux choix de livres d'enfant, de romans, d'essais ainsi qu'un large rayon de livres de voyage comme on en trouve peu en ville. Le personnel est charmant, érudit et serviable. Achetez-y un roman de Jane Austen à lire dans le beau square Manchester devant la Wallace Collection.

3   Fishmonger & Restaurant/Fischhändler & Restaurant/Poissonnerie & Restaurant

FishWorks

89 Marylebone High Street
London W1U 4QW
Tel: +44 20 7935 9796
www.fishworks.co.uk
Tube: Baker Street/Bond Street

FishWorks is charming in that it is both a

fishmongers and a restaurant all rolled into one. Walk by the deep blue exterior, stop and gaze at the variety of fresh fish staring back at you, asking you to eat them. Drop in for fabulous seafood in the café-style restaurant for lunch. Or, better yet, get a takeaway and have a picnic in one of the beautiful parks of London.

FishWorks ist ein reizendes Lokal zwischen Fischhändler und Restaurant. Schon nur das meerblaue Äußere macht Lust auf den frischen Fisch, der in der Auslage darauf wartet, gegessen zu werden. Ob Fisch oder Meeresfrüchte, die Gerichte in diesem einfachen Café-Restaurant sind einfach köstlich. Wer Lust auf ein Picknick in einer der wunderbaren Parkanlagen Londons hat, kann ein Takeaway-Menü bestellen.

Le charme de FishWorks est que c'est à la fois une poissonnerie et un restaurant. Longez sa façade bleue et admirez la variété de poissons frais qui ne demandent qu'à être mangés. Puis dégustez-les dans le formidable petit restaurant sans prétention ou, mieux encore, faites emballer votre repas pour pique-niquer dans un des beaux parcs de Londres.

4   Restaurant/Restaurant/Restaurant

Odin's

27 Devonshire Street
London W1G 6PL
Tel: +44 20 7935 7296
Fax: +44 20 7493 8309
Tube: Baker Street

The first thing that you should know about Odin's is that it is closed on weekends. It has been around since 1966 so, really, it doesn't need to worry. Odin's is as perfect for a serious business meeting as for a romantic dinner a deux. The food is beautifully prepared English fare (beef, oysters, game) and puddings are not to be missed. Service is impeccable.

Das Wichtigste, das man über Odin's wissen sollte: An Wochenenden bleibt das Restaurant geschlossen. Das ist bereits seit 1966 so und hat seinem Erfolg keinen Abbruch getan. Perfekt für ein geschäftli-

4

5

6

ches Treffen, aber auch für ein romantisches Dinner zu zweit. Hier gibt's schön
zubereitete englische Gerichte mit Rind,
Austern und Wild, und natürlich Puddings.
Nicht nur das: Der Service ist tadellos.

Avant tout, sachez qu'Odin's est fermé le
week-end ; toutefois, pas de panique, ce
restaurant existe depuis 1966. C'est l'endroit idéal pour un rendez vous d'affaires
sérieux comme pour un dîner romantique
en tête à tête. La cuisine anglaise (bœuf,
huîtres, gibier) est superbement présentée
et les puddings sont un must. Le service
est impeccable.

---

5   Shoes/Schuhe/Chaussures

TN_29
29 Marylebone Lane
London W1U 2NQ
Tel: +44 20 7935 0039
www.TN29.com
Tube: Bond Street

Nestled amongst the traditional sausage
shops, delicatessens and furniture stores
on Marylebone Lane is Tracey Neuls' seriously groovy shoe shop, TN_29, which
opened in 2005. Originally from Vancouver
Island in Canada, Neuls hangs her fusion
of dressy/sneaker shoes on ribbons from
the ceiling rather than sitting them on
shelves. Who said Canadians are boring?

Nicht nur die Lage zwischen althergebrach-
ten Wurstereien, Delikatessläden und
Möbelgeschäften ist außergewöhnlich: In
Tracey Neuls Schuhboutique TN_29 bau-
meln ihre individuellen bequemen Kreationen
an Bändern von der Decke. Die Designerin
stammt ursprünglich aus Vancouver Island
in Kanada und hat 2005 an der Marylebone
Lane ihr erstes Geschäft eröffnet.

Blottie entre des charcuteries, des épice-
ries et des magasins de meubles, la formidable boutique de chaussures de Tracey
Neul, TN_29, a ouvert en 2005. Originaire
de Vancouver, Neul suspend ses souliers
mi-soirée mi-baskets au plafond avec des
rubans plutôt que de les présenter sur des
étagères. Qui a dit que les Canadiens
manquaient d'originalité?

6   Buttons/Knöpfe/Boutons

The Button Queen
19 Marylebone Lane
London W1U 2NF
Tel: +44 20 7935 1505
www.thebuttonqueen.co.uk
Tube: Bond Street

Rows and rows of browning paper boxes
hold thousands and thousands of buttons
(new and antique) at The Button Queen,
which has been in this location since the
1960s. It started as a market stall in
south London by Mrs Frith, who was
nicknamed The Button Queen. Her son,
Martyn, now runs the shop and counts
American button collectors, fashion designers and costume designers amongst
his loyal clientele.

Seit den 1960ern reihen sich in diesem
Geschäft zahlreiche braune, mit Tausenden alten und neuen Knöpfen gefüllte,
Pappschachteln. The Button Queen war
ursprünglich ein Marktstand in Südlondon
und gehörte einer Mrs Frith, die als
„Button Queen" (Knopfkönigin) bekannt
war. Heute führt ihr Sohn Martyn das
Geschäft. Zur treuen Kundschaft zählen
amerikanische Knopfsammler genau so
wie Mode- und Kostümdesigner.

Après avoir commencé avec un étal sur un
marché du sud de Londres, Mme Frith, «
la reine du bouton », a ouvert sa boutique
dans les années 60, tenue aujourd'hui par
son fils Martyn. Collectionneurs américains,
créateurs de mode et costumiers hantent
régulièrement ses rayons croulant sous les
boîtes en papier jauni qui renferment des
milliers et des milliers de boutons, nou-
veaux et anciens.

Personal Finds/Eigene Entdeckungen/
Découvertes personnelles:

Montagu Place

2 Montagu Place, London W1H 2ER
☏ +44 20 7467 2777 ☐ +44 20 7467 2778
stay@montagu-place.co.uk
www.montagu-place.co.uk
Tube: Baker Street
Booking: www.great-escapes-hotels.com

Montagu Place

If less really is more, then Montagu Place has it right. Opened in 2006, this small, simple hotel has three types of rooms: Comfy, Fancy and Swanky, with Fancy being larger than Comfy and Swanky being the largest of all. The hotel occupies a grade II listed Georgian townhouse that was once gutted in a fire. It has been refurbished and fitted with super modern bathrooms, and decorated with contemporary furniture with warm browns and whites on the walls and floors. The prices are as accessible as the decor and the hotel is right in Marylebone, one of the best residential neighbourhoods in the city. The restaurant serves a delicious breakfast, with organic and fair trade options, all of which can also be brought up to guest bedrooms. The lobby bar is also great for a cocktail. If you possibly can, spring for a spacious Swanky room with views of Montagu Place.

Im Montagu Place gilt die Maxime „weniger ist mehr". Das kleine, schlichte Hotel liegt in einem denkmalgeschützen georgianischen Stadthaus, das während eines Feuers fast abbrannte. Nachdem es instand gesetzt wurde, konnte es 2006 eröffnet werden. Die Zimmer-Typen comfy (klein), fancy (mittelgroß) und swanky (groß) sind mit ultramodernen Badezimmern und zeitgemäßen Möbeln ausgestattet. Als Farbthema wurde ein warmes Braun und Weiß gewählt. Obschon das Hotel in einem der besten Wohnquartiere der Stadt, Marylebone, liegt, sind die Preise durchaus vernünftig. Im Restaurant wird ein deliziöses Bio-Frühstück (mit Fair-Trade-Produkten) serviert, das man auch mit aufs Zimmer nehmen kann, und in der Lobby lädt die Bar zum Cocktail ein. Die beste Wahl sind die luftigen Zimmer der Kategorie „swanky": Sie haben einen schönen Blick auf Montagu Place.

Le Montagu Place a tout compris du minimalisme. Inauguré 2006, ce petit hôtel simple est situé dans un ancien hôtel particulier classé du XVIIIe siècle autrefois détruit par un incendie. Entièrement restauré et équipé de salles de bains ultramodernes, il propose à des prix accessibles trois types de chambres, par ordre de taille : Comfy, Fancy et Swanky. Le décor, avec un mobilier contemporain aux tons bruns chauds, des murs et des sols blancs, cadre parfaitement avec Marylebone, un des meilleurs quartiers résidentiels de la ville. Le restaurant vous propose un délicieux petit-déjeuner bio (avec des produits du commerce équitable), que vous pourrez prendre aussi dans votre chambre. Le bar du lobby est idéal pour prendre l'apéritif. Si vous le pouvez, optez pour une spacieuse Swanky avec vue sur Montagu Place.

Rates: From 188 € (129 GBP) excl. VAT.
Rooms: 16.
Restaurant: The restaurant serves breakfast and there is 24-hour room service available.
History: The hotel is housed in a grade II listed Georgian townhouse.
X-Factor: It is lovely to see that the building's original features have been so painstakingly restored.
Internet: WiFi is available in the lounge and wired broadband access is available in the bedrooms. Charges for either are 2 GBP for one hour or 9 GBP per day.

Preise: ab 188 € (129 GBP) exkl. VAT.
Zimmer: 16.
Restaurant: Im Restaurant wird Frühstück serviert. 24-Stunden-Zimmerservice.
Geschichte: Das Hotel befindet sich in einem denkmalgeschützten georgianischen Stadthaus.
X-Faktor: Das Haus wurde originalgetreu mit viel Liebe zum Detail restauriert.
Internet: WiFi in der Lounge und Breitbandanschluss in den Zimmern. Beides für 2 GBP/Stunde oder 9 GBP pro Tag.

Prix : À partir de 188 € (129 GBP), TVA non comprise.
Chambres : 16.
Restauration : Le restaurant ne sert que le petit-déjeuner mais le service dans les chambres est assuré 24h/24.
Histoire : L'hôtel est situé dans un hôtel particulier du XVIIIe siècle classé.
Le « petit plus » : Le soin avec lequel les détails du bâtiment original ont été restaurés.
Internet : WiFi disponible dans le grand salon et accès haut débit dans les chambres. Les prix vont de 2 GBP l'heure à 9 GBP par jour.

1

2

3

---

1   Market/Markt/Marché

Marylebone Farmers' Market
Cramer Street Car Park
(just off Marylebone High Street)
London W1U 4EA
Tel: +44 20 7704 9659
www.lfm.org.uk
Tube: Baker Street/Bond Street

Thanks to Marylebone Farmers' Market, the area has become foodie central. At this rain-or-shine Sunday market, fresh produce, English cheeses and free-range meat and eggs come from mainly Kent, Surrey and Sussex, where suppliers bake artisanal breads and cakes as a bonus. Get there early: the farmers pack up around 2pm. Shop for a picnic at St James's Park for a perfect afternoon.

Dank dem Marylebone Farmers' Market ist dieses Viertel zu einem Food-Mekka geworden. Sonntags wird bei jedem Wetter frische Ware, wie Käse aus England, Freiland-Fleisch und -Eier, feilgeboten. Fast alle Lieferanten kommen aus Kent, Surrey und Sussex und bringen auch handgemachtes Brot und leckere Kuchen mit. Zeitig vorbeikommen: Die Bauern packen um zwei Uhr nachmittags zusammen. Ideal, um sich für ein Picknick im St James's Park einzudecken.

Ce marché dominical est devenu le repaire des amateurs de bonne chère. Par tous les temps, des producteurs du Kent, du Surrey et du Sussex viennent y vendre leurs produits frais, leurs fromages, leurs œufs, leurs viandes, leurs pains et leurs gâteaux artisanaux. Allez-y tôt, ils replient leurs étals dès 14h. Idéal pour s'approvisionner avant un pique-nique à St James's Park.

---

2   Food & Café/Feinkost & Café/
Épicerie fine et café

La Fromagerie
2–4 Moxon Street
London W1U 4EW
Tel: +44 20 7935 0341
www.lafromagerie.co.uk
Tube: Baker Street/Bond Street

La Fromagerie is the perfect pit stop for when shopping in Marylebone starts hurting. Patricia Michelson is the brains behind this Mecca to cheese and not only is it a delicatessen with fresh groceries, but a gorgeous lunch is served in the petite dining room to showcase the quality food. French cheeses prevail here and you can taste before you buy if you're not sure which sort you'd like best.

Shopping in Marylebone kann sehr anstrengend sein, und da kommt ein Lokal wie La Fromagiere gerade recht. Im Käseparadies von Patricia Michelson gibt es nicht nur Feinkost und frische Lebensmittel, sondern auch köstliche Mittagsmahlzeiten, die in einem Miniatur-Esssaal serviert werden. Große Auswahl an französischen Käsen, die man vor dem Kauf probieren kann.

Quand vos pieds crient au secours après des heures de shopping dans Marylebone, c'est qu'il est temps de faire une halte à la Fromagerie. Conçu par Patricia Michelson, ce temple du fromage (surtout français) est aussi une épicerie fine et un traiteur. Testez les produits au cours d'un délicieux déjeuner dans la petite salle à manger.

---

3   Beauty Products/Kosmetik/Produits
de beauté

Fresh
92 Marylebone High Street
London W1U 4RD
Tel: +44 20 7486 4100
www.fresh.com
Tube: Baker Street/Bond Street

Started by the husband and wife team of Lev Glazman and Alina Roytberg in 1991, Fresh sells gorgeous skincare products, make-up, fragrance, haircare and bodycare products as well as scents and soaps for the home. Beautifully clean packaging and a smart white shop (the only store in London) make trying and buying these products an engaging few hours of fun.

Bei Fresh gibt's himmlische Hautpflegeprodukte, Make-ups, Parfüms, Haar- und Körperpflegeprodukte, Seifen, Raumdüfte, und das alles erst noch in wunderschöner Verpackung. Dahinter steckt das Ehepaar Lev Glazman und Alina Roytberg, die das Label 1991 gegründet haben. Stundenlanges Ausprobieren macht in diesem schicken Geschäft in Weiß – dem einzigen in London – richtig Spaß.

Lancé en 1991 par Lev Glazman et Alina Roytberg, Fresh propose une excellente ligne de cosmétiques, de maquillage, de parfums, de lotions capillaires ainsi que des senteurs d'ambiance et des savons, le tout dans un emballage superbe. On passerait des heures dans cette jolie boutique blanche (leur unique à Londres) à essayer et acheter les produits.

---

4   Scandinavian Design/Skandinavisches Design/Design scandinave

Skandium
86 Marylebone High Street
London W1U 4QS
Tel: +44 20 7935 2077
Fax: +44 20 7224 2099
www.skandium.com
Tube: Baker Street/Bond Street

This store on fashionable Marylebone High Street defines Scandinavian chic and is a destination for furniture and design nuts. From Arne Jacobsen kitchenware and chairs, to Marimekko fabrics and cool children's tableware, this place is heaven for modernists in search of something gorgeous.

Skandinavischer Schick an der angesagten Marylebone High Street: Unwiderstehlich für Design-Aficionados und Modernisten auf der Suche nach dem Besonderen. Das Angebot zwischen Arne-Jacobsen-Stühlen und -Küchenware, Marimekko-Textilien und trendy Kindergeschirr ist fantastisch.

Cette boutique, repaire des mordus du design, définit le chic scandinave. Depuis les chaises et ustensiles de cuisine d'Arne Jacobsen aux textiles et à la vaisselle pour enfants de Marimekko, c'est le paradis des modernistes en quête de l'objet rare.

4

5

6

Fish'n'Chips/Fish'n'Chips/
Fish'n'Chips

The Golden Hind
3 Marylebone Lane
London W1U 2PN
Tel: +44 20 7486 3644
Tube: Bond Street

A chippie that is reminiscent of another
era altogether, The Golden Hind has been
a fixture on Marylebone Lane since 1914.
Locals are religious followers and Londoners travel from far and wide to come and
try its trademark cod and chips. The
restaurant itself has an Art Deco fish fryer,
the wooden tables are simple and sparse,
and the vibe is pure London.

Die Fish'n'Chips-Bude erinnert an längst
vergangene Zeiten. Seit 1914 ist The Golden
Hind fester Bestandteil der Marylebone
Lane, und die Bewohner des Viertels haben eine fast religiöse Beziehung zum
Lokal. Es gibt sogar Londoner, die quer
durch die Stadt fahren, um in den Genuss
der Hausspezialität, Kabeljau und Pommes
frites, zu kommen. Typisches Londoner
Lokal mit einfachen Holztischen und original Art-Deco-Friteuse.

Vrai fish'n'chips qui rappelle un autre
temps, le Golden Hind existe sur Marylebone Lane depuis 1914. Les gens du
quartier le vénèrent et les Londoniens
viennent de loin pour savourer sa fameuse
morue agrémentée de frites. Avec sa fri-
teuse Art Deco, ses tables en bois, son décor dépouillé et son ambiance bon enfant,
c'est du Londres pur jus.

Italian Restaurant/Italienisches
Restaurant/Restaurant italien

Caffè Caldesi
118 Marylebone Lane
London W1U 2QF
Tel: +44 20 7935 1144
www.caffecaldesi.com
Tube: Bond Street

Caffè Caldesi is the only place to come in
Marylebone for Saturday and Sunday

brunch (have the Big Tuscan) or lunch.
This place is staffed by proper Italians so
you could just as well be in a square somewhere in Tuscany for all you know. The cof-
fees are divine, the service brisk and the
people-watching provides countless hours
of entertainment. Dinners upstairs are also
worth a look-in, too.

Ein besseres Lokal für den Wochenend-
Brunch (empfehlenswert ist The Big
Tuscan) oder -Lunch als das Caffè Caldesi
gibt's nirgends in Marylebone. Hier wird
man von echten Italienern bedient, und
so fühlt man sich wie irgendwo in der
Toskana. Der Kaffee schmeckt zudem
himmlisch. Nicht zu schlagen ist das Lokal
auch als Beobachtungsposten: Man kann
hier locker stundenlang People-Watching
betreiben. Im oberen Stock gibt's übrigens
auch Abendessen.

C'est le seul endroit à Marylebone où prendre son brunch ou déjeuner le samedi et le
dimanche (optez pour le Big Tuscan). Avec
son personnel entièrement italien, on se
croirait sur une petite place toscane. Les
cafés sont divins, le service rapide et on ne
se lasse pas d'observer la clientèle. Les salles à l'étage valent également le coup d'œil.

Personal Finds/Eigene Entdeckungen/
Découvertes personnelles:

HYDE PARK

KENSINGTON GARDENS

The Ring

Serpentine Road

● BOAT HOUSE

THE SERPENTINE

West Carriage Drive

● SERPENTINE GALLERY

Rotten Row

South Carriage Drive

Kensington Road

Knightsbr

Ennismore Gdns

Trevor Place

Knightsbridg

ROYAL ALBERT HALL

THE CAPITAL RESTAURANT

Rutland Gate

Rutland Gate

● HARRODS

Hans

THE GORE

Princes

Exhibition Road

Queen's Gate

ROYAL COLLEGE OF MUSIC

Gardens

Brompton Square

Hans Rd

Road

Beauchamp Pl

Imperial College Rd

● THE BUNCH OF GRAPES

Pont

SCIENCE MUSEUM

Egerton Terr

NATURAL HISTORY MUSEUM

Egerton Gdns

Walton Street

Hasker St

Milner St

Cromwell Road

Queens Gate

VICTORIA & ALBERT MUSEUM

Egerton Gdns

South Terr

Thurloe Pl

Thurloe St

Thurloe Sq

South Kensington

SW7

& SW3
South Kensington
Chelsea

1 Gallery/Galerie/Galerie
Serpentine Gallery

2 Rowing/Rudern/Promenade en barque
Serpentine Lake, Boat House

3 Museum Garden/Museums-Garten/Jardin de musée
Victoria & Albert Museum

4 Pub/Pub/Pub
The Bunch of Grapes

5 Department Store/Kaufhaus/Grand magasin
Harrods

6 Restaurant/Restaurant/Restaurant
The Capital Restaurant

1 Books/Bücher/Librairie
Waterstone's

2 French Restaurant/ Französisches Restaurant/Restaurant française
La Bouchée

3 Traditional Paint/Tradtionelle Farbwaren/Peintures traditionnelles
Farrow & Ball

4 Furniture & More/Möbel & More/Meubles & plus
The Conran Shop

5 Polish Restaurant/Polnisches Restaurant/Restaurant polonais
Daquise

6 Botanical Garden/Botanischer Garten/Jardin botanique
Royal Botanical Gardens, Kew

1 Furniture & Café/Möbel & Café/Mobilier & Café
Searcy's GTC Café

2 Knitwear/Strickwaren/Lainages
Pringle

3 Perfume & Cosmetics/ Düfte & Hautpflege/Parfumerie et cosmétiques
Jo Malone

4 Shoes/Schuhe/Chaussures
French Sole

5 Café/Café/Café
Oriel

6 Shoes/Schuhe/Chaussures
Emma Hope

7 Kitchen Ware/Küchenutensilien/Ustensiles de cuisine
David Mellor

8 Dog's & Cat's Fashion/Haustier-Boutique/Mode pour chiens et chats
Mungo & Maud

9 Hats/Hüte/Modiste
Philip Treacy

10 Chocolate/Schokolade/Chocolat
The Chocolate Society

11 Pub/Pub/Pub
The Grenadier

12 Italian Restaurant/Italienisches Restaurant/Restaurant italien
Daphne's

NUMBER SIXTEEN HOTEL

Exhibition Road

SCIENCE MUSEUM

Imperial College Road

Queen's Gate

VICTORIA & ALBERT MUSEUM

BROMPTON ORATORY

Brompton Square

Cheval Place

Beauchamp

Yeoman's Rd

NATURAL HISTORY MUSEUM

Cromwell Road

Egerton Terr

Walton

Brompton Rd

Thurloe Place

Thurloe St

DAQUISE

DAPHNE'S

Harrington Rd

South Kensington

Deny

Dray

Stanhope Gdns

Onslow Sq

Sloan

LA BOUCHÉE

THE CONRAN SHOP

Summer Pl

Old Brompton Road

Onslow Gdns

Ixworth Place

Elystan St

WATERSTONE'S

Cranley Gdns

Onslow Road

Fulham Road

Sydney Street

Cale Street

Britten st

Jubilee Pl

Dovehouse Street

Drayton Gdns

Old Church Street

FARROW & BALL

Flood

ROYAL BOTANIC GARDENS

THE GRENADIER

Hans Crescent

Basil St

's Rd

Hans Place

Pont Street

Pont Street

Stoane Street

Pavilion Road

Lowndes St

Pont Street

Cadogan Place

Cadogan Lane

Chesham St

Lyall St

Eaton Place

King's Road

Belgrave Square

Belgrave Pl

Eaton Pl

Eaton Square

Upp Belgrave St

Belgrave Road

Eaton Square

ELEVEN CADOGAN GARDENS

FRENCH SOLE

JO MALONE

PRINGLE

Cadogan Street

Draycott Place

Avenue

Road

THE CHOCOLATE SOCIETY

Elizabeth Street

MUNGO & MAUD

Eaton Terr

DAVID MELLOR

EMMA HOPE

ORIEL

Stoane Square

Sloane Square

Chester Row

Elizabeth Street

PHILIP TREACY

SEARCY'S GTC CAFÉ

Lower Sloane Street

Ebury

Pimlico Rd

Bloomfield Terrace

Ranelagh Gr

Cheltenham Terrace

Franklin's Row

Hospital Road

St Leonard's Terr

Smith Street

Tedworth Sq

Royal

Chelsea Bridge Road

Ebury Bridge Road

ROYAL HOSPITAL CHELSEA

© MICHAEL A HILL

The Gore

190 Queen's Gate, London SW7 5EX
☎ +44 20 7584 6601   🖷 + 44 20 7589 8127
reservations@gorehotel.co.uk
www.gorehotel.co.uk
Tube: South Kensington/Gloucester Road
Booking: www.great-escapes-hotels.com

The Gore

Walking into The Gore is like visiting a loopy uncle's house. The walls of the chandeliered reception are covered in gilt-framed artwork. There are pictures of Queen Victoria and Prince Albert, of children in buckled shoes and paintings of farm animals. It would all be overkill if it wasn't so very whimsical and delightful. The hotel's busy restaurant, 190 Queens Gate, serves food sourced from UK farms. The Gore's clientele are as eclectic as the decor. Supermodels and their rock star boyfriends hide out here when press intrusion gets too much. At the same time, you'll find businessmen tapping away at their laptops; or you could come across an elegant woman, lashed in diamonds, mysteriously accompanied by a three-tonne bodyguard. The rooms at The Gore are quirky and eccentric furnished with an amazing collection of English and French antiques. The deluxe Venus Room has a huge antique bed, topped with raw silk swag and tails, which apparently belonged to Judy Garland.

Im Gore ist es wie zu Besuch bei einem exzentrischen Onkel. Die Rezeption ist vollgestopft mit Leuchtern und goldgerahmten Kunst-Bildern von Königin Victoria, Prinz Albert, Kindern in Schnallenschuhen und Bauernhof-Tieren. Zum Glück spürt man hier ein Augenzwinkern, sonst wäre das ganze Dekor etwas zu viel des Guten. Die buntgemischte Klientel passt perfekt in die Szenerie: Supermodels in Begleitung von Rockstar-Boyfriends suchen hier Zuflucht vor der neugierigen Journaille, diamantenübersäte Damen stolzieren vor ihren drei Tonnen schweren Bodyguards, dazwischen sieht man auch ein paar mit Laptops ausgerustete Geschäftsleute. Die Gästezimmer mit englischen und französischen Antiquitäten sind so eigenwillig wie der Rest. So protzt im luxuriösen Venus Room ein riesiges antikes Bett (es soll Judy Garland gehört haben) mit rohseidenen Vorhängen und Girlanden. 190 Queen's Gate, das Hotelrestaurant allerdings setzt auf natürlich und verwendet lokale Landwirtschaftsprodukte.

En entrant au Gore, on se croirait chez un vieil oncle un peu fou. Le hall, orné d'un lustre, est tapissé de tableaux dans des cadres dorés. On y trouve des portraits de la reine Victoria et du prince Albert, d'enfants aux souliers à boucle et d'animaux de ferme. Cela paraîtrait trop chargé si ce n'était aussi fantasque et plein d'humour. Le restaurant très prisé de l'hôtel, le 190 Queens Gate, s'approvisionne directement dans des fermes du pays. La clientèle est aussi éclectique que le décor. On y croise des top-modèles avec leurs fiancés rock stars fuyant les paparazzis, des hommes d'affaires pianotant sur leur ordinateur ou des élégantes couvertes de diamants flanquées d'un garde du corps pesant trois tonnes. Les chambres merveilleusement excentriques sont meublées d'antiquités françaises et anglaises. La luxueuse Venus Room possède un immense lit ancien surmonté d'un drapé en soie sauvage qui aurait appartenu à Judy Garland.

Rates: From 190 € (130 GBP) excl. VAT.
Rooms: 50 (1 suite).
Restaurants: 190 Queen's Gate, Bar 190.
History: The Gore has two rooms dedicated to Miss Fanny and Miss Ada, who once lived in the hotel and ran it as a lodging house when all the family's men were lost to war.
X-Factor: The Green Room, which is actually pink, is a lovely place to have a drink and relax.
Internet: Complimentary WiFi access.

Preise: ab 190 € (130 GBP) exkl. VAT.
Zimmer: 50 (1 Suite).
Restaurants: 190 Queen's Gate, Bar 190.
Geschichte: The Gore hat zwei seiner Zimmer Miss Fanny und Miss Ada gewidmet. Die beiden Frauen betrieben das Haus als Pension, nachdem sie ihre Ehemänner im Krieg verloren hatten.
X-Faktor: The Green Room ist ein wunderbarer Ort zum Entspannen. Übrigens ist der Raum ganz in Rot – trotz des Namens.
Internet: Kostenloser WiFi-Zugang.

Prix : À partir de 190 € (130 GBP), TVA non comprise.
Chambres : 50 (1 suite).
Restauration : 190 Queen's Gate, Bar 190.
Histoire : Le Gore conserve deux chambres consacrées à Miss Fanny et Miss Ada, qui vivaient autrefois dans la maison et la transformèrent en pension après que tous les hommes de la famille furent morts à la guerre.
Le « petit plus » : La Green Room, qui en fait est rose, est un endroit charmant où prendre un verre et se détendre.
Internet : Accès WiFi gratuit.

1

2

3

1   Gallery/Galerie/Galerie

Serpentine Gallery
Kensington Garden
London W2 3XA
Tel: +44 20 7402 60 75
www.serpentinegallery.org
Tube: Lancaster Gate/Knightsbridge

Famed for its summer party full of starry guests, the Serpentine Gallery, originally built as a tea room in 1934, was given a new lease of life when Julia Peyton-Jones took over its directorship in 1991 and turned it into a destination museum for fans of contemporary art, right in the middle of Hyde Park. Londoners now look forward to which big-name architect will build the summer pavilion each year. Perfect combination of nature and art.

Die Sommerpartys der Serpentine Gallery (1934 als Teehaus gebaut) sind legendär und gespickt mit Prominenz. Seit Julia Peyton-Jones 1991 die Direktion und einen lebenslangen Mietvertrag übernommen hat, ist die Galerie mitten im Hyde Park zu einer Zieladresse für Liebhaber zeitgenössischer Kunst geworden. Das Sommerpavillon wird jedes Jahr von einem anderen Stararchitekten gestaltet, was jeweils für viel Aufsehen sorgt. Hier trifft Kunst auf Natur.

Célèbre pour sa party estivale très people, cet ancien salon de thé inauguré en 1934 a connu une nouvelle vie sous la direction de Julia Peyton-Jones qui, en 1991, l'a transformé en destination de choix pour les amateurs d'art contemporain en plein cœur de Hyde Park. Chaque année, les Londoniens attendent avec impatience de savoir quel grand architecte bâtira le pavillon d'été. Une combinaison parfaite de nature et d'art.

2   Rowing/Rudern/Promenade en barque

Serpentine Lake, Boat House
Hyde Park
Tel: +44 20 7262 1330
www.bluebirdboats.co.uk
Tube: Hyde Park Corner

If the noise and traffic fumes of London get to be too much, there is one thing to do: seek respite in one of the parks. Hyde Park is a lush, green space in which to cycle, ride, run and, believe it or not, go for a row in the Serpentine. For a mere 6 GBP per hour, you can rent a boat and swoosh around. For those with a penchant for swimming, the Lido is open from June to September.

Wem Lärm und Abgase in London zu viel werden, hat nur eine Möglichkeit: ab in eine der Parkanlagen und tief durchatmen. Der Hyde Park ist nicht nur lauschig, hier kann man auch fahrradfahren, reiten, joggen und im Serpentine Lake sogar rudern. Für 6 GBP die Stunde ein Boot mieten und damit über den See gleiten. Wer schwimmen möchte: Das Strandbad ist von Juni bis September geöffnet.

Si le bruit et les odeurs de Londres vous suffoquent, une seule solution : cherchez le répit dans un de ses parcs. Hyde Park est un espace vert luxuriant où faire du vélo, du cheval, du footing ou, croyez-le ou non, pour 6 GBP de l'heure, louer une barque sur le Serpentine. Pour les nageurs, le Lido est ouvert de juin à septembre.

3   Museum Garden/Museums-Garten/ Jardin de musée

Victoria & Albert Museum
The John Madejski Garden
Cromwell Road
London SW7 2RL
Tel: +44 20 7942 2000
www.vam.ac.uk
Tube: South Kensington

The V&A was founded in 1852 as a museum devoted to the best in art and design. If the multitude of collections are too much, head straight for the shop and its amazing offering of wonderful gifts. Also, don't miss The John Madejski Garden in the courtyard. Prince Charles opened it on 5 July 2005. The two-metre high sculpture "Diamond (pink/gold)" by Jeff Koons is spectacular and on public display for the first time.

Das V&A Museum zeigt seit 1852 das Beste aus Kunst und Design. Wem die zahlreichen Sammlungen zu viel sind: unbedingt den Museumsshop besuchen. Hier findet man tolle Geschenke. Auch der John-Madejski-Garten im Hof, der von Prinz Charles am 5. Juli 2005 eröffnet wurde, ist eine Besichtigung wert. Hier wird die zwei Meter hohe Skulptur „Diamond (pink/gold)" von Jeff Koons zum ersten Mal öffentlich ausgestellt.

Fondé en 1852, le V&A est un musée consacré au meilleur des arts décoratifs. Si vous êtes submergé par la multitude de collections, rabattez-vous sur la boutique, ses superbes cadeaux. N'oubliez pas le jardin John Madejski, inauguré par le prince Charles le 5 juillet 2005. La sculpture de deux mètres „Diamond (pink/gold)" réalisée par Jeff Koons y est exposé pour la première fois au public.

4   Pub/Pub/Pub

The Bunch of Grapes
207 Brompton Road
London SW3 1LA
Tel: +44 20 7589 4944
Tube: Knightsbridge/South Kensington

Locals, tourists and everything in between congregate at this pub – which dates back to 1844 – not only to gather round a pint, but because it offers a lovely food menu in its upstairs restaurant. A cut above the normal grease and starch fare, the fish and chips are particularly popular because of the light batter and not-so-oily chips.

Einheimische, Zugewanderte und Besucher treffen sich in diesem Pub seit 1844. Man kommt nicht bloß hierher um sich bei einem Bier zu erfrischen, sondern auch weil das Essen im Restaurant im oberen Stockwerk wunderbar schmeckt – jedenfalls viel besser als die üblichen fettigen Gerichte in anderen Pubs. Besonders beliebt sind die „Fish and Chips" – der Teig ist leicht und die Pommes Frites überhaupt nicht ölig.

Les locaux, les touristes et tous les autres se rassemblent dans ce pub qui remonte

4

5

6

ux années 1844, non seulement pour
bière mais aussi pour son charmant
estaurant à l'étage, un cran au-dessus
u troquet habituel. Les fish'n chips y sont
ès prisés parce que la pâte à frire est
gère et les frites pas trop grasses.

Department Store/Kaufhaus/Grand
magasin

Harrods
7–135 Brompton Road
ondon SW1X 7XL
el: +44 20 7730 1234
ww.harrods.com
ube: Knightsbridge

Vhen Charles Henry Harrod opened the
oors of this store in 1849, it's safe to say
e had no idea that he'd started what was
o be a London icon. The department store
o rival all department stores, Harrods has
verything you could want under one roof:
om fridges, to boats, to fine china and on
nd on. The Food Hall is one of the most
pectacular in the world.

Is Charles Henry Harrod 1849 dieses
Kaufhaus gründete, hatte er bestimmt kei-
e Ahnung, dass er damit den Grundstein
ür ein Londoner Wahrzeichen legte. Das
Kaufhaus gilt als das Nonplusultra aller
Kaufhäuser. Bei Harrods findet man alles,
vas man braucht: Kühlschränke, Boote,
Porzellan und vieles mehr. Die „Food Hall"
t eine der schönsten der Welt.

n ouvrant son établissement en 1849,
Charles Henry Harrod n'imaginait pas
naugurer un futur monument de Londres.
Le » grand magasin par excellence, Harrods
assemble tout ce que vous pouvez désirer
ous un même toit : des frigos aux yachts
n passant par la vaisselle, les restaurants,
tc. Les Food Halls sont spectaculaires.

Restaurant/Restaurant/Restaurant

The Capital Restaurant
he Capital Hotel
2–24 Basil Street
ondon SW3 1AT
el: +44 20 7589 5171

www.capital-london.net
Tube: Knightsbridge

Located on an unassuming little street off
Sloane Street, right near Knightsbridge
Tube station and Harrods, The Capital
Restaurant is one of those rare gems in
gastronomy that serious foodies hanker after. Eric Chavot, the head chef, has a quietly
illustrious reputation for his innovative style.

Das Capital Restaurant liegt an einer kleinen, unauffälligen Seitenstraße der Sloane
Street, ganz in der Nähe der Knightsbridge
Tube Station und von Harrods. Das Capital
ist eine dieser seltenen Gastro-Trou vaillen,
die bei echten Gourmets hoch im Kurs
stehen. Der innovative Kochstil von Küchenchef Eric Chavot genießt einen ausgezeichneten Ruf.

Dans une petite rue discrète donnant sur
Sloane street, tout près du métro Knightsbridge et d'Harrods, le restaurant Capital
est un de ces joyaux rares qui font saliver
les gastronomes sérieux. Eric Chavot, le
chef principal, s'est forgé une solide réputation grâce à sa cuisine inventive.

Personal Finds/Eigene Entdeckungen/
Découvertes personnelles:

Number Sixteen Hotel

16 Sumner Place, London SW7 3EG
☎ +44 20 7589 5232   📠 +44 20 7584 8615
reservations@numbersixteenhotel.co.uk
www.numbersixteenhotel.co.uk
Tube: South Kensington
Booking: www.great-escapes-hotels.com

Number Sixteen Hotel

The sparkling white row of Victorian townhouses that make up Number Sixteen give away little about how fantastic this hotel really is. Compact but perfectly formed, this little jewel of an inn in South Kensington boasts a near-perfect London location, right near the V&A and great shopping. Decorated by owner Kit Kemp in what is best described as South Kensington chic – a bit flowery, a bit contemporary, very London – Number Sixteen is bright, modern and very fresh. The two drawing rooms have fluffy sofas and sun streaming in through the windows. Then there is the conservatory, decorated with African and Asian prints collected by Kemp on her travels round the world; it is light, airy and leads out to the piece de resistance at Number Sixteen: the lush garden replete with fountain and perky carp swimming around. Whatever you do, don't leave London before you have sat out here with a full afternoon tea (the delicious scones are home-made) and a good English newspaper.

Das Number Sixteen besteht aus einer Reihe zuckergussweißer viktorianischer Stadthäuser. Wie fantastisch das Hotel tatsächlich ist, lässt sich von außen kaum erahnen. Hinter der Fassade verbirgt sich ein kleines Juwel und erst noch an bester Lage in South Kensington: der nahezu perfekte Aufenthaltsort in London. Gleich in der Nähe befindet sich das V&A Museum, die Shoppinggelegenheiten sind erstklassig. Besitzerin Kit Kemp hat die Inneneinrichtung (ein Stil, den man mit „South Kensington Chic" bezeichnen könnte) selbst entworfen – ein bisschen floral, ein bisschen zeitgemäß, sehr frisch und vor allem typisch London. Das Haus verfügt über zwei helle Salons mit superbequemen Sofas und einen Wintergarten, dekoriert mit afrikanischen und asiatischen Prints, die Kemp von ihren Reisen mitgebracht hat. Das Prachtstück ist der lauschige Garten mit Karpfen Brunnen. Die Stadt kann man unmöglich verlassen, ohne hier einen Afternoon Tea mit den deliziösen hausgemachten „Scones" genossen zu haben.

La rangée de maisons victoriennes d'un blanc étincelant qui constituent le Number Sixteen ne laisse pas deviner à quel point cet hôtel est magique. Compact mais parfaitement aménagé, ce petit bijou jouit d'un emplacement quasi parfait : à deux pas du V&A et des meilleures boutiques. Décoré par sa propriétaire Kit Kemp dans ce qu'on pourrait appeler le style « South Kensington chic » (un peu floral, un peu contemporain, très londonien), il est lumineux, moderne et très frais. Les deux salons inondés de lumière possèdent des canapés douillets ; le jardin d'hiver est décoré d'imprimés africains et asiatiques glanés par Kemp au fil de ses voyages. Mais la pièce de résistance, c'est le jardin luxuriant avec sa fontaine et son bassin où nagent des carpes. Ne quittez pas Londres avant d'y avoir pris le thé (les délicieux scones sont faits maison) devant un bon journal anglais.

Rates: From 145 € (100 GBP) excl. VAT.
Rooms: 42.
Restaurants: None but there is 24-hour room service.
History: The property was a hotel before the Firmdale group purchased it and redecorated it in its own style.
X-Factor: The tranquil garden is simply amazing and the beds are amazingly comfortable.
Internet: Broadband access at 20 GBP per day.

Preise: ab 145 € (100 GBP) exkl. VAT.
Zimmer: 42.
Restaurants: Keines. 24-Stunden-Zimmerservice.
Geschichte: Das Haus war bereits ein Hotel, bevor es die Firmdale-Gruppe übernommen und renoviert hat.
X-Faktor: Die Stille im Garten ist wunderbar, und die Betten in den Zimmern unglaublich bequem.
Internet: Breitbandanschluss für 20 GBP pro Tag.

Prix : À partir de 145 € (100 GBP), TVA non comprise.
Chambres : 42.
Restauration : Aucune, mais service assuré dans les chambres 24h/24.
Histoire : L'établissement était déjà un hôtel avant d'être racheté et réaménagé par le groupe Firmdale dans son propre style.
Le « petit plus » : Le jardin tranquille est magnifique et les lits sont d'un confort indécent.
Internet : Accès haut débit pour 20 GBP par jour.

1

2

1   Books/Bücher/Librairie

Waterstone's
99–101 Old Brompton Road
London SW7 3LE
Tel: +44 20 7581 8522
Tube: South Kensington

Waterstone's may be a chain of book-shops around the UK but it is a good one, catering to the very neighbourhoods in which it resides. This Waterstone's, like the others, has wood-pannelled shelves and cosy nooks. Here you will also find plenty of books about the history of London and books about Chelsea. Also, check out the shelf where staff recommend their favourite books. Read them in the pleasant, beautiful garden of Number Sixteen Hotel.

Waterstone's ist zwar eine Kette, doch die Buchhandlungen gehören zu den besten des Landes. Der Waterstone's an der Old Brompton Road ist mit Holzpaneelen und Ecken genau so gemütlich wie alle anderen, und die Auswahl an Büchern über die Geschichte Londons und über Chelsea ist fantastisch. Unbedingt das Regal mit den Empfehlungen der Buchhändler durchstöbern, dann eines dieser Bücher im wunderschönen Garten des Number Sixteen Hotels lesen.

Certes, c'est une chaîne répandue dans tout le Royaume-Uni mais elle est excellente et chaque enseigne est adaptée à son quartier. Celle-ci, comme les autres, a des rayonnages en bois et des recoins cosy. Vous y trouverez plein d'ouvrages sur l'histoire de Londres et sur Chelsea. Le personnel entrepose sur une étagère ses lectures favorites. À lire tranquillement dans le beau jardin du Number Sixteen Hotel.

2   French Restaurant/Französisches Restaurant/Restaurant français

La Bouchée
56 Old Brompton Road
London SW7 3DY
Tel: +44 20 7589 1929
Tube: South Kensington

It's a good thing La Bouchée exists, otherwise where would the countless French expatriates living in Chelsea go to eat? Or where would the would-be aristocrats of this district have their romantic dinners? Known for its rustic French cooking, La Bouchée does not disappoint with dishes that include juicy snails and the traditional coq au vin.

Ein Glück für alle nach Chelsea ausgewanderten Franzosen, dass es La Bouchée gibt. Wo sonst würden sie essen gehen? Auch die aristokratisch angehauchten Bewohner des Viertels finden hier das ideale Lokal für ein romantisches Dinner. La Bouchée bringt rustikale französische Gerichten auf den Tisch, wie saftige Schnecken oder traditionellen Coq au Vin. Die Küche enttäuscht nie.

Si La Bouchée n'existait pas, où irait manger les nombreux expatriés français de Chelsea ? Où les aristos du quartier iraient-ils pour leurs dîners romantiques ? Spécialisée dans la cuisine française rustique, La Bouchée est à la hauteur de sa réputation avec une carte incluant de succulents escargots et le traditionnel coq au vin.

3   Traditional Paint/Tradtionelle Farbwaren/Peintures traditionnelles

Farrow & Ball
249 Fulham Road
London SW3 6HY
Tel: +44 20 7351 0273
www.farrow-ball.com
Tube: South Kensington

Farrow & Ball is testament to the British talent for creating exquisite products for the home. The paint company was founded in the 1930s by chemists John Farrow and Richard Ball and all products are still made in Dorset. Farrow & Ball still provide paints for National Trust properties but new, contemporary colours were added to suit modern tastes. Get the most subtle shades you will not find elsewhere to paint your home at home.

Die Briten sind bekannt für die Herstellung bester Haushaltsprodukte. Dazu ge-

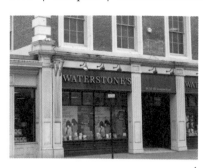

hören auch die Farbwaren von Farrow & Ball. Das Unternehmen wurde in den 1930ern von den Chemikern John Farrow und Richard Ball in Dorset gegründet, wo bis heute alle Produkte hergestellt werden, und liefert die Farben für die Gebäude des National Trust. Doch man findet auch aktuelle, zeitgemäße Farben: Subtilere Farbtöne findet man sonst nirgends, da macht es Spaß einen neuen Farbanstrich für zuhause zu planen.

Les Britanniques n'ont pas leur pareil pour créer des produits exquis pour la maison. Cette entreprise fondée dans les années 30 par John Farrow et Richard Ball fabrique encore toutes ses peintures dans le Dorset et fournit le National Trust, la fondation qui restaure les demeures historiques. De nouvelles couleurs modernes ont été ajoutées à son nuancier. Vous y trouverez les tons les plus subtils pour redécorer votre intérieur.

4   Furniture & More/Möbel & More/Meubles & plus

The Conran Shop
Michelin House
81 Fulham Road
London SW3 6RD
Tel: +44 20 7589 7401
www.conranshop.co.uk
Tube: South Kensington

The Conran Shop is best described as furniture heaven and it's located in Michelin House which was built in 1909. Sir Terence Conran has one of the best-bought and designed collections of furniture, home accessories, boys' toys, tableware and rugs that any shop could offer. Don't miss out on eating oysters at Bibendum next door or simply buy a coffee and some flowers to take back to the hotel.

Der Conran Shop im Michelin-Haus, Baujahr 1909, ist ein Einrichtungs-Nirvana mit Designer-Möbeln, Wohnaccessoires, Spielzeugen, Geschirr und Teppichen. Die Auswahl von Sir Terence Conran ist fantastisch und gehört zum Besten überhaupt. Im Bibendium gleich nebenan unbedingt ein paar Austern schlürfen oder

4

5

6

einfach auch nur einen Kaffee genießen. Auch schön: hier Blumen kaufen und mit ns Hotelzimmer nehmen.

Située dans l'immeuble Michelin bâti en 1909, la boutique Conran est le paradis du meuble. Sir Terence Conran y propose ses collections merveilleusement pensées et dessinées de mobilier, de linge de maison, de gadgets, de vaisselle et de tapis. Profitez-en pour dégustez des huîtres chez Bibendum à côté, ou prenez simplement un café et achetez un bouquet pour votre chambre d'hôtel.

5　Polish Restaurant/Polnisches Restaurant/Restaurant polonais

Daquise
20 Thurloe Street
London SW7 2LT
Tel: +44 20 7589 6117
Tube: South Kensington

Daquise is the kind of restaurant that makes eating out fun. This Polish eatery has been in South Kensington since 1947 and its popularity – with Poles and non-Poles alike – has not eased up. Go on a busy Friday night and try the pierogi, the potato pancakes, dumplings and finish off with apple cakes. (Those on an Atkins diet need not enter the doors.) Best of all, prices are reasonable.

Hier macht es richtig Spaß, auswärts zu essen. Das polnische Restaurant Daquise in South Kensington gibt es seit 1947 und ist bei Polen und Nicht-Polen genau so beliebt. Am besten an einem Freitag hingehen, dann ist besonders viel los, und Piroggen, Kartoffelpuffer, Knödel und zum Abschluss Apfelkuchen kosten. Wer sich eine Atkins-Diät verschrieben hat, bleibt besser draußen. Und: Die Preise sind durchaus vernünftig.

Dîner chez Daquise est une vraie fête. Depuis son ouverture en 1947, ce restaurant polonais ne désemplit pas de Polonais comme de non Polonais. Allez-y un vendredi soir, quand il y a foule. Goinfrez-vous de pierogi, de galettes de pommes de terre, de boulettes et finissez avec un gâteau aux pommes. Si vous êtes au régime,

n'entrez pas ! En outre, les prix sont raisonnables.

6　Botanical Garden/Botanischer Garten/Jardin botanique

Royal Botanic Gardens, Kew
Richmond
Surrey TW9 3AB
Tel: +44 20 8332 5655
www.rbgkew.org.uk
Tube: Kew Gardens

It may sound like a trek to Richmond but the District Line takes you to one of the most wonderful places in London: Kew Gardens, home to the largest collection of living plants on the planet. Pack a picnic and head down to see one of the World Heritage Sites as inscribed by UNESCO. Kew has been leading the world in botanical and environmental science since 1759 and if you love plants, you must go.

Was zunächst aussieht wie eine gewöhnliche Fahrt nach Richmond mit der District Lane, entpuppt sich als Ausflug an einen der schönsten Orte Londons, den Kew Gardens. Hier befindet sich die weltweit größte Pflanzensammlung. Am besten einen Picknick-Korb packen und ab zu der UNESCO-Weltstätte, die seit 1759 führend in Botanik und Umweltwissenschaften ist. Ein Muss für Pflanzenliebhaber.

Ne vous laissez pas décourager par la distance, la District Line vous mènera droit dans l'un des lieux les plus magiques de Londres : Kew Gardens, qui abrite la plus vaste collection de plantes au monde. Emportez votre pique-nique sur un site inscrit au patrimoine mondial de l'UNESCO. Kew est à la pointe de la science botanique et écologique depuis 1759. Si vous aimez les plantes, c'est un must.

Personal Finds/Eigene Entdeckungen/
Découvertes personnelles:

Eleven Cadogan Gardens

11 Cadogan Gardens, London SW3 2RJ
☎ +44 20 7730 7000   🖷 + 44 20 7730 5217
reservations@number-eleven.co.uk
www.number-eleven.co.uk
Tube: Sloane Square
Booking: www.great-escapes-hotels.com

Eleven Cadogan Gardens

here is a refreshing air of English exclusivity about Eleven Cadogan Gardens that doesn't exist at any other London hotel. One can rely on a certain type of experience here that is highly satisfying for a stay in an English city. Discreetly hidden in the leafy streets of Chelsea, it is the hotel of choice for super-chic Europeans and those who visit London from their country estates. Guests are greeted at the front door by a butler, a chauffeur-driven car is available for airport pick-ups or shopping expeditions and guests' privacy is fiercely guarded. Decorated in an understated English style – with floral textiles, rich oil paintings and beautiful antiques – this place really is for the discerning traveller. Number Eleven also has the most wonderful rituals in place: guests who are back from shopping or sightseeing are treated to afternoon tea, with delicious oatmeal biscuits and freshly baked cake. And, just before dinner, they partake in canapés and sherry, just as they would at home.

Ein Aufenthalt im Eleven Cadogan Gardens ist etwas Besonders. Die wohltuend erfrischend englische Exklusivität, die hier herrscht, findet man in keinem anderen Londoner Hotel. Das diskret gelegene Haus mitten in den belaubten Straßen Chelseas wird von eleganten europäischen Landhausbesitzern auf Besuch in London bevorzugt. Am Eingang begrüßt ein Butler die Gäste, die mit einem Wagen von Flughafen abgeholt wurden (Wagen und Chauffeur stehen auch für Shoppingtouren zur Verfügung). Angenehm: Auf die Privatsphäre der Gäste wird äußerst Wert gelegt. Das Dekor repräsentiert englisches Upper-Class-Understatement: Textilien mit Blumenmustern, üppige Ölgemälde, prächtige Antiquitäten – perfekt für die anspruchsvolle Klientel. Wunderbar sind die Rituale des Hauses: der Afternoon Tea mit köstlichen Haferbiscuits und frisch gebackenem Kuchen, besonders nach einer anstrengenden Shoppingtour, und die Canapés, die man vor dem Dinner mit einem Glas Sherry genießt. Fast wie zuhause.

Eleven Cadogan Gardens dégage une aura d'exclusivité typiquement anglaise qu'on ne trouve dans aucun autre hôtel à Londres, une expérience hautement gratifiante quand on séjourne dans une ville britannique. Caché dans les rues ombragées de Chelsea, c'est l'hôtel de choix des Européens ultrachics ou de ceux qui descendent à Londres depuis leurs grandes propriétés à la campagne. On est accueilli à la porte par le majordome, une voiture avec chauffeur vous attend à l'aéroport ou vous conduit faire du lèche-vitrine. L'intimité des clients est férocement protégée. Décoré dans un style anglais sobre, avec des tissus fleuris, de beaux tableaux et des antiquités exquises, l'endroit satisfera le voyageur avisé. On y entretient de merveilleux rituels : de retour de shopping ou de visites, un thé vous attend avec de délicieux biscuits à l'avoine et un cake tout juste sorti du four. Juste avant le dîner, on fait la causette avec les autres clients devant des canapés et un verre de sherry comme à la maison.

---

ates: From 210 € (145 GBP) excl. VAT.
ooms: 60.
estaurant: There is a dining room for guests serving breakfast, lunch and dinner.
History: Lord Chelsea built the Victorian mansions on his cricket ground near Buckingham Palace. The hotel was established in 1949.
X-Factor: Views of beautiful Cadogan Gardens.
Internet: Complimentary WiFi access.

Preise: ab 210 € (145 GBP) exkl. VAT.
Zimmer: 60.
Restaurant: Ein Speisesaal für Frühstück, Mittagessen und Abendessen.
Geschichte: Lord Chelsea hatte die viktorianischen Mansions in der Nähe des Buckingham Palace auf seinem Cricket Platz erbauen lassen. 1949 wurde daraus ein Hotel.
X-Faktor: Ausblick auf die wunderbaren Cadogan Gardens.
Internet: Kostenloser WiFi-Zugang.

Prix : À partir de 210 € (145 GBP), TVA non comprise.
Chambres : 60.
Restauration : Le restaurant réservé aux clients de l'hôtel sert les petits-déjeuners, les déjeuners et les dîners.
Histoire : Lord Chelsea a construit les maisons victoriennes sur son terrain de cricket près du palais de Buckingham. L'hôtel a été inauguré en 1949.
Le « petit plus » : Les vues sur le beau parc de Cadogan.
Internet : Accès WiFi gratuit.

1

2

3

1   Furniture & Café/Möbel & Café/
    Mobilier & Café

Searcy's GTC Café
at the General Trading Company
2 Symons Street
London SW3 2TJ
Tel: + 44 20 7730 5271
www.searcys.co.uk
Tube: Sloane Square

The General Trading Company, launched
in 1920 but in its current location since
2001, is the ideal place to buy furniture
and furnishings for the perfect Chelsea
townhouse. And when the credit card is
worn out, rest your weary self at Searcy's
GTC Café. If it's lunch you're after, the fish
of the day or a simple salad is how the lady
keeps her shape.

Die General Trading Company gibt's seit
1920, am heutigen Standort ist sie allerdings erst seit 2001. Möbel, Einrichtungs-
gegenstände: Hier findet man alles für die
Einrichtung eines typischen Chelsea-Stadt-
hauses. Wer seine Kreditkarte bis zum Limit
benutzt hat, kann sich im Searcy's GTC Café
von der anstrengenden Aktion erholen. Der
Tagesfisch zusammen mit einem einfachen
Salat ist der ideale Lunch für Linienbewusste.

La General Trading Company, fondée en
1920 mais dans son emplacement actuel
depuis 2001, est l'endroit idéal où acheter
du mobilier pour son hôtel particulier à
Chelsea. Et quand votre carte de crédit
sera morte, reprenez vos esprits au café.
Si c'est l'heure du déjeuner, sachez que les
ladys gardent leur ligne grâce au poisson
du jour ou une simple salade.

2   Knitwear/Strickwaren/Lainages

Pringle
141–142 Sloane Street
London SW1X 9AY
Tel: +44 20 7881 3060
www.pringlescotland.com
Tube: Sloane Square

Hawick in Scotland is the centre of the
British knitwear industry and where

Pringle got its illustrious beginnings in
1815. This is the brand that first managed
to knit cashmere and turn it into the
world's most luxurious material. By 2000,
it looked like Pringle had had its day but
a significant re-think turned the company
around into the hip knitwear label it has
once again become, contemporary twist in
old quality.

Das schottische Hawick ist das Zentrum
der britischen Strickwaren-Industrie und
die Heimat des 1815 gegründeten Lables
Pringle. Pringle war das erste Unternehmen, das aus Kaschmir Strick herstellte
und zu einem der weltweit luxuriösesten
Materialien machte. Allerdings hatte das
Unternehmen um 2000 seine besten Tage
hinter sich, doch dank einer Neupositionie-
rung ist das Label wieder hip und verbindet
Zeitgeist gekonnt mit guter alter Qualität.

Pringle a vu le jour en 1815 à Hawick en
Écosse, le centre du tricot britannique.
Elle fut la première à tricoter du cachemire
et à en faire le lainage le plus luxueux du
monde. En 2000, ses jours paraissaient
comptés mais un important remaniement
en a fait à nouveau une marque branchée,
avec un look contemporain dans une
qualité du bon vieux temps.

3   Perfume & Cosmetics/ Düfte & Haut-
    pflege/Parfumerie et cosmétiques

Jo Malone
150 Sloane Street
London SW1X 9BX
Tel: +44 20 7730 2100
www.jomalone.co.uk
Tube: Sloane Square

Jo Malone launched her business out of
her flat in the 1980s and her facials quickly became cult treatments with models
such as Yasmin Le Bon and her friends.
She opened up shop in 1994 and expanded to include fragrances – the Grapefruit
is delicious – and wonderfully light make-
up. Products come in many price ranges
and it's hard to resist the butter yellow-
and-black packaging.

Jo Malone legte den Grundstein für ihr Ge-

schäft in den 1980ern – in ihrer Wohnung.
Ihre Gesichtsbehandlungen begeisterten
Kundinnen wie Model Yasmin Le Bon und
wurden so Kult. 1994 eröffnete Malone
den ersten Laden; gleichzeitig erweiterte
sie ihr Angebot mit Düften (der Grapefruit-
Duft ist himmlisch) und traumhaft leichten
Make-ups. Beim Anblick der buttergelb-
schwarzen Verpackungen fällt es einem
schwer, dem Angebot zu widerstehen.

Jo Malone a commencé dans son appartement dans les années 80 et ses masques
sont vite devenus culte auprès de mannequins comme Yasmin Le Bon et ses amies.
Elle a ouvert sa boutique en 1994, élargis-
sant sa gamme aux parfums (le pample-
mousse est divin) et au maquillage léger
et sublime. Il y en a pour toutes les bourses.
Son packaging jaune beurre et noir est
irrésistible.

4   Shoes/Schuhe/Chaussures

French Sole
6 Ellis Street
London SW1X 9AL
Tel: +44 20 7730 3771
www.frenchsole.com
Tube: Sloane Square

Flat shoes are always in fashion for shoe
designer Jane Winkworth, who founded
French Sole in 1980 after designing for
various companies (including Biba and
Gamba) starting in 1968. French Sole
started as a mail order and was followed
by this delicious store, which stocks over
400 designs of ballet shoes in everything
from animal print, to metallic and polka-dot
prints. The question is: which to choose?

Für Schuhdesignerin Jane Winkworth, die
seit 1968 für verschiedene Labels (darun-
ter Biba und Gamba) entwarf, sind flache
Schuhe immer im Trend. 1980 lancierte sie
French Sole zunächst als Katalogversand.
Heute verkauft sie in diesem herrlichen
Laden über 400 Varianten ihres klassischen
Ballettschuhs: Animalprints, Metallic, Tup-
fenmuster – man hat die Qual der Wahl.

Pour Jane Winkworth, qui a lancé French
Sole en 1980 après avoir été styliste pour

4

5

6

plusieurs autres marques (dont Biba et Gamba), les semelles plates ne se démodent pas. Opérant d'abord par correspondance, puis dans cette délicieuse boutique, la marque décline la ballerine sous plus de 400 formes, de l'imprimé animal au métallique en passant par les petits pois. La question est : lesquelles choisir ?

---

5   Café/Café/Café

Oriel
50–51 Sloane Square
London SW1W 8AX
Tel: +44 20 7730 2804
Tube: Sloane Square

With a perfect view of Sloane Square and all around it, it's no wonder that Oriel is almost always full to the hilt. This café/restaurant is as close you get to a French brasserie in London – grumpy service included – and is super popular with locals and tourists alike. Opt for a big English breakfast, or just go for coffee. Either way, there is plenty to look at.

Vom Oriel hat man einen tollen Blick auf den Sloane Square. Kein Wunder, ist das Café/Restaurant meist zum Bersten voll. Es ist genau so, wie man sich in London eine französische Brasserie vorstellt; dazu gehört auch der unfreundliche Service. Bei Einheimischen und Besuchern ist es dennoch beliebt. Unbedingt das große englische Frühstück ausprobieren – oder einfach einen Kaffee genießen. Egal was, zu sehen gibt es hier allemal viel.

Avec sa vue imprenable sur Sloan Square, il ne faut pas s'étonner qu'Oriel soit toujours bondé. Ce café/restaurant, très prisé des locaux et des touristes, est ce qui se rapproche le plus d'une brasserie parisienne à Londres, les serveurs grognons inclus. Que vous preniez un copieux breakfast anglais ou un simple café, vous ne vous y ennuierez pas.

---

6   Shoes/Schuhe/Chaussures

Emma Hope
53 Sloane Square

London SW1W 8AX
Tel: +44 20 7259 9566
www.emmahope.co.uk
Tube: Sloane Square

Emma Hope's shoes are like a party for feet: decorative, boisterous and colourful. Her first shop opened in Islington in 1986 and her company has gone from strength to strength. While she does beautiful, dainty shoes for women in great hues and decorated with pretty detailing, she also does a lovely sneaker collection for men who like a bit of attention drawn to their feet.

Schuhe von Emma Hope haben eine tolle Eigenschaft: Sie versetzen in Festlaune. Ihr erstes Geschäft eröffnete sie 1986 in Islington und eilt seither von Erfolg zu Erfolg. Kein Wunder: Ihre Schuhe sind effektvoll und etwas unverfroren. Hope hat sich einen Namen mit zierlichen Damenschuhen in wunderbaren Farbtönen und mit hübschen Details gemacht, entwirft aber auch eine Turnschuh-Kollektion für Herren, die das Augenmerk gerne auf ihre Füße richten.

Les souliers d'Emma Hope sont une fête pour les pieds : décoratifs, tapageurs et colorés. Depuis l'ouverture de sa première boutique à Islington en 1986, sa maison n'a cessé de gagner en puissance. Outre ses ravissantes créations aux couleurs superbes pour les dames, elle propose une ligne de baskets pour les messieurs qui aiment attirer l'attention sur leurs pieds.

Personal Finds/Eigene Entdeckungen/
Découvertes personnelles:

_____

_____

_____

_____

_____

_____

_____

7

8

9

7 Kitchen Ware/Küchenutensilien/
Ustensiles de cuisine

David Mellor
4 Sloane Square
London SW1W 8EE
Tel: +44 20 7730 4259
www.davidmellordesign.com
Tube: Sloane Square

This shop is pure hedonism for those obsessed with cooking and anything to do with kitchens. David Mellor's career was kicked off when his Pride cutlery (now a modern classic) was put into production in 1953 when he was still a student at the Royal College of Art. The Sloane Square shop has been keeping Chelsea kitchens looking gorgeous since it opened in 1969.

Wer gerne kocht und viel Zeit in der Küche verbringt, wird in diesem Geschäft schwelgen. David Mellor machte sich 1953 einen Namen mit der Lancierung der Pride Messer, die er noch als Student am Royal College of Art entwickelte. Heute sind die Messer ein Klassiker. Und seit 1969 sorgt sein Geschäft am Sloane Square dafür, dass Küchen in Chelsea gut aussehen.

Une boutique qui fera fondre tous les mordus de cuisine. La carrière de David Mellor a démarré en flèche en 1953 quand ses couverts Pride (désormais un classique) ont été produits en série alors qu'il était encore étudiant au Royal College of Art. Depuis son ouverture en 1969, les plus belles cuisines de Chelsea s'équipent dans sa boutique de Sloane Square.

8 Dog's & Cat's Fashion/Haustier-
Boutique/Mode pour chiens et chats

Mungo & Maud
79 Elizabeth Street
London SW1W 9PJ
Tel: +44 20 7952 4570
www.mungoandmaud.com
Tube: Sloane Square/Victoria

There are many ways to spoil a child and, now, thanks to Mungo & Maud, there are an equal number of ways to spoil a pet.

This pretty shop on Elizabeth Street offers just about everything under the blue sky that a dog or cat (or its owner) should need or want, be it towels, toys, raincoats or treats. You must buy something for Spot or Fluffy, a biscuit might do.

Nicht nur Kinder, sondern auch die geliebten Vierbeiner kommen heutzutage in den Genuss eines gepflegten Lifestyles. An der Elizabeth Street bietet Mungo & Maud so ziemlich alles an, was Hund, Katze und Besitzer brauchen oder unbedingt haben müssen: Tücher, Spielzeuge, Regenmäntel oder Leckerbissen. Ein Biscuit sollte man für Fido oder Mieze schon kaufen.

Il y a mille manières de gâter son enfant et, désormais, grâce à Mungo & Maud, il y en existe autant de combler son animal chéri. Cette jolie boutique contient tout ce dont un chien ou un chat (ou leur maître) peut avoir besoin : serviettes, jouets, imperméables ou friandises. Médor et Minou se contenteront peut-être d'un biscuit.

9 Hats/Hüte/Modiste

Philip Treacy
69 Elizabeth Street
London SW1W 9PJ
Tel: +44 20 7730 3992
www.philiptreacy.co.uk
Tube: Sloane Square/Victoria

Irish-born Philip Treacy is not just a milliner, he is an artist. This is the view taken by his many fans who rely on his creations to make them look smashing at Ascot. His biggest fan, of course, is the eccentric stylist Isabella Blow in whose basement his business started. This shop opened in 1994 and nobody can resist going in to admire or – if they are feeling brave – to try on one of his splendid creations.

Der Ire Philip Treacy ist nicht nur Hutmacher, sondern auch Künstler. So sehen das die Kunden, die sich für einen effektvollen Auftritt in Ascot hundertprozentig auf ihn verlassen. Treacys größter Fan ist allerdings die exzentrische Stylistin Isabella Blow. Seine Karriere startete er in ihrem Keller, seit 1994 hat er ein eigenes Ge-

schäft. Es ist unmöglich, dort vorbeizulaufen, ohne die prachtvollen Kreationen bewundert oder anprobiert zu haben.

L'Irlandais Philip Treacy n'est pas un simple modiste, c'est un artiste. Croyez-en ses nombreux clients qui comptent sur lui pour briller à Ascot. Son premier atelier était situé dans le sous-sol de son plus grand fan, la styliste excentrique Isabella Blow. On ne peut s'empêcher d'entrer dans sa boutique, ouverte en 1994, pour admirer ses splendides créations et, si on s'en sent le courage, en essayer une.

10 Chocolate/Schokolade/Chocolat

The Chocolate Society
36 Elizabeth Street
London SW1W 9NZ
Tel: +44 20 7259 9222
www.chocolate.co.uk
Tube: Sloane Square/Victoria

It's so great that something as wonderful as chocolate should have its own society just to make its power official. The society says it "was formed in 1991 to promote the consumption and pure enjoyment of the finest quality chocolates". Not ones to argue, we are grateful that one can also buy chocolate at the premises to consume and enjoy. The gold-leaf choccies are particularly indulgent and hard to resist.

Toll, dass etwas so Wunderbares wie Schokolade in einem eigenen Verein gefeiert wird. Der Verein „Chocolate Society" wurde 1991 gegründet, um nach eigenen Aussagen „den Genuss allerfeinster Schokolade" zu fördern. Ein edler Vorsatz, der dadurch noch versüßt wird, dass man hier auch noch diese Schokoladen kaufen kann. Die Schokoladen mit echtem Blattgold sind besonders köstlich und ihnen ist schwer zu widerstehen.

N'est-il pas merveilleux qu'un produit aussi divin que le chocolat ait sa propre société afin d'officialiser son pouvoir ? Cette dernière a été « fondée en 1991 afin de promouvoir la consommation et le plaisir pur des meilleurs chocolats ». Qui contestera un tel programme ? Par chance, on peut même

10

11

12

n acheter sur place. Les petits chocolats
nrobés de feuille d'or sont irrésistibles.

1 Pub/Pub/Pub

The Grenadier

8 Wilton Row
London SW1X 7NR
Tel: +44 20 7235 3074
Tube: Hyde Park Corner/Knightsbridge

For a pub with local history, look no further
than The Grenadier, which sits in very posh
Wilton Row and is painted British red,
white and blue. The interior pays homage
to its military past: the Duke of Wellington's troops used it as their mess.

The Grenadier, in den britischen Farben
Rot, Weiß und Blau, ist ein Pub voller
Lokalgeschichte. Die Einrichtung ist eine
Hommage an die militärische Vergangen-
heit des Lokals. Es diente den Truppen
des Duke of Wellington als Messe.

Pour un pub chargé d'histoire locale, rendez-vous au Grenadier peint aux couleurs
du drapeau britannique. Le décor rend
hommage à son passé militaire : c'était
autrefois le messe des troupes du duc de
Wellington.

2 Italian Restaurant/Italienisches Res-
    taurant/Restaurant italien

Daphne's

12 Draycott Avenue
London SW3 3AE
Tel: +44 20 7589 4257
www.daphnes-restaurant.co.uk
Tube: South Kensington

Tucked away in one of South Ken's
smartest streets, Daphne's is the antithe-
sis of peasant Italian cooking. Ever since
opening its chic doors in 1964, Daphne's
has been pulling in the glossy ladies
who lunch during the day and the stars
in the evening with its delicious seasonal
menu of seafood, pasta and light meat
dishes. Don't be surprised to find the
likes of Elizabeth Hurley there with her
cohorts.

Das Daphne's liegt etwas versteckt an einer der elegantesten Straßen von South
Kensington und ist das genaue Gegenteil
eines einfachen, bäuerlichen italienischen
Restaurants. Seit 1964 wird Daphne's von
gepflegten Damen bevorzugt, die sich zum
Lunch treffen. Abends trifft sich die Prominenz zu köstlichem Fisch, feiner Pasta und
leichten Fleischgerichten. Gut möglich, hier
Elizabeth Hurley mit ihrem Gefolge anzutreffen.

Niché dans l'une des rues les plus sélectes
de South Ken, le Daphne's est l'antithèse
de la cuisine paysanne italienne. Depuis
son inauguration en 1964, les élégantes
dames de la haute viennent y déjeuner et
les stars y dîner, attirées par sa délicieuse
carte saisonnière de fruits de mer, de pâ-
tes et de plats de viande légers. Ne soyez
pas surpris si vous y croisez Elizabeth
Hurley et sa clique.

Personal Finds/Eigene Entdeckungen/
Découvertes personnelles:

Fashion/Mode/Mode
Paul Smith

Brasserie/Brasserie/Brasserie
Notting Hill Brasserie

Pub/Pub/Pub
The Cow

Vintage Furniture/Vintage-Möbel/Mobilier vintage
Themes & Variations

Food Heaven/Gourmettempel/Café traiteur
Tom's Deli

Shop Café/Boutique-Café/Boutique café
Nicole Farhi

Beauty Products & spa/Kosmetik & Spa/Produits de beauté & spa
SPACE.NK

Chocolate/Schokolade/Chocolatier
Melt

Bags/Handtaschen/Sacs
Anya Hindmarch

Café & Delis/Café & Delikatessengeschäft/Café & traiteur
Ottolenghi

Fashion/Mode/Mode
Matches

Patisserie/Patisserie/Pâtisserie
Lisboa Patisserie

Shopping Centre/Shopping Center/Galerie marchande
Whiteleys

Restaurant/Restaurant/Restaurant
Raoul's Café & Bar

Burger/Burger/Hamburger
Gourmet Burger Kitchen

Dim Sum/Dim Sum/Dim Sum
Ping Pong

Vintage Furniture/Vintage-Möbel/Mobilier vintage
Domus Gallery

Restaurant/Restaurant/Restaurant
The Ledbury

W2

Notting Hill
Bayswater

LISBOA PATISSERIE

Gotborne Rd
Wornington Rd
Bevington Rd
Westway
Portobello Road
Basing St
Tavistock Road
All Saints' Rd
Westbourne Park
Blenheim Cres
Talbot Rd
Elgin Cres
Ladbroke
Lansdowne Crescent
Grove
Westbourne Park
Leamington Rd Villas
Aldridge Road Villas
Great Western Road
Westbourne Park Road
Ledbury Road
Talbot Road
Chepstow Road

THE COW

THE LEDBURY

RAOUL'S CAFÉ & BAR

OTTOLENGHI

DOMUS

ANYA HINDMARCH
NICOLE FARHI
TOM'S DELI

GALLERY
MATCHES
SPACE

Artesian Rd
Grove

MELT

Westbourne Road
Villas

PAUL SMITH

THEMES & VARIATIONS

NOTTING HILL BRASSERIE

Kensington Park
Portobello
Chepstow Road
Pembridge Cres
Pembridge Road
Pembridge Gdns

Pembridge Square

THE

Ladbroke Square
Ladbroke Terrace
Lansdowne Walk

Notting Hill Gate
Nottin Ga

©MICHAEL A HILL

Delamere Terrace
Howley P
Bourne Terrace
Road
Harrow Road
Westway
Park Villas
Royal Oak
Park Road
Porchester Rd
Gloucester Terrace
Bishop's Bridge Road
Eastbourne Terrace
Westbourne Terrace
Paddington
Terrace
GOURMET BURGER KITCHEN
Westbourne Grove
Gloucester Terrace
Cleveland Gdns
WHITELEYS
THE HEMPEL
Craven Road
Queensway
Porchester Gdns
Porchester Gdns
Leinster Gdns
Craven Hill Gdns
Craven Hill
Inverness Terrace
Hereford Rd
Moscow Road
St Petersburgh Pl
Bayswater
Lancaster Gate
Bayswater Road
Queensway
KENSINGTON PALACE
KENSINGTON GARDENS

The Lennox Hotel

34 Pembridge Gardens, London W2 4DX
☎ +44 20 7229 9977   🖷 +44 20 7727 4982
info@thelennox.com
www.thelennox.com
Tube: Notting Hill Gate
Booking: www.great-escapes-hotels.com

The Lennox Hotel

When it comes to hotels in London, the very British expression "cheap and cheerful" rarely applies. The Lennox, however, is an exception in that it's a reasonably priced hotel in an expensive city, and staff members are, quite literally, cheerful. The Lennox is a five-minute walk to Notting Hill Gate station and mere seconds from Portobello Road and its eponymous market. The Lennox was once the popular but badly decorated Pembridge Court Hotel. It was refurbished, had its name changed and reopened in 2006 with a clean, contemporary new look – simple white walls, dark woods, neutral textiles – and hasn't looked back. It is as popular with music industry professionals, model agencies and other fashion types as it is with regular travellers and families. With the cool cafes and shops of Notting Hill so close by, and transport links so convenient, it is a lovely hotel in which to set up base and explore the city.

Hotels in London sind alles, nur nicht billig. Eine der wenigen Ausnahmen ist das Lennox. Nicht nur sind die Preise hier sehr vernünftig, auch das Personal ist äußerst zuvorkommend. Das Hotel ist nur gerade fünf Gehminuten von der Notting Hill Gate Station entfernt und ein paar Sekunden von der Portobello Road und dem gleichnamigen Markt. Früher hieß das Lennox Pembridge Court Hotel – ein beliebtes, aber nicht besonders nett eingerichtetes Hotel. Mit der Renovierung von 2006 erhielt es seinen neuen Namen und einen neuen Look. Das Dekor mit weißen Wänden, dunklem Holz und Textilien in Neutral-Tönen wirkt sehr zeitgemäß, und von der Vergangenheit ist hier nichts mehr zu sehen. Die Gäste sind Leute aus dem Musikbusiness, von Modelagenturen und Fashionistas, aber auch ganz normale Vielreisende und sogar Familien. Nett: In Notting Hill gibt's viele coole Cafés und Läden und dank der guten Verkehrsverbindungen kann man von diesem reizenden Hotel aus die Stadt gut erkundschaften.

L'expression très british « pas cher et joyeux » s'applique rarement aux hôtels londoniens. Le Lennox fait exception, pratiquant des prix raisonnables dans une ville chère et possédant un personnel littéralement enjoué. Il est situé à cinq minutes à pied de la station de métro Notting Hill Gate et à quelques secondes du marché aux puces de Portobello Road. Anciennement le Pembridge Court Hotel, c'était un hôtel populaire mais laid. Réaménagé, rebaptisé, il a rouvert ses portes en 2006 avec une décoration fraîche et contemporaine : murs blancs, boiseries sombres, tissus neutres. Il est très apprécié des musiciens, des agences de mannequin, des gens de la mode, comme des touristes voyageant en famille. À proximité des cafés et boutiques branchés du quartier et pratique pour les transports, c'est un endroit charmant où s'établir pour explorer la ville.

Rates: From 140 € (100 GBP) excl. VAT.
Rooms: 20 (4 junior suites).
Restaurant: The Lennox Bar.
History: The hotel used to be the chintz-filled Pembridge Court Hotel but was refurbished and reopened in 2006 in its new format.
X-Factor: Miniature teddy bears are complimentary to guests.
Internet: Complimentary WiFi and broadband access.

Preise: ab 140 € (100 GBP) exkl. VAT.
Zimmer: 20 (4 Junior Suiten).
Restaurant: The Lennox Bar.
Geschichte: Das verstaubte Pembridge Court Hotel wurde renoviert und 2006 als The Lennox wiedereröffnet.
X-Faktor: Miniatur-Teddybären als Gast-Geschenk.
Internet: Kostenloser WiFi-Zugang und Breitbandanschluss.

Prix : À partir de 140 € (100 GBP), TVA non comprise.
Chambres : 20 (4 junior suites).
Restauration : The Lennox Bar.
Histoire : L'hôtel s'appelait autrefois le Pembridge Court Hotel et était tapissé de chintz du sol au plafond. Réaménagé, il a rouvert en 2006.
Le « petit plus » : Les nounours miniatures offerts aux clients.
Internet : Accès WiFi et haut débit gratuit.

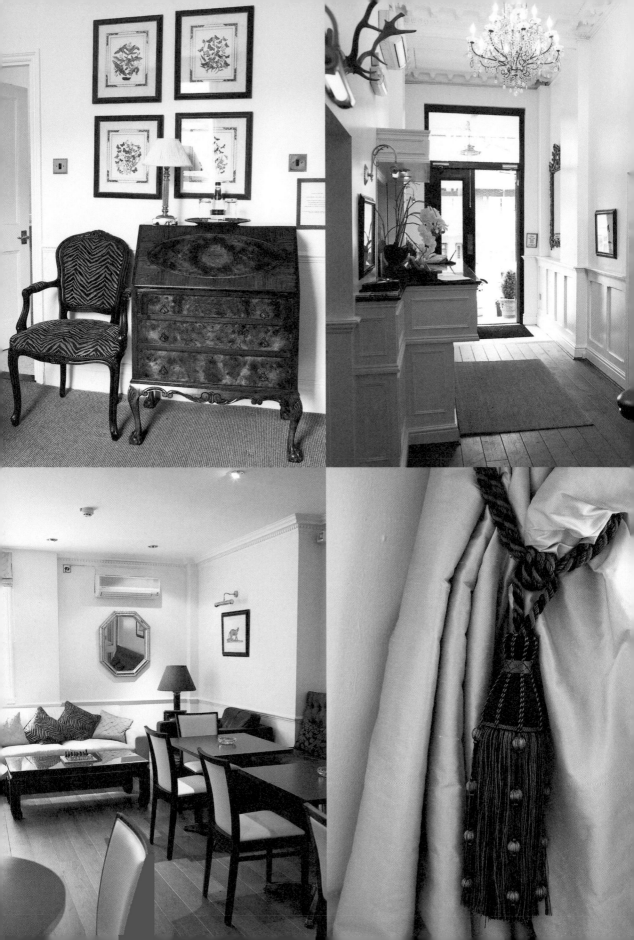

1

2

3

---

1   Fashion/Mode/Mode

Paul Smith
Westbourne House
122 Kensington Park Road
London W11 2EP
Tel: +44 20 7727 3553
www.paulsmith.co.uk
Tube: Notting Hill Gate

This enormous villa that was converted into a shop in the late 1990s provides one
of the most incredible retail experiences in
London. In fact, it was Sir Paul Smith's
shop that was instrumental in the gentrifi-
cation of this area in the past decade. Over
three floors, choose from Smith's finely tailored suits, feminine dresses, accessories,
vintage toys and books – all quirky and
English, like Smith himself.

Aus einer riesigen Villa wird eine Boutique:
In den späten 1990ern eröffnete hier Sir
Paul Smith sein Geschäft und löste damit
im Viertel einen Boom aus. Über drei Stockwerke verteilt findet man seine fantastisch
geschnittenen Anzüge, feminine Kleider,
Accessoires, Vintage-Spielzeug und Bücher. Alles sehr eigenwillig gemischt und
englisch, genau wie Smith. Eines der span-
nendesten Einkaufserlebnisse in London.

Cet hôtel particulier converti en boutique à
la fin des années 90 offre une expérience
unique à Londres. De fait, il a sérieusement
contribué à l'embourgeoisement du quartier. Sur trois étages, vous pouvez flâner
entre les costumes superbement taillés,
les robes féminines, les jouets anciens et
les livres, tous excentriques et très british,
à l'image de sir Paul Smith lui-même.

---

2   Brasserie/Brasserie/Brasserie

Notting Hill Brasserie
92 Kensington Park Road
London W11 2PN
Tel: +44 20 7229 4481
Tube: Notting Hill Gate

Popular with Notting Hill residents and
Holland Park dwellers alike, the Notting
Hill Brasserie housed in three converted
Victorian townhouses is an elegant slice of
French in the chicest part of west London.
Yet, although it caters to a sophisticated
crowd, the vibe is very laid-back and staff
are super friendly. Duck, fish and seafood,
done contemporary French-style, feature
heavily on the menu.

Die Notting Hill Brasserie, die bei den Bewohnern von Notting Hill und Holland Park
sehr beliebt ist, bringt ein Stück französische Eleganz ins schicke Westlondon. Dafür wurden drei viktorianische nebeneinander liegende Stadthäuser umgebaut. Die
Gäste sind zwar mondän, dennoch ist das
Ambiente sehr entspannt und das Personal
außergewöhnlich freundlich. Ente, Fisch
und Meeresfrüchte nach moderner franzö-
sicher Art dominieren die Speisekarte.

Très prisée des habitants de Notting Hill et
d'Holland Park, cette brasserie occupant
trois maisons victoriennes constitue une
élégante touche de France dans la partie
la plus chic de l'ouest de Londres. La
clientèle est sophistiquée mais l'ambiance
très décontractée et le personnel adorable.
La carte, très moderne, met à l'honneur le
canard, les poissons et les fruits de mer.

---

3   Pub/Pub/Pub

The Cow
89 Westbourne Park Road
London W2 5QH
Tel: +44 20 7221 0021
Tube: Westbourne Park

As far as pubs go, it doesn't get much
cooler than this. The gorgeous people of
Notting Hill crowd into the Cow every day
of the week either to chat over a pint, or to
eat its delicious food in the upstairs dining
room. It's no ordinary pub grub, either.
We're talking beautiful seafood platters,
fish, risotto… you get the picture. Book
or you'll never get a table.

Dieser Pub gehört so ziemlich zum Angesagtesten, was Notting Hill zu bieten hat.
Die schicken Bewohner pilgern tagtäglich
hierher, um sich bei einem Bier zu unterhal-
ten oder oben im Speisesaal ein gutes Essen zu genießen. Selbstverständlich gibt es
hier keine gewöhnliche Pub-Gerichte,
sondern Dinge wie Meeresfrüchte, Fisch
und Risotto. Unbedingt reservieren. Sonst
wird man garantiert keinen Tisch finden.

Vous ne trouverez pas un pub plus cool.
Tout le gratin de Notting Hill s'y presse
tous les jours pour papoter devant une
pinte de bière ou déguster sa délicieuse
cuisine dans la salle à manger à l'étage.
Superbes plateaux de fruits de mer, poisson, risotto… inutile de vous faire un des-
sin. Réservez, sinon vous n'aurez jamais
une table.

---

4   Vintage Furniture/Vintage-Möbel/
     Mobilier vintage

Themes & Variations
231 Westbourne Grove
London W11 2SE
Tel: +44 20 7727 5531
www.themesandvariations.com
Tube: Notting Hill Gate

Set designers, interior designers and modernists flock to Themes & Variations to
check out its exquisite collection of high-
est quality post-war and contemporary
design furnishings and decorative art for
inspiration. It opened in 1984 and has
been showing off its mix of mainly (but
not exclusively) Scandinavian and Italian
pieces ever since. Designers represented
include the likes of Tom Dixon, Gio Ponti
and Mark Brazier-Jones.

Bühnenbildner, Inneneinrichter und Modernisten lieben Themes & Variations. Hier
finden sie seit 1984 auserlesene Möbel
und dekorative Kunstobjekte, zeitgenös-
sisch oder aus der Nachkriegszeit. Der
Schwerpunkt liegt vor allem auf skandina-
vischem und italienischem Design, aber
auch Designer wie Tom Dixon und Mark
Brazier-Jones sind hier vertreten.

Les décorateurs de cinéma et d'intérieur,
comme les modernistes, hantent cette
boutique en quête d'inspiration. Ouverte
en 1984, sa superbe collection de meubles
et d'art décoratif de grande qualité des
années 50 à aujourd'hui, principalement
scandinaves et italiens mais pas seule-

4

5

6

ment, inclut des grands noms du design tels que Tom Dixon, Gio Ponti et Mark Brazier-Jones.

---

5 Food Heaven/Gourmettempel/Café traiteur

Tom's Deli
226 Westbourne Grove
London W11 2RH
Tel: +44 20 7221 8818
Tube: Notting Hill Gate

You know a restaurant is good when you can't get a seat. Tom's is one such place, so popular with locals that there are normally queues of people waiting to get in on a weekend. Tom Conran (son of Sir Terence) offers gorgeous brunches and lunches in the tiny café bit upstairs, but also beautiful baked goods, cheeses and fresh takeaway meals for busy Notting Hillers. This is simply food heaven.

Ein gutes Restaurant erkennt man daran, dass es (fast) unmöglich ist, einen Tisch zu ergattern. In Tom's Delikatessen sind die Warteschlangen besonders an den Wochenenden endlos lang. Doch die Brunches und Mittagessen von Tom Conran (Sir Terence Conrans Sohn) sind super köstlich – da nimmt man die Warterei gerne in Kauf. Es gibt auch herrliche Backwaren, köstliche Käse und frische Takeaway-Mahlzeiten. Hier fühlt sich jeder Gourmet wie im Himmel.

Vous savez qu'un restaurant est bon quand il est toujours plein. Tom est tellement prisé des Londoniens qu'ils font la queue devant la porte le week-end. Tom Conran (fils de sir Terence) propose des brunchs et des déjeuners délicieux dans le minuscule café à l'étage mais également des plats à emporter, des fromages et des produits frais pour les gens pressés. Une véritable manne.

---

6 Shop & Café/Boutique & Café/ Boutique & café

Nicole Farhi
202 Westbourne Grove
London W11 2RH

Tel: +44 20 7792 6888
www.nicolefarhi.com
Tube: Notting Hill Gate

Is it a shop or is it a café? The answer is: both. Taking inspiration from the Bond Street shop and café, Nicole Farhi opened up 2002 (there's also one in Chelsea Market New York) in what is pretty much a dead zone in terms of places to eat. Now, weekends are bursting at the seams with people eating outside and lining up near the mannequins and accessories to get a table inside. Shop while you wait.

Hier sind Café und Boutique ein und dasselbe. 2002 hat das Konzept von Nicole Farhi Café-Boutique an der Bond Street auf diese Location in Notting Hill (und übrigens auch im New Yorker Chelsea Market) übertragen. Da es in dieser Gegend kaum ein Restaurant gibt, ist es hier an Wochenenden zum Bersten voll. Das Schöne daran: Während man in der langen Schlange auf seinen Tisch wartet, kann man nebenbei noch etwas einkaufen.

Est-ce une boutique ou un café ? Les deux. S'inspirant du café/boutique de Bond Street, Nicole Farhi a ouvert le 2002 (elle en a un autre à Chelsea à New York) dans un coin qui manquait cruellement de restaurants. Désormais, sa terrasse est toujours pleine et on se presse entre les robes et les accessoires pour obtenir une table à l'intérieur. En attendant d'être assis, faites quelques emplettes.

Personal Finds/Eigene Entdeckungen/ Découvertes personnelles:

_____

_____

_____

_____

_____

Miller's Residence

111a Westbourne Grove, London W2 4UW
☎ +44 20 7243 1024   📠 +44 20 7243 1064
enquiries@millersuk.com
www.millersuk.com
Tube: Bayswater/Notting Hill Gate
Booking: www.great-escapes-hotels.com

Miller's Residence

Miller's Residence in Notting Hill is for the unashamed maximalist in all of us. Just about every millimetre of the walls, ceilings and floors is covered by something: antique furniture, dried flowers, gilt-framed paintings, more antique furniture… you get the picture. Its location is excellent – it is right off Westbourne Grove above a row of shops and it is, without a doubt, the most bohemian hotel in town. Owned by Martin Miller, a renowned antiques dealer, Miller's Residence is very much a work-in-progress and furniture is constantly being moved around and re-arranged. The lounge, where guests take their breakfast, is as busy as the rest of the house and yet as cosy as your own living room. Rooms at Miller's Residence are comfortable, clean and come with a small bathroom. If you want a trip to London with a good dose of English eccentricity thrown in, it doesn't get better than this.

„Nur nichts übertreiben" ist man versucht, beim Anblick der Miller's Residence in Notting Hill auszurufen: Wände, Decken und Böden – jeder Millimeter ist vollgestopft mit Antiquitäten, getrockneten Blumen, goldgerahmten Bildern und noch mehr Antiquitäten. Mit Sicherheit ist dies das verrückteste Hotel der Stadt. An ausgezeichneter Lage, gleich beim Westbourne Grove, besetzt es den zweiten Stock über einer ganzen Reihe von Läden. Angetrieben vom Besitzer Martin Miller, einem bekannten Antiquitätenhändler, werden hier ständig Möbel verschoben und Bilder umgehängt. Die Lounge, in der die Gäste jeweils ihr Frühstück einnehmen, ist so opulent wie der Rest des Hauses und so gemütlich wie ein Wohnzimmer. Die Gästezimmer sind behaglich, blitzblank und verfügen über ein eigenes Badezimmer. Liebhaber englischer Exzentrik sind hier genau richtig. Besser als hier wird's garantiert nirgends.

Miller's Residence à Notting Hill s'adresse au maximaliste éhonté qui sommeille en chacun de nous. Du sol au plafond, il n'y pas un centimètre carré qui ne soit occupé par des tableaux, des antiquités, des bouquets séchés… et encore des antiquités. L'emplacement est idéal, sur Westbourne Grove au-dessus d'une rangée de boutiques. C'est sans conteste l'hôtel le plus bohème de Londres. Martin Miller, son propriétaire, est un célèbre antiquaire. Il entretient son établissement en évolution constante, déplaçant sans cesse les meubles. Le salon cosy, où l'on prend ses petits-déjeuners, est aussi chargé que le reste de la maison mais vous vous y sentirez chez vous. Les chambres sont confortables, propres et équipées d'une petite salle de bains. Si vous souhaitez insuffler une bonne dose d'excentricité britannique dans votre séjour à Londres, il n'y a pas mieux.

Rates: From 220 € (150 GBP) excl. VAT.
Rooms: 8.
Restaurants: None.
History: The hotel opened in 1995. Before that the location was derelict.
X-Factor: The abundant wrapped sweets available at every turn.
Internet: Complimentary WiFi and broadband access.

Preise: ab 220 € (150 GBP) exkl. VAT.
Zimmer: 8.
Restaurants: Keines.
Geschichte: Das Hotel wurde 1995 eröffnet. Zuvor war das Gebäude vom Zerfall bedroht.
X-Faktor: Überall im Haus findet man zum Naschen hübsch verpackte Süßigkeiten.
Internet: Kostenloser WiFi-Zugang und Breitbandanschluss.

Prix : À partir de 220 € (150 GBP), TVA non comprise.
Chambres : 8.
Restauration : Aucune.
Histoire : Inauguré en 1995. Avant cela, le bâtiment n'était qu'une ruine.
Le « petit plus » : L'abondance de bonbons mis à disposition dans tous les coins.
Internet : Accès WiFi et haut débit gratuit.

1

2

3

1 Beauty Products & Spa/Kosmetik & Spa/Produitsde beauté & Spa

SPACE.NK
127–131 Westbourne Grove
London W2 4UP
Tel: +44 20 7727 8002
www.spacenk.co.uk
Tube: Royal Oak

When Nicky Kinnaird launched Space.NK in Covent Garden in 1993, she was onto a good thing: a one-stop shop for cool beauty and skincare products you can't find elsewhere in London. Others may have copied the idea since but Space.NK is still the leader of the pack with its selection of over 60 brands – Chantecaille, NARS, Stila, Dr. Sebagh, Elizabeth Arden, the list could go on and on. This Notting Hill branch also offers spa services.

Space.NK wurde 1993 von Nicky Kinnaird in Covent Garden gegründet. Ihr Konzept: hippe Kosmetik- und Hautpflegeprodukte anzubieten, die man sonst nirgends findet. Die Idee war so gut, dass Kinnaird zahlreiche Nachahmer fand. Doch Space.NK bleibt die beste Adresse für Produkte wie Chantecaille, NARS, Stila, Dr. Sebagh und Elizabeth Arden. Die Auswahl umfasst über 60 Produktlinien. Im Geschäft in Notting Hill gibt's auch Spa-Treatments.

En ouvrant Space.NK à Covent Garden en 1993, Nicky Kinnaird a eu du flair. On ne trouve ses formidables produits de beauté et de soin nulle part ailleurs à Londres. D'autres ont copié le concept depuis mais Space.NK reste le leader, avec plus de 60 marques dont Chantecaille, NARS, Stila, Dr. Sebagh, Elizabeth Arden. La branche de Notting Hill fait également spa.

2 Chocolate/Schokolade/Chocolatier

Melt
59 Ledbury Road
London W11 2AA
Tel: +44 20 7727 5030
www.meltchocolates.com
Tube: Notting Hill Gate

Notting Hill ladies may be famously trim

but even they can't resist Melt, a shop that gives chocolate addicts no hope for reform. Started in 2006 by Louise Nason, Melt's chocolates are made on-site and displayed in pristine white surroundings that only emphasise the beauty of the craft of chocolate-making by hand. Jasmine-tea truffles are particularly irresistible, but then so is everything else.

Selbst die notorisch figurbewussten Damen in Notting Hill können Melt nicht widerstehen. Schokoldensüchtige kann man hier schon gar nicht mehr retten. In der minimalistischen milchweißen Schokoladen-Boutique, die Louise Nason 2006 gegründet hatte, kommen die haus- und handgemachten Kreationen besonders gut zur Geltung. Die Trüffel mit Jasmintee sind besonders unwiderstehlich, alles andere jedoch auch.

Les dames de Notting Hill sont réputées pour leur minceur mais même elles ne résistent pas à Melt, la boutique où les accros au chocolat n'ont aucun espoir de rémission. Ouvert en 2006 par Louise Nason, tous les produits sont faits sur place et présentés dans un décor à la blancheur immaculée qui met en valeur leur beauté. Les truffes au thé au jasmin sont à se damner, comme tout le reste.

3 Bags/Handtaschen/Sacs

Anya Hindmarch
63a Ledbury Road
London W11 2AD
Tel: +44 20 7792 4427
www.anyahindmarch.com
Tube: Notting Hill Gate

You may well tell yourself you don't need any more handbags but wait until you enter Anya Hindmarch's shop and then try and resist. From washbags to tote bags, there is something luxurious in here for everyone. London society girls wouldn't be caught dead going to work without one of her solid leather day bags and her gimmicky "Be a Bag" collection seems to have a life of its own.

Mit dem Vorsatz, nicht schon wieder eine

Tasche zu kaufen, kommt man bei Anya Hindmarch nicht sehr weit. Ihre luxuriöse Taschenkollektion, die von Kulturbeutel bis Einkaufstasche reicht, ist einfach zu verführerisch. Das wissen bereits die Society-Töchter Londons: Ohne eine der soliden Lederhandtaschen von Hindmarch verlassen sie schon gar nicht erst das Haus. Hübsch: die verspielte „Be a Bag"-Kollektion.

Vous croyiez ne pas avoir besoin d'un sac à main de plus ? Attendez d'être entrée dans la boutique d'Anya Hindmarch. De la trousse au fourre-tout, il y en a pour tous les goûts. Les mondaines londoniennes préféreraient mourir que d'être vues sans un de ses solides sacs du jour en cuir. Les cabas imprimés avec votre photo favorite sont à mourir de rire.

4 Café & Delis/Café & Delikatessengeschäft/Café & traiteur

Ottolenghi
63 Ledbury Road
London W11 2AD
Tel: +44 20 7727 1121
www.ottolenghi.co.uk
Tube: Notting Hill Gate

Is it a café or a deli? Who cares as long as it's this yummy. Ottolenghi is like a boudoir of delicious, hand-crafted food. From the pastries displayed like jewels to the delicious, fresh salads overflowing in huge white bowls, it's difficult to know where to start. Or finish. Get a selection of salads and quiche as a takeaway or jostle with the Notting Hill yummy mummies for a seat in the café section.

Café oder Delikatessengeschäft? Das Ottolenghi ist nicht nur beides, sondern auch ein Schlaraffenland mit köstlichen, von Hand zubereiteten Spezialitäten. Feingebäck wird wie Schmuckstücke ausgestellt, die frischen Salate in großen, weißen Schüsseln präsentiert. Alles sieht so lecker aus, dass die Wahl schwer fällt. Im Café angelt man sich einen Tisch neben all den schicken Notting-Hill-Bewohnern. Für ein Takeaway empfiehlt sich Salat mit Quiche.

4

5

6

Café ou traiteur ? Peu importe tant que c'est bon. Ottolenghi est un boudoir de mets divins faits maison. Des pâtisseries présentées comme des bijoux aux immenses bols blancs débordant de salades exquises, on ne sait plus où donner de la tête. Emportez un choix de salades et une quiche ou battez-vous avec les jolies jeunes mamans de Notting Hill pour une table dans le coin café.

---

5   Fashion/Mode/Mode

Matches
60–64 Ledbury Road
London W11 2AJ
Tel: +44 20 7221 0255
www.matchesfashion.com
Tube: Notting Hill Gate

For those who hate shlepping around huge department stores in search of designer duds, Matches is a brilliant option. Small but perfectly formed, Matches offers beautiful, expensive clothing and accessories from mainstream and unusual labels. It has a brilliantly edited selection from the likes of Jovovich Hawk, Vanessa Bruno, Phi, Marc Jacobs the list goes on. Suffice it to say, the buyers are genius.

Kilometerlanger Streckenlauf mit schweren Einkaufstüten: Die Suche nach Designerklamotten in großen Kaufhäusern kann ganz schön anstrengend sein. Zum Glück gibt es Alternativen wie Matches. Hier findet man schöne, teure Kleider und Accessoires von etablierten, aber auch unkonventionellen Labels. Jovovich Hawk, Vanessa Bruno, Phi, Marc Jacobs und mehr – die Auswahl ist fantastisch und die Einkäufer sind einfach genial.

Pour ceux qui détestent errer dans les grands magasins en quête de nippes de créateur, Matches est la solution. Petite mais parfaitement conçue, la boutique propose des vêtements et accessoires beaux et chers de marques connues et plus rares. Elle présente une sélection brillante des collections de Jovovich Hawk, Vanessa Bruno, Phi, Marc Jacobs, et ainsi de suite. Ses acheteurs sont de vrais génies.

---

6   Patisserie/Patisserie/Pâtisserie

Lisboa Patisserie
57 Golborne Road
London W10 5NR
Tel: +44 20 8968 5242
Tube: Westbourne Park

Lisboa Patisserie is a slice of Portugal – Lisbon, presumably – in West London. Packed with Portuguese expat families, older men and ladies, youth and those in search of an exotic place to try something different, this café/restaurant has been plying its trade in the same location since 1978. Join the local Notting Hillbillies for a frothy coffee and a custard pastry, and pretend you're on holiday.

Ein Stück Portugal, besser Lissabon, in London: In der Patisserie Lisboa versammeln sich portugiesische Auswanderer-Familien, altere Semester genauso wie jüngere, und Leute, auf der Suche nach dem Anderen, Außergewöhnlichen. Das Café/Restaurant ist seit 1978 fester Bestandteil von Notting Hill, und viele Bewohner kommen hierher, um sich bei schaumigem Kaffee und Gebäck ein bisschen wie im Urlaub zu fühlen.

Une tranche de vie portugaise (ou lisboate) dans l'ouest de Londres. Bondé d'expatriés portugais de tout âge et de gens en quête d'un peu d'exotisme, ce café-restaurant existe depuis 1978. Mêlez-vous aux babas cool de Notting Hill devant un café et une pâtisserie à la crème, vous vous croirez en vacances.

Personal Finds/Eigene Entdeckungen/
Découvertes personnelles:

_____
_____
_____
_____
_____

The Hempel

31–35 Craven Hill Gardens, London W2 3EA
☎ +44 20 7298 9000   📠 +44 20 7102 4666
hotel@the-hempel.co.uk
www.the-hempel.co.uk
Tube: Bayswater
Booking: www.great-escapes-hotels.com

The Hempel

White, white and more white, The Hempel is an exercise in 1990s minimalism, but somehow retains a currency despite its homage to neutrals. Anouska Hempel knocked together five houses to create the hotel and her design is, without a doubt, the strongest statement here, but one must not overlook its amazing location mere minutes from Hyde Park. Service can be patchy but the rooms are peaceful, particularly those that look onto the square, and the Eastern influence in the interior lends it a Zen quality. The lobby is particularly impressive, created entirely from white Portland stone with elegant fireplaces and sunken seating areas. The Hempel's perfectly manicured garden square is one of its big selling points, especially during warm summer evenings when it is filled with candles and guests are invited to sit out there for dinner or to knock back a cocktail or two. I-Thai, The Hempels' Japanese-Thai-Italian fusion restaurant, offers a unique dining experience and is worth a visit, too.

Überall wo man hinblickt, sieht man nur Weiß. Das Hempel ist der Inbegriff des Minimalismus der 1990er. Trotz monochronen Dekors ist das Hotel ein klares Statement, für das Designerin Anouska Hempel fünf nebeneinander stehende Häuser zusammenlegen ließ. Natürlich ist ihr Design der wichtigste Grund, hier abzusteigen. Doch auch die Lage, ein paar Minuten vom Hyde Park entfernt, ist ein großes Plus. Die Gästezimmer sind alle sehr ruhig, besonders diejenigen auf der Seite des Hofes. Mit fernöstlich inspiriertem Dekor vermitteln sie zudem ein zen-buddhistisches Ambiente. Die Lobby aus weißem Portland-Gestein mit eleganten Kaminen und Sitzecken wirkt besonders beeindruckend. Toll ist auch der perfekt manikürte Garten: Besonders schön ist es, an einem lauen Sommerabend bei Kerzenlicht draußen zu dinieren oder an einem Cocktail zu nippen. Das Hempel-Restaurant I-Thai mit japanisch-thailändischer Fusion-Küche ist außergewöhnlich. Einziger Minuspunkt im Haus: Der Service ist mal so, mal so.

Du blanc, encore du blanc, rien que du blanc. Le Hempel est un exercice en minimalisme des années 90 avec quelques concessions aux tons neutres. Anouska Hempel a rassemblé cinq maisons pour créer son hôtel et apposé son style inimitable à la décoration, ce qui en fait son attrait outre son emplacement idéal à quelques minutes de Hyde Park. Le service n'est pas toujours à la hauteur mais les chambres sont tranquilles, notamment celles donnant sur le jardin, et l'influence orientale crée une ambiance zen. Le hall est particulièrement impressionnant, tout en pierre blanche de Portland avec d'élégantes cheminée et des banquettes encastrées. Le square/jardin carré parfaitement manucuré est l'un de ses principaux atouts, notamment les soirs chauds d'été quand il est illuminé de bougies et que l'on peut y dîner ou y prendre un verre. L'excellent restaurant I-Thai, avec sa cuisine fusion japonaise-thaï-italienne, mérite le détour.

Rates: From 390 € (265 GBP) excl. VAT.
Rooms: 35 rooms (6 suites, 6 private apartments).
Restaurant: I-Thai.
History: Five Georgian houses were knocked together in 1998 to create the hotel.
X-Factor: The garden square is, without a doubt, the best thing about this hotel.
Internet: WifFi in all rooms at 15 GBP per day.

Preise: ab 390 € (265 GBP) exkl. VAT.
Zimmer: 35 (6 Suiten, 6 Privat-Apartments).
Restaurant: I-Thai.
Geschichte: Fünf georgrianische Häuser wurden 1998 zu diesem Hotel zusammengefügt.
X-Faktor: Der rechteckig angelegte Garten ist zweifellos die größte Attraktion des Hotels.
Internet: WiFi-Zugang in allen Zimmern für 15 GBP pro Tag.

Prix : À partir de 390 € (265 GBP), TVA non comprise.
Chambres : 35 (6 suites, 6 appartements privés).
Restauration : I-Thai.
Histoire : Cinq maisons datant du XVIIIe siècle ont été reliées en 1998 pour créer cet hôtel.
Le « petit plus » : Le jardin carré est sans aucun doute le point fort de cet hôtel.
Internet : WiFi dans toutes les chambres pour 15 GBP par jour.

1

2

1   Shopping Centre/Shopping Center/ Galerie marchande

Whiteleys
151 Queensway
London W2 4QS
Tel: +44 20 7229 8844
www.whiteleys.com

Reflexology Shop
first floor, Fountain Atrium
Tel: +44 20 7792 9492
www.reflexshop.com

Viktorija at World of Feng Shui
Unit 113
Tel: +44 20 7034 0388
Tube: Bayswater

Whiteleys was the first shopping centre when it opened its Edwardian doors back in 1912 with its beautiful colonnade facade. After the restauration in 1989 it still keeps its old-time charme. Once you've done enough credit card damage, stop off at Reflexology Shop for a walk-in seated shoulder massage or reflexology on aching feet. It's affordable at 25 GBP for half an hour of bliss. And if it's your tarot cards you need read, head for Unit 113 and ask Viktorija about your future.

Whiteleys war, als es 1912 seine Tore in einem Gebäude mit wunderbarer Kolonnaden-Fassade öffnete, das erste Shopping Center Londons. 1989 renoviert, hat es seinen altmodischen Charme beibehalten. Wer sich seinem Kreditkartenlimit nähert, dem sei zur Beruhigung ein Stop im Reflexshop für eine Rücken- oder Fußreflexzonenmassage (25 GBP die halbe Stunde) empfohlen. Oder man schaut bei Viktorija in der „Unit 113" für einen Blick in die Tarotkarten vorbei.

Whiteleys était la première galerie marchande de Londres quand elle a ouvert ses portes en 1912 avec sa façade Belle Époque à colonnade. Restaurée en 1989, elle a conservé son charme d'antan. Une fois votre carte de crédit épuisée, faites une halte au Reflexshop pour faire masser vos épaules et vos petits pieds meurtris. Il ne vous en coûtera que 25 GBP

pour une demi-heure de béatitude. Et si l'avenir vous préoccupe, demandez à Viktorija, Unit 113, de vous tirer le tarot.

2   Burger/Burger/Hamburger

Gourmet Burger Kitchen
50 Westbourne Grove
London W2 5SH
Tel: +44 20 7243 4344
www.gbkinfo.co.uk
Tube: Bayswater/Royal Oak

London was hit by a wave of burger chains in about 2004 and Gourmet Burger Kitchen is one of the best. Burgers are made from 100% Aberdeen-Angus Scotch beef and are incredibly thick and juicy as burgers should be. The chicken and veggie options are equally yummy and none of these dishes would be complete without the perfectly cooked chips and a nice fresh salad.

Um 2004 schwappte über London eine Burger-Welle. Zu den besten Lokalen gehört Gourmet Burger Kitchen mit unglaublich dicken und saftigen Burgern aus 100 % schottischem Aberdeen-Angurs Rind – genau so wie richtige Burger sein sollten. Die Varianten mit Huhn und Gemüse schmecken genau so lecker. Dazu gibt's perfekt gebackene Pommes Frites und frische Salate.

Vers 2004, une vague de chaînes de hamburgers a déferlé sur Londres. Gourmet Burger est l'une des meilleures, avec des hamburgers 100% pur bœuf écossais incroyablement épais et juteux comme il se doit. Les options poulet et végétarienne sont également succulentes. Aucun de ces plats ne serait complet sans les frites dorées à point et une bonne salade.

3   Dim Sum/Dim Sum/Dim Sum

Ping Pong
74–76 Westbourne Grove
London W2 5SH
Tel: +44 20 7313 9832
www.pingpongdimsum.com
Tube: Bayswater/Royal Oak

Dim sum and cocktails sound like a rather strange combination but at Ping Pong, it somehow works. Dim sum is essentially a steamed dumpling filled with meat, seafood or vegetables and a staple Chinese dish. Ping Pong employs the best dim sum chefs in London as well as hot mixologists who prepare zingy cocktails to accompany the food. The simple modern design of the restaurant also adds to the experience.

Dim Sum und Cocktails klingt nach einer seltsamen Kombination. Doch im Ping Pong geht das ganz gut zusammen. Chinesische Dim Sum sind gedämpfte Teigtaschen mit Fleisch-, Fisch- oder Gemüsefüllung. Bei Ping Pong arbeiten die besten Dim-Sum-Köche und Barkeeper Londons – ein Besuch im Restaurant mit dem einfachen, modernen Look ist ein Erlebnis.

L'association de dim sum et de cocktails peut surprendre mais chez Ping Pong, elle marche. Ces raviolis à la vapeur au porc, aux crevettes ou aux légumes, plat de base de la cuisine chinoise, sont préparés par les meilleurs spécialistes de Londres et accompagnés de cocktails détonants mixés par des barmen experts. Le décor design simple et moderne ajoute à l'expérience.

4   Vintage Furniture/Vintage-Möbel/ Mobilier vintage

Domus Gallery
15 Needham Road
London W11 2RP
Tel: +44 20 7221 1666
Tube: Notting Hill Gate/Bayswater

This is modernism done in the most elegant way possible by Gary De Sparham and Nigel Wells, who have 15 years' experience in dealing in 20th-century furniture. The vintage pieces are exhibited over two floors with work by designers including George Nelson, Fontana Arte, Gio Ponti and Eames. Opened in 2005, this gallery has a vast following from all over the world.

Gary De Sparham und Nigel Wells haben aus ihrer 15-jährigen Erfahrung mit Designermöbeln des 20. Jahrhunderts die Domus

4   5   6

allery und damit eine elegante Oase der
oderne geschatten. Die Vintage-Objekte
n Designern wie George Nelson, Font-
a Arte, Gio Ponti und Eames werden auf
vei Stockwerken ausgestellt. Seit 2005
t Domus bei einer internationalen Kund-
:haft ein Begriff.

ary De Sparham et Nigel Wells, qui s'oc-
upent de mobilier du XXe siècle depuis
5 ans, ont l'art de présenter le modernis-
e avec élégance. Signées George Nelson,
ntana Arte, Gio Ponti et Eames, leurs
èces sont exposées sur deux étages.
uverte en 2005, cette galerie attire les
ollectionneurs des quatre coins du monde.

Restaurant/Restaurant/Restaurant

he Ledbury
27 Ledbury Road
ondon W11 2AQ
el: +44 20 7792 9090
ww.theledbury.com
ube: Westbourne Park

was given a Michelin star and several
ther awards in 2006 but if that isn't
nough to convince you of how fabulous
his elegant restaurant is, then let it be
nown that the chic customers have to
ook months in advance to get in here.
Opened in 2005 by Nigel Platts-Martin
nd Philip Howard, the French-influenced
ooking by Australian chef Brett Graham
as won fans far and wide.

Das elegante Ledbury konnte 2006 einen
Michelin-Stern und zahlreiche andere Aus-
eichnungen entgegennehmen, und selbst
ie schicke Stammkundschaft muss Mo-
nate auf einen freien Tisch warten. Nigel
Platts-Martin und Philip Howard haben das
antastische Lokal 2005 eröffnet. Küchen-
:hef ist der Australier Brett Graham. Mit
seiner französisch inspirierten Küche hat
:r sich weitum einen Namen gemacht.

l a reçu une étoile Michelin et plusieurs
autres prix en 2006 mais si cela ne suffit
pas à vous convaincre que cet élégant
restaurant est fabuleux, sachez qu'il faut
réserver des mois à l'avance. Ouvert en
2005 par Nigel Platts-Martin et Philip

Howard, la cuisine aux accents français
du chef australien Brett Graham a fait des
adeptes dans le monde entier.

6   Restaurant/Restaurant/Restaurant

Raoul's Café & Bar
105 –107 Talbot Road
London W11 2AT
Tel: +44 20 7229 2400
Tube: Notting Hill Gate/Bayswater

This Notting Hill favourite is the cousin of
the Raoul's in Maida Vale and just as roar-
ingly popular. The place is packed on
weekends with locals jostling for a table so
they can chow down on the full breakfasts
(the eggs Benedict are rather good).
Evenings are just as fun with great menu
featuring fish, beautifully cooked meats
and a few good veggie options.

Der Notting-Hill-Ableger von Raoul's ist
genauso beliebt wie das deliziöse Orignal
im Stadtteil Maida Vale. Besonders an den
Wochenenden ist das Café zum Bersten
voll mit Anwohnern, die sich für eine Früh-
stücks-Mahlzeit um einen freien Tisch
rangeln. Besonders gut schmecken die
pochierten Eier „Benedict". Abends wählt
man zwischen leckeren Fisch- und
Fleischgerichten oder Vegetarischem.

Ce haut-lieu culinaire de Notting Hill est
aussi populaire que son cousin de Maida
Vale. Le week-end, les habitués s'y bous-
culent pour déguster ses brunchs (les
oeufs Benedict sont particulièrement
prisés). Le soir, ambiance tout aussi
sympathique avec un belle carte offrant
du poisson, des viandes succulentes et
quelques bons plats végétariens.

Personal Finds/Eigene Entdeckungen/
Découvertes personnelles:

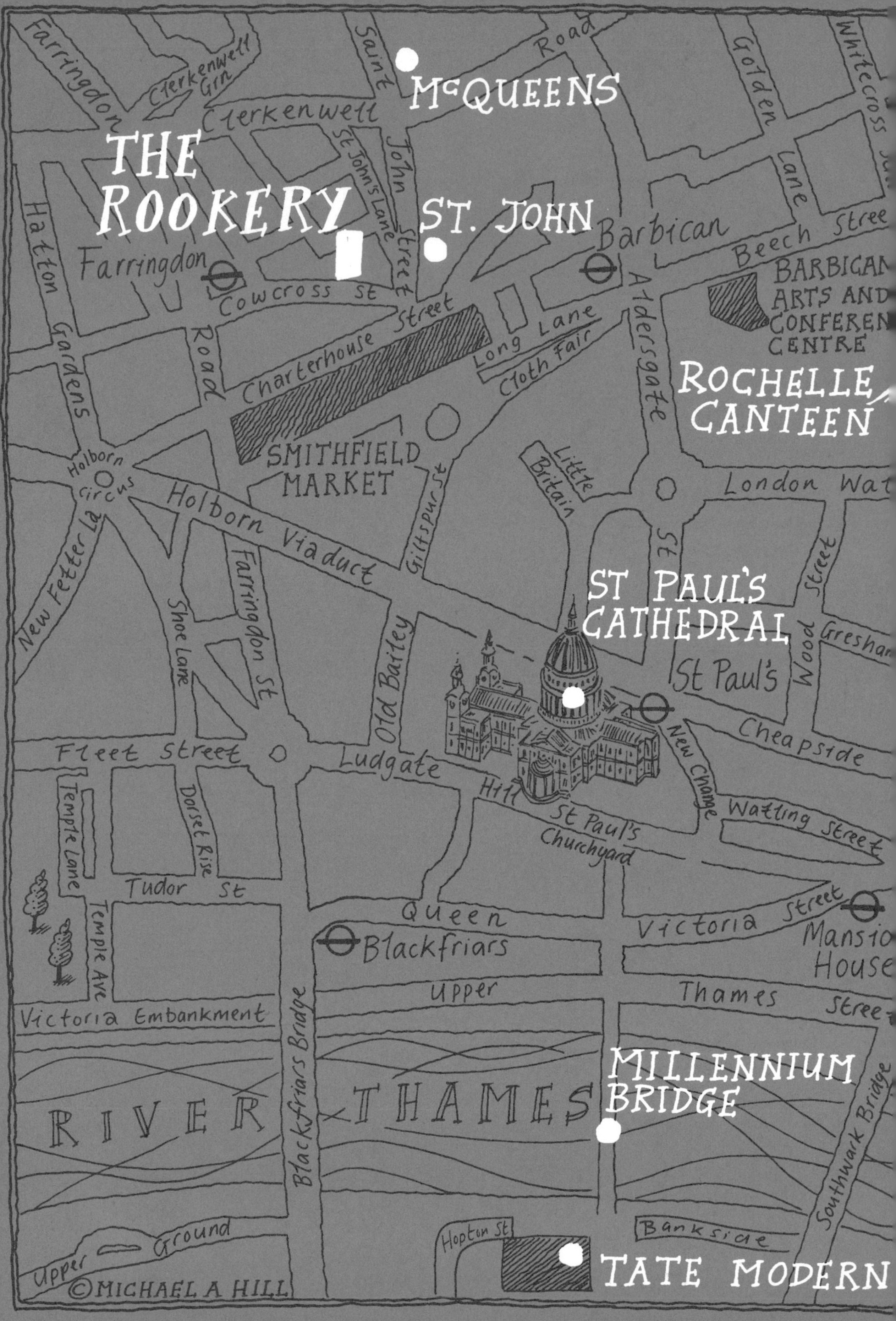

THE ROOKERY

McQUEENS

ST. JOHN

Barbican

BARBICAN ARTS AND CONFERENCE CENTRE

ROCHELLE CANTEEN

Farringdon

Clerkenwell Grn

Clerkenwell

St Johns Lane Street

Saint John Street

Road

Golden Lane

Whitecross St

Beech Stree

Cowcross St

Charterhouse Street

Long Lane

Cloth Fair

Aldersgate

London Wal

Hatton Gardens

Farringdon Road

SMITHFIELD MARKET

Giltspur St

Little Britain

St Pauls St

Wood Street

Gresham

Holborn Circus

New Fetter la

Holborn Viaduct

Farringdon St

Shoe Lane

Old Bailey

ST PAUL'S CATHEDRAL

St Paul's

New Change

Cheapside

Watling Street

Fleet Street

Temple Lane

Dorset Rise

Tudor St

Temple Ave

Ludgate

Hill

St Paul's Churchyard

Queen

Victoria Street

Mansio House

Blackfriars

Upper

Thames Stree

Victoria Embankment

Blackfriars Bridge

MILLENNIUM BRIDGE

Southwark Bridge

R I V E R   T H A M E S

Upper Ground

Hopton St

Bankside

TATE MODERN

© MICHAEL A HILL

EC1

Clerkenwell

Restaurant/Restaurant/Restaurant
St. John

Flowers/Blumen/Fleurs
McQueens

Church/Kathedrale/Église
Whispering Gallery at St Paul's Cathedral

Bridge/Brücke/Pont
Millennium Bridge

Turbine Hall/Turbinenhalle/Centrale électrique
Tate Modern

Restaurant/Restaurant/Restaurant
Rochelle Canteen
(Map on page 194/195)

Restaurant/Restaurant/Restaurant
Smiths of Smithfields

Night Club/Club/Night-Club
Fabric

Restaurant/Restaurant/Restaurant
The Comptoir Gascon

Church/Kirche/Église
Temple Church

Skincare/Kosmetik/Soins de beauté
Ren

Gallery/Galerie/Galerie
Whitechapel Art Gallery

Pub/Pub/Pub
Three Kings

Restaurant/Restaurant/Restaurant
Moro

Pub/Pub/Pub
The Eagle

Gallery/Galerie/Galerie
White Cube Gallery

Delicatessen/Delikatessen/Produits fins
Food Hall

Restaurant/Restaurant/Restaurant
Fifteen

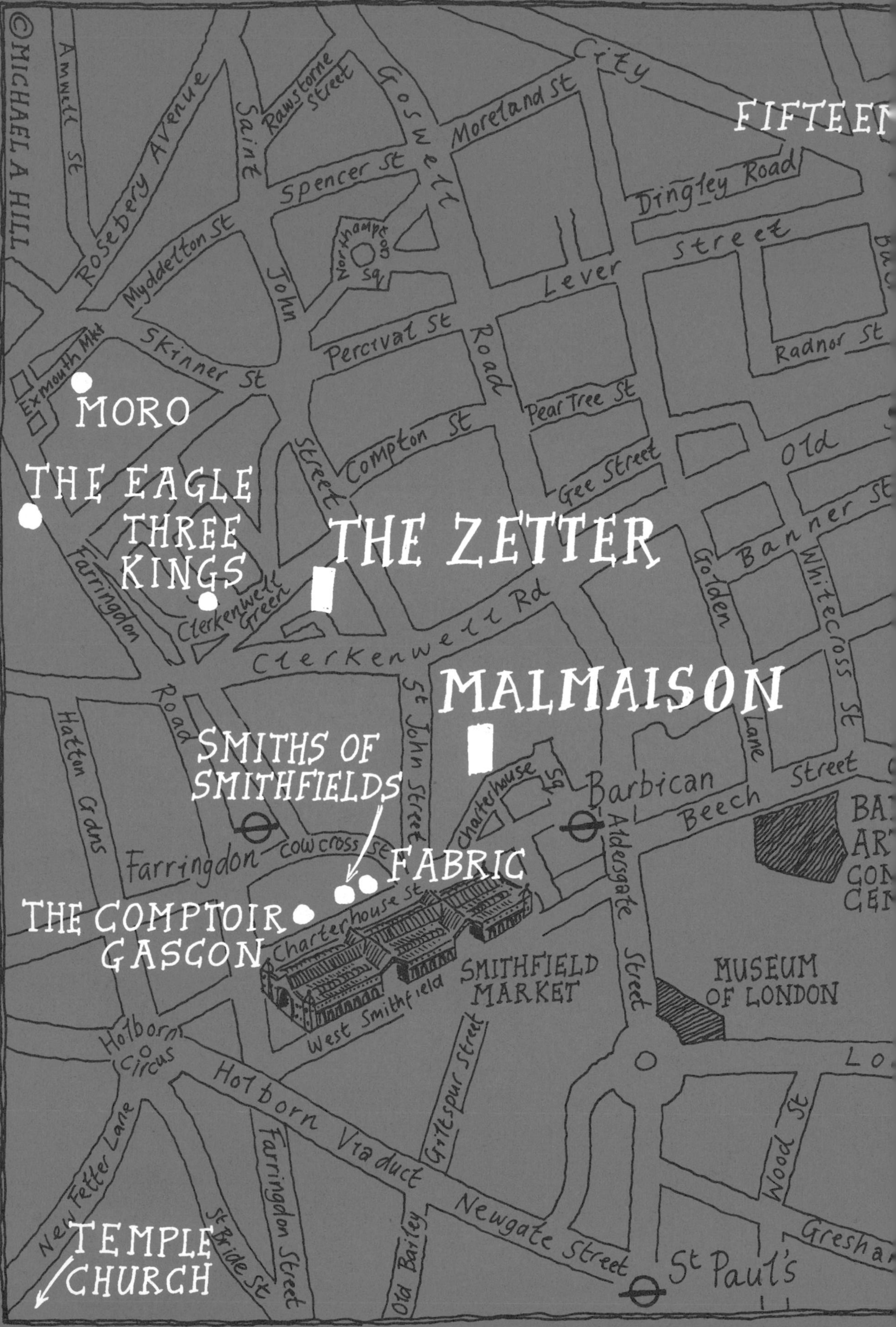

© MICHAELA HILL
FIFTEEN
MORO
THE EAGLE
THREE KINGS
THE ZETTER
MALMAISON
SMITHS OF SMITHFIELDS
FABRIC
THE COMPTOIR GASCON
SMITHFIELD MARKET
MUSEUM OF LONDON
TEMPLE CHURCH
Amwell St
Rosebery Avenue
Saint John Street
Rawstorne Street
Goswell Road
Moreland St
City
Dingley Road
Spencer St
Myddelton St
Northampton Sq
Lever Street
Percival St
Skinner St
Exmouth Mkt
Radnor St
Pear Tree St
Compton St
Gee Street
Old
Banner St
Golden Lane
Whitecross St
Farringdon Road
Clerkenwell Green
Clerkenwell Rd
St John Street
Hatton Grdns
Cowcross St
Farringdon
Charterhouse Sq
Barbican
Beech Street
Aldersgate Street
Charterhouse St
West Smithfield
Giltspur Street
Holborn Circus
Holborn Viaduct
New Fetter Lane
St Bride St
Farringdon Street
Old Bailey
Newgate Street
St Paul's
Wood St
Gresham

WHITE CUBE GALLERY

FOOD HALL

ROCHELLE CANTEEN

Pitfield St

Chart St

East Road

Hoxton Sq

Old Street

Kingsland Road

Hackney Road

Columbia Rd

Calvert Ave

Arnold Circus

Rivington Street

Shoreditch High Street

Club Row

Green

Rd

Leonard Street

Street

Street

Great Eastern Street

Bethnal

Sclater St

Tabernacle Street

Paul Street

Scrutton St

Curtain Road

Quaker Street

Brick Lane

City Road

Clifton Street

Appold Street

CHRIST CHURCH

Street

Sun St

Wilson St

OLD SPITALFIELDS MARKET

Lamb St

Commercial Street

Fashion St

Moorgate

Finsbury Circus

Liverpool Street

Liverpool Street

Brushfield Street

REN

Wall

Old Broad St

Bishopsgate

SWISS RE BUILDING

Middlesex St

Wentworth Street

WHITECHAPEL ART GALLERY

Aldgate East

Aldgate

Whitechapel High St

E ate

The Rookery

Cowcross Street, London EC1M 6DS
☎ +44 20 7336 0931　　☐ +44 20 7336 0932
reservations@rookery.co.uk
www.rookeryhotel.com
Tube: Farringdon
Booking: www.great-escapes-hotels.com

The Rookery

In the mid-18th century the word 'rookery' was used to describe a notorious neighbourhood known for criminal activity. Clerkenwell, where The Rookery hotel is located, is a very different place than it once was, though it is no less colourful. It is a one-minute walk from Smithfield Market, one of Europe's largest meat markets, and it's an area full of lively wine bars, pubs, restaurants and cafés. During the week, it hosts creatives in town for business; at weekends, a more fun and indulgent crowd, including Hollywood royalty, checks in. Rooms are spacious and lush, with antiques, dark walls, rich fabrics, beds with four posters or giant wooden headboards. The suite called The Rook's Nest is the cherry on top of the sundae: it is a loft room, replete with Victorian roll-top bathtub cum shower in the middle of the room, kinky mirrored headboard and, best of all, a ceiling that electronically slides open to reveal a living room/office balcony up above.

Mitte des 18. Jahrhunderts nannte man in London berüchtige Stadtteile „Rookery". Obschon in Clerkenwell immer noch ein buntes Treiben herrscht, ist von diesem rauen Geist nicht mehr viel übrig geblieben. Das Hotel liegt eine Gehminute vom Smithfield Market, einem der größten Fleischmärkte Europas und einer belebten Gegend mit Weinbars, Pubs, Restaurants und Cafés. Unter der Woche steigen im Rookery vor allem Reisende aus dem Kreativbusiness ab, und an den Wochenden nistet sich hier eine unternehmenslustige Gästeschar ein, darunter auch Hollywood-Prominenz. Die Zimmer bieten viel Platz und sind opulent luxuriös: dunkle Wände, üppige Stoffe, Antiquitäten und Himmelbetten. Die Perle ist die Suite „The Rooks Nest". Sie ist vollgestopft mit Möbeln, Stoffen und Objekten, darunter eine viktorianische Badewanne und ein verspiegeltes Kopfbrett. Damit nicht genug: Wie bei „Sesam öffne dich" schiebt sich die Decke auf Knopfdruck auf die Seite und gibt den Blick frei nach oben ins Arbeitszimmer.

Au milieu du XVIIIe siècle, le terme « rookery » désignait un coin malfamé. Clerkenwell a bien changé depuis tout en restant toujours aussi pittoresque. À une minute à pied de Smithfield Market, un des marchés de viande les plus grands d'Europe, ce quartier animé abonde de bars à vin, de pubs, de restaurant et de cafés. Pendant la semaine, l'hôtel accueille surtout des créatifs en ville pour affaires. Le week-end, il voit débarquer une clique plus festive et indulgente, dont des stars de Hollywood. Les chambres sont spacieuses et luxueuses, meublées d'antiquités, décorées de murs sombres, d'étoffes précieuses, de baldaquins ou de têtes de lit monumentales. La suite Rook's Nest est la cerise sur le gâteau : un loft avec une grande baignoire/douche à cylindre au milieu de la chambre, une tête de lit coquine en miroir et, surtout, un plafond qui s'ouvre électroniquement pour révéler un salon/bureau en mezzanine.

Rates: From 255 € (175 GBP) excl. VAT.
Rooms: 33 (1 suite).
Restaurants: None but there is 24-hour room service and lots of restaurants in the area. Breakfast is served in your room.
History: The three houses date back to the mid-18th century and were once three shops: a baker's, a butcher's and a pharmacy. Each of the 33 rooms is named after locals of the time: knights, prostitutes etc.
X-Factor: Delicious-smelling Aveda products in all the bathrooms.
Internet: Complimentary WiFi access for all guests.

Preise: ab 255 € (175 GBP) exkl. VAT.
Zimmer: 33 (1 Suite).
Restaurants: Keines. Jedoch viele Restaurants in der Umgebung und 24-Stunden-Zimmerservice. Das Frühstück wird aufs Zimmer gebracht.
Geschichte: Die drei Häuser stammen aus dem 18. Jahrhundert: Eine Bäckerei, eine Metzgerei und eine Apotheke. Jedes der 33 Zimmer wurden nach den Bewohnern der damaligen Zeit benannt: Ritter, Kurtisanen usw.
X-Faktor: In den Badezimmern stehen fein riechende Produkte von Aveda.
Internet: Kostenloser WiFi-Zugang.

Prix : À partir de 255 € (175 GBP), TVA non comprise.
Chambres : 33 (1 suite).
Restauration : Service dans les chambres 24h/24. Le quartier abonde en restaurants. Petit-déjeuner servi dans les chambres.
Histoire : Les trois maisons datent du milieu du XVIIIe siècle et abritaient autrefois un boulanger, un boucher et une pharmacie. Chacune des 33 chambres porte le nom d'occupants d'antan : chevalier, prostituée, etc.
Le « petit plus » : Les produits Aveda sentant délicieusement bon dans les salles de bain.
Internet : Accès WiFi gratuit.

1

2

---

1   Restaurant/Restaurant/Restaurant

St. John
26 St John Street
London EC1M 4AY
Tel: +44 20 7251 0848
www.stjohnrestaurant.co.uk
Tube: Farringdon/Barbican

Fergus Henderson's former smokehouse put St John Street on the culinary map. When he launched St John in 1994, this Clerkenwell thoroughfare got very little evening trade and this city had little reliable nose-to-tail eating. But Henderson made offal cool during the 1990s, and that's some accomplishment. But just because cows and pigs are sold nearby does not mean you'll get a simple chop here.

Fergus Henderson machte 1994 aus dieser ehemaligen Räucherei an der St John Street einen kulinarischen Begriff. Damals war an dieser Durchgangsstraße in Clerkenwell nicht sehr viel los. Auch bodenständiges Essen, wie Henderson es auf den Tisch brachte, kannte man in London damals noch nicht. Dank ihm wurde ein neues Bewußtsein geschaffen – eine respektable Leistung. Einfache Küche auf hohem Niveau.

En transformant cet ancien fumoir en 1994, Fergus Henderson a placé St John Street sur la carte des gastronomes. Jusque là, Clerkenwell ne disposait pas de bonne table digne de ce nom et les bonnes tripes était rares à Londres. Henderson a su rendre les abats chics pendant les années 90, et ce n'est pas parce que le marché aux bestiaux est à côté qu'on vous servira une simple côtelette.

---

2   Flowers/Blumen/Fleurs

McQueens
126 St John Street
London EC1V 4JS
Tel: +44 20 7251 5505
www.mcqueens.co.uk
Tube: Farringdon/Barbican

McQueens is a first-rate neighbourhood florist – that grew through word of mouth into a destination from this little but beautifully decorated shop on St John Street which Kally Ellis opened in 1994. After her huge success, the bigger shop on 70-72 Old Street followed. Now a fashion posse including Naomi Campbell, Alexander McQueen (no relation) and Gwyneth Paltrow use its services. And when Vanity Fair throws a party, McQ is on call. If you want your room at The Zetter, Malmaison or The Rookery to look more like home, just take a simple but wonderful bouquet back with you.

McQueens, 1994 an der St John Street von Kally Ellis gegründet, ist eines der aufregendsten Blumengeschäfte überhaupt und so erfolgreich, dass es nun auch ein zweites, größeres Ladenlokal an der Old Street 70–72 gibt. Als Hoflieferant der Mode und des Entertainments zählt McQueens Naomi Campbell, Alexander McQueen (nicht verwandt), Gwyneth Paltrow und das Magazin Vanity Fair zu seinen Kunden. Tipp: einen der wunderbaren Sträuße von McQueens erstehen und damit sein Zimmer im Zetter, Malmaison oder The Rookery verschönern.

Tout a commencé par cette jolie petite boutique ouverte par Kally Ellis en 1994. Le bouche-à-oreille a fonctionné et McQueens, qui a ouvert une enseigne plus grande au 70-72 d'Old Street, est désormais le fleuriste attitré des stars de la mode dont Naomi Campbell, Alexander McQueen (sans lien de parenté) ou des stars tout court comme Gwyneth Paltrow. Quand Vanity Fair organise une soirée, c'est à lui qu'on fait appel. Rien de tel qu'un superbe petit bouquet pour personnaliser votre chambre d'hôtel.

---

3   Church/Kathedrale/Église

Whispering Gallery at St Paul's Cathedral
Ludgate Hill
London EC4M 8AD
Tel: +44 20 7236 4128
www.stpauls.co.uk
Tube: St Paul's

The site of Christopher Wren's St Paul's dates back to Roman times, but this magnificent structure was built in the early 17th century, after the original was destroyed in the Great Fire of 1666, after which Wren was commissioned to build 51 new churches and this cathedral. Since then, tourists and locals love climbing the 259 stairs to the Whispering Gallery. Here, you can whisper at the wall and someone on the dome's opposite side can hear you, so perfect are the acoustics.

St Paul's geht auf römische Zeiten zurück, wurde aber während des großen Feuers von 1666 zerstört. Der Wissenschaftler und Architekt Sir Christopher Wren bekam im frühen 18. Jahrhundert den Auftrag, 51 Kirchen und die St-Paul's-Kathedrale wiederaufzubauen. Seither klettern Londoner und Besucher die 259 Stufen hoch zur Whispering Gallery. Man flüstert an eine Wand und wird auf der anderen Seite des Doms gehört. Perfekte Akustik.

Le premier édifice, érigé sur un site romain, fut détruit lors du grand incendie de Londres en 1666, à la suite duquel Christopher Wren fut chargé de bâtir 51 nouvelles églises plus cette magnifique cathédrale. Depuis, les touristes et les Londoniens ne se lassent pas de gravir les 259 marches jusqu'à la galerie des chuchotements. Ici, l'acoustique est si parfaite que vous pouvez susurrer des mots doux à votre dulcinée se tenant de l'autre côté du dôme.

---

4   Bridge/Brücke/Pont

Millennium Bridge
Between St Paul's Cathedral and Tate Modern
Tube: Blackfriars

This elegant footbridge was the laughing stock of London when it had to be closed three days after opening in 2000 because it was wobbly and dangerous. After two years and 5million GBP spent on repairs, the 320-metre long structure re-opened and thank goodness for that. The design bySir Anthony Caro and Sir Norman Foster is magic at night where you can stand in the middle and watch the city twinkle

4

5

6

around you, the view from Tate Modern on St Paul's has become one of London's iconic images. When you cross on a night when museums have long nights you can even visit the Tate Modern at the same time.

Diese elegante Fußgängerbrücke wurde drei Tage nach der Eröffnung bereits zum Gegenstand des Gespötts. Sie musste geschlossen werden, weil sie wacklig und gefährlich war. Ein Glück, dass zwei Jahre und 5 Millionen GBP später die 320 Meter lange Brücke wiedereröffnet wurde. Die von Sir Anthony Caro und Sir Norman Foster entworfene Struktur ist, besonders nachts, magisch. Von der Mitte sieht man die Lichter Londons glitzern, und der Blick von der Tate Modern auf St Paul's ist zu einem Symbol der Stadt geworden. Während der langen Museumsnacht kann man auch noch die Tate Modern besichtigen.

En 2000, tout Londres s'est esclaffé quand cette élégante passerelle a fermé trois jours après son inauguration parce qu'elle tremblait trop. Deux ans et 5 millions de livres plus tard, cette structure de 320 m de long de sir Anthony Caro et lord Norman Foster a rouvert. C'est tant mieux car elle est désormais devenue un emblème de la ville, s'intégrant magistralement dans la vue sur St Paul depuis la Tate Modern. Elle est magique la nuit quand on se tient au milieu et que la ville scintille autour de soi ; profitez-en pour la traverser et aller visiter la Tate Modern en nocturne.

5   Turbine Hall/Turbinenhalle/Centrale
     électrique

Tate Modern
Bankside
London SE1 9TG
Tel: +44 20 7887 8888
www.tate.org.uk
Tube: Blackfriars/Southwark

The most successful Millennium project on the Southbank was the transformation of this power station by Swiss architects Herzog & de Meuron into a slick exhibition space for the more contemporary works in the Tate collection. Make sure to check out at least the gigantic ground-floor 100-ft

high Turbine Hall, the cavernous show space for the world's best installation artists. There are also nice coffee bars on the 4th and 7th floors with great views.

Für die Tate-Sammlung zeitgenössischer Kunst haben die Schweizer Architekten Herzog & de Meuron aus einem Elektrizitätswerk elegant-reduzierte Ausstellungsräumlichkeiten gemacht – es ist das erfolgreichste Milleniums-Projekt der Southbank. Der Besuch der über 30 Meter hohen Turbinenhalle im Erdgeschoss ist ein Muss. Hier werden die besten internationalen Installationskünstler ausgestellt. Cafébars mit toller Aussicht in der 4. und 7. Etage.

Le projet du Millennium le plus réussi sur la Southbank fut la reconversion de cette centrale électrique par les architectes suisses Herzog & de Meuron en vaste espace d'exposition pour les œuvres les plus modernes de la collection Tate. Ne manquez pas la gigantesque salle des turbines de 30 mètres de haut qui accueille les meilleurs artistes d'installation du monde. Les cafétérias fort sympathiques du 4e et 7e étage ont des vues superbes.

6   Restaurant/Restaurant/Restaurant

Rochelle Canteen
Rochelle School
Arnold Circus
London E2 7AS
Tel: +44 20 7729 5677
Tube: Shoreditch
(Map on page 194/195)

Run by Melanie Arnold and Margot Henderson, who have their own catering company, this lovely lunchtime venue serves the creative workers (think art, fashion, music) whose offices, workshops and studios occupy this former school. It looks like a proper school canteen but the food is British with a European edge – seasonal, simple (that is the secret), always fresh and changing daily.

Die Rochelle Canteen liegt in einem ehemaligen Schulhaus und wird von den Catering-Unternehmerinnen Melanie Arnold und Margot Henderson geführt. Das rei-

zende Mittagslokal sieht zwar immer noch wie eine Schulkantine aus, wird aber heute von Gästen aus Kunst, Mode und Musik besucht, die hier ihre Büros, Ateliers und Studios eingerichtet haben. Die Küche ist britisch mit kontinentaleuropäischem Einschlag: saisonal, einfach und stets frisch. Das Menü wechselt täglich.

Dirigée par les traiteurs Melanie Arnold et Margot Henderson, c'est la cantine des créatifs (de l'art, de la mode et de la musique) dont les bureaux et ateliers se trouvent dans cette ancienne école. La salle rappelle toujours un réfectoire mais la cuisine (anglaise avec une touche européenne) est saisonnière, simple et toujours fraîche. Le menu change quotidiennement.

Personal Finds/Eigene Entdeckungen/
Découvertes personnelles:

_____

_____

_____

_____

_____

_____

_____

_____

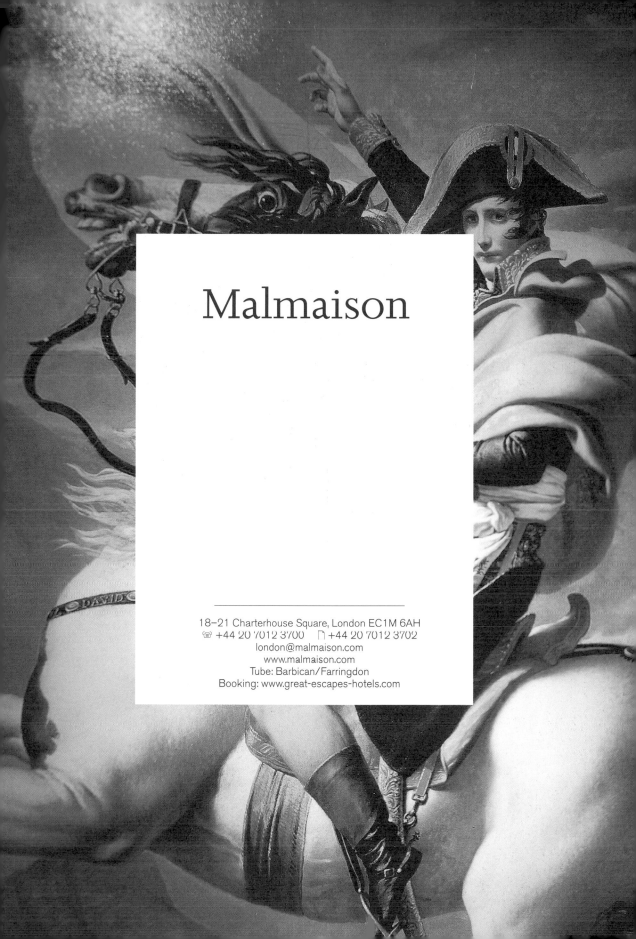

Malmaison

18–21 Charterhouse Square, London EC1M 6AH
☎ +44 20 7012 3700 📠 +44 20 7012 3702
london@malmaison.com
www.malmaison.com
Tube: Barbican/Farringdon
Booking: www.great-escapes-hotels.com

Malmaison

The clever folk behind the Malmaison chain, which started in the north of England, have stayed true to their philosophy of "real places for real people" with a hotel that provides comfortable, modern rooms at reasonable prices. Malmaison London is in busy Clerkenwell, right in quiet Charterhouse Square, nestled among the enormous trees and next to the Chapel of Sutton's Hospital, which dates back to the 17th century. The lobby looks serious at first glance, with its dark velvet chairs, the low lighting and the Veuve Cliquot Champagne bar. But the bust of Napoleon leading to the lifts hints at something a bit more playful. There are also photographs of London scenes peppered on the walls so there is plenty to admire. During the week Malmaison hosts business people but the weekends are when lovestruck couples set up base for gallery-hopping and sampling the wine bars around the area. Make sure to try one of the Malmaison's own Bellinis and don't miss the Sunday brunch.

Die Malmaison-Gruppe aus dem Norden Englands ist glücklicherweise ihrer Philosophie „kein Firlefanz" treu geblieben. Das fängt bei den Preisen an: die elegant-modernen Zimmer kosten nicht alle Welt. In London liegt das Malmaison zwischen riesigen Bäumen am ruhigen Charterhouse Square gleich neben der Kapelle des Sutton's Hospital aus dem 17. Jahrhundert. Ein Privileg im sonst so belebten Clerkenwell. Die Lobby wirkt auf den ersten Blick etwas förmlich: Die Stühle sind mit dunklem Samt bezogen und das Licht an der Veuve Cliquot Bar wirkt gedämpft. Doch eine Napoleon-Büste beim Fahrstuhl und Fotografien von London verraten, dass das Hotel durchaus eine spielerische Seite hat. Unter der Woche steigen im Malmaison vor allem Geschäftsleute ab. An den Wochenenden dient es als Basisstation für Paare, die die Galerien der Gegend besuchen oder die umliegenden Weinbars entdecken wollen. Im Malmaison unbedingt ausprobieren: die ausgezeichneten Bellinis und den Sonntagsbrunch.

Les petits malins derrière la chaîne Malmaison, qui a vu le jour dans le nord de l'Angleterre, sont restés fidèles à leur devise « des lieux authentiques pour des gens authentiques ». Leur hôtel londonien offre des chambres confortables et modernes à des prix raisonnables. Il est situé dans le quartier animé de Clerkenwell mais sur le square paisible de Charterhouse à l'ombre d'arbres géants près de la chapelle de l'hôpital Sutton, qui date du XVIIe siècle. Avec ses fauteuils en velours sombre, son éclairage tamisé et son bar à champagne Veuve Cliquot, le hall paraît sérieux mais le buste de Napoléon menant aux ascenseurs est un clin d'œil. Les murs sont tapissés de vues de Londres. En semaine, la Malmaison accueille surtout des hommes d'affaires mais, le week-end, des couples d'amoureux viennent s'y poser pour faire le tour des galeries et essayer les bars à vin du quartier. Goûtez les Bellini faits maison et ne ratez pas le brunch du dimanche.

Rates: From 182 € (125 GBP) excl. VAT.
Rooms: 97 (2 suites).
Restaurants: Brasserie.
History: Malmaison is named after the chateau that Napoleon built for Josephine. The Malmaison's red brick building was once home to the nurses of nearby St Bartholomew's Hospital.
X-Factor: Own-brand Malmaison bathroom products are great and can be taken along when you leave.
Internet: Complimentary broadband connections in rooms; WiFi in the lobby and Brasserie.

Preise: ab 182 € (125 GBP) exkl. VAT.
Zimmer: 97 (2 Suiten).
Restaurants: Brasserie.
Geschichte: Das Hotel wurde nach Schloss Malmaison benannt – ein Geschenk Napoleons an Joséphine. Einst diente es als Unterkunft für die Schwestern des nahe gelegenen Krankenhauses St Bartholomew's.
X-Faktor: Die feinen, eigens für Malmaison hergestellten Badeprodukte kann man mit nach Hause nehmen.
Internet: Kostenloser Breitbandanschluss in allen Zimmern; WiFi in der Lobby und der Brasserie.

Prix : À partir de 182 € (125 GBP), TVA non comprise.
Chambres : 97 (2 suites).
Restauration : La Brasserie.
Histoire : Malmaison doit son nom au château construit par Napoléon pour Joséphine. Le bâtiment abritait autrefois les infirmières de l'hôpital St Bartholomew.
Le « petit plus » : La Malmaison a sa propre marque de produits de salle de bain que vous pouvez emporter avec vous en partant.
Internet : Accès haut débit gratuite dans les chambres ; WiFi dans le lobby et la Brasserie.

1

2

---

1   Restaurant/Restaurant/Restaurant

Smiths of Smithfields
67–77 Charterhouse Street
London EC1M 6HJ
Tel: +44 20 7251 7950
www.smithsofsmithfields.co.uk
Tube: Farringdon

The Victorian meat market on Charterhouse Street is still in operation, but the cold-storage houses across the street have been funked up. Smiths, however, has kept its warehouse feel and stainless-steel accents. The four floors are structured in the manner of the old English classes, with a casual diner and pub on the main floor and a posh organic dining room at the top.

Den Fleischmarkt an der Charterhouse Street gibt's bereits seit viktorianischen Zeiten und er ist heute noch in Betrieb. Allerdings wurden die Kühllager auf der gegenüber liegenden Seite der Straße modernisiert. Umso schöner, dass das Smiths immer noch den Look einer alten Lagerhalle mit den typischen Chrom-Akzenten beibehalten hat. Das Lokal ist in vier Stockwerke aufgeteilt. Unten kann man im Pub einen kleinen Imbiss genießen, oben gibt's schicke Bio-Gerichte.

Le marché de la viande victorien sur Charterhouse Street existe toujours mais ses chambres froides en face ont été reconverties. Smiths a néanmoins conservé des éléments du décor original (fonte, brique et acier) ainsi qu'un esprit de classes bien anglais, avec un café et un pub décontractés au rez-de-chaussée et un restaurant chic et bio au dernier étage.

---

2   Night Club/Club/Night-Club

Fabric
77a Charterhouse Street
London EC1M 3HN
Tel: +44 20 7336 8898
www.fabriclondon.com
Tube: Farringdon

In a city where night-time venues come and go faster than London buses, Fabric is the most established and the coolest club in town, with its own record label and a consistent line-up of the world's best underground DJs and live dance acts. Fabric is housed in a former meat market and is super popular so party-goers need to arrive early to avoid the queues of cool kids lined up for the music.

Auch wenn in London Nachtlokale so schnell auftauchen, wie sie wieder verschwinden, bleibt Fabric ein Fixstern und der coolste Club der Stadt. Fabric betreibt nicht nur ein eigenes Plattenlabel, sondern hat stets die besten Underground-DJs und Live Dance Acts im Programm. Der Club in einem ehemaligen Fleischmarkt ist so beliebt, dass Partygänger gut daran tun, rechtzeitig zu erscheinen. Die Schlange voller „Cool Kids" kann nämlich ziemlich lange sein.

Dans une ville où les nouvelles boîtes de nuit se succèdent plus rapidement que les bus, Fabric est le club le plus établi et le plus cool de la capitale, avec son propre label de disques, les meilleurs DJ underground du monde et des démonstrations de danse. Situé dans une ancienne halles aux viandes, Fabric est pris d'assaut tous les soirs alors arrivez tôt pour éviter les queues de jeunes clubeurs branchés.

---

3   Restaurant/Restaurant/Restaurant

The Comptoir Gascon
63 Charterhouse Street
London EC1M 6HJ
Tel: +44 20 7608 0851
Tube: Farringdon

The English may still pretend to hate the French but they will always admit to liking their food. Hence the success of this little gem of a restaurant that has garnered positive commentary from even the most jaded of reviewers. In typical French style, duck and pig feature heavily on the menu as do delicious after-dinner treats like apricot tarts and home-made ice cream.

Zwar kokettieren die Engländer immer noch damit, die Franzosen nicht zu mögen. Doch gegen ihr Essen haben sie überhaupt nichts einzuwenden. Das Comptoir Gascon, ein kleines Juwel, wird selbst von den snobistischsten Restaurantkritikern gelobt. Auf der Menükarte findet man typisch französische Gerichte mit viel Ente und Schwein. Auch die Nachspeisen wie Aprikosen-Tarte und hausgemachtes Eis sind köstlich.

Les Anglais ont beau prétendre détester les Français, ils ne peuvent résister à leur cuisine. D'où le succès de ce petit bijou qui s'est attiré les éloges des critiques les plus blasés. La carte typiquement français se met l'accent sur le canard et le porc et inclut de délicieux desserts comme les tartes aux abricots et les crèmes glacées faites maison.

---

4   Church/Kirche/Église

Temple Church
Fleet Street
London EC4Y 7BB
Tel: +44 20 7353 3470
www.templechurch.com
Tube: Temple/Blackfriars

This church is steeped in history and is worth a trip to the area even if you aren't staying anywhere nearby. It was built by the Knights Templar (think The DaVinci Code) in the 12th century in a circular design to mimic the Church of the Holy Sepulchre at Jerusalem where Jesus was buried. Come and see the choir and marvel at how advanced acoustics were even 800 years ago

Die Temple Church ist voller Historie. Unbedingt einen Ausflug hierher einplanen, auch wenn man nicht in der Gegend weilt. Sie stammt aus dem 12. Jahrhundert und wurde von Tempelrittern gebaut, die den Tempel der Heiligen Grabstätte in Jerusalem, in der Christus begraben wurde, zum Vorbild nahmen. Wie das Original ist der Grundriss der Kirche rund. Besonders beeindruckend Chor und Akustik: Erstaunlich, wie fortgeschritten man vor 800 Jahren war.

Cette église historique vaut le détour même si vous ne logez pas dans le quartier. Construite par les Templiers au XIIe siècle (pensez DaVinci Code), sa forme circulaire

4

5

6

prend celle de la basilique du Saint-Sépulcre à Jérusalem qui abrite le tombeau du Christ. Admirez le chœur qui démontre à quel point la science acoustique était développée il y a 800 ans.

Skincare/Kosmetik/Soins de beauté

en
0 Liverpool Street
London EC2M 7QN
el: +44 20 7618 5353
www.renskincare.com
be: Liverpool Street

ot often is a skincare line so successful ith women and men alike but we've eard of at least one gentleman who loved s Ren products so much, he had them edEx'd to his ski chalet when he forgot em. The all-natural, GM-free range is ondon-based, but named for the Swedish ord for "clean" – which initially attracted e likes of Kate Moss and Uma Thurman efore seducing the world.

autpflegeprodukte, die sogar Männer egeistern, sind eine Seltenheit. Doch gibt s die Geschichte eines Kunden, der ohne en-Produkte nicht mehr sein konnte: Er eß sie sogar per Kurier in sein Ski-Chalet ingen. Das Label stammt aus London, der ame jedoch ist schwedisch und bedeutet auber", da die Produkte aus rein natür- chen Inhaltsstoffen hergestellt sind. Seit ate Moss und Uma Thurman sie benutzen, ollen sie nun alle haben.

est rare qu'une ligne de cosmétiques aise autant aux femmes qu'aux hommes. lous connaissons au moins un monsieur ui aimait tant ses produits Ren 100% aturel et sans OGM qu'il se les a fait nvoyer par FedEx dans son chalet de ki après les avoir oubliés. Cette marque nglaise qui signifie « propre » en suédois d'abord séduit Kate Moss et Uma hurman avant de conquérir le monde.

Gallery/Galerie/Galerie

Vhitechapel Art Gallery
0–82 Whitechapel High Street

London E1 7QX
Tel: +44 20 7522 7888
www.whitechapel.org
Tube: Aldgate East

Small and perfectly formed, the century-old Whitechapel Art Gallery is off the beaten path (at least for the mainstream art crowd). And we prefer it that way. Frida Kahlo, Jackson Pollock and even Picasso showed their work here in their time, and new sensations such as Paul McCarthy, Albert Oehlen and David Adjaye are the kind you can see here now, showing experimental, didactic works, often in several media.

Die kleine, gut geformte hundertjährige Whitechapel Galerie kennen eigentlich nur Insider. Und das ist gut so. Hier haben große Namen wie Frida Kahlo, Jackson Pollock und auch Picasso ausgestellt, aber auch zeitgenössische Künstler wie Paul McCarthy, Albert Oehlen und David Adjaye. Die experimentellen, didaktischen Arbeiten werden oft mit unterschiedlichen Medien dargestellt.

Petite et parfaite, la Whitechapel a plus d'un siècle. Située hors des sentiers battus de l'art, Frida Kahlo, Jackson Pollock et même Picasso y ont exposé leurs œuvres en leur temps. Aujourd'hui, c'est au tour des nouvelles vedettes de l'art contemporain comme Paul McCarthy, Albert Oehlen ou David Adjaye d'y présenter leurs travaux expérimentaux, didactiques et souvent multimédia.

Personal Finds/Eigene Entdeckungen/
Découvertes personnelles:

The Zetter

86–88 Clerkenwell Road, London EC1M 5RJ
☎ +44 20 7324 4444   ☐ +44 20 7324 4445
reservations@thezetter.com
www.thezetter.com
Tube: Farringdon
Booking: www.great-escapes-hotels.com

Original and affordable, contemporary but not minimalist, The Zetter Restaurant & Rooms is a modern-day inn with a light-hearted attitude. The Zetter is located in a former 19th-century warehouse and attracts those who want to stay well away from the tourist trail. Its quirky, cosy rooms and rooftop studios, which come with patios looking over the city and St John's Square (St John's Gate, now called the Priory Gate, was built in 1504 and its gateway is still in the square) set it apart from traditional hotels. Furthermore, rooms are decorated with colourful Eley Kishimoto textiles, unique furniture and Penguin Classics on bedside tables. Each bed is decorated with a cute Zetter throw but please avoid putting these in your bag when you leave. Don't miss out on chef Megan Jones's seasonal, light modern Italian menu. Also, sample the delicious Zetter water, collected from the hotel's well, 1500ft underground.

The Zetter Restaurant & Rooms ist die zeitgemäße – aber nicht übertrieben minimalistische – Version des guten alten Gasthauses. Es liegt in einem ehemaligen Lagerhaus aus dem 19. Jahrhundert und zieht Leute an, die das Außergewöhnliche suchen, ohne dabei allzu tief in die Tasche greifen zu müssen, und vor allem die üblichen Touristenpfade meiden. Von den kuschligen Zimmern und Dachterrassen-Studios mit ungewöhnlichem Möbel-Mix kann man über die City und den St John's Square blicken. (Das Tor des St John's Gate, heute Priory Gate, wurde übrigens 1504 gebaut und befindet sich heute noch auf dem St John's Square). Besonders schön: die farbigen Textilien von Eley Kishimoto, die Literatur-Klassiker auf dem Nachttisch und die bunten Bettdecken mit Zetter-Logos. Auf jeden Fall im Restaurant Megan Jones' leichte italienische Saisonküche ausprobieren. Dazu Zetter Wasser bestellen: Es stammt aus der hoteleigenen Quelle – sie liegt 457 Meter unter der Erde.

Original et abordable, contemporain sans être minimaliste, le Zetter est une auberge décontractée des temps modernes. Située dans un ancien entrepôt du XIXe siècle, elle accueille ceux qui préfèrent éviter les sentiers battus touristiques. Elle se distingue des hôtels traditionnels par ses chambres douillettes décorées de tissus colorés d'Eley Kishimoto, de meubles uniques, de classiques en livre de poche sur les tables de chevet, ainsi que par ses studios sur le toit agrémentés de terrasses dominant St Johns Square (bâti en 1504, la porte de St John, aujourd'hui The Priory Gate, se dresse toujours au milieu du square). Chaque lit est orné d'un charmant plaid Zetter que l'on évitera de glisser dans ses bagages. Ne manquez pas la cuisine italienne légère et moderne à base de produits de saison du chef Megan Jones, ainsi que la délicieuse eau Zetter, puisée dans le puits de l'hôtel, profond de 457 mètres.

Rates: From 205 € (140 GBP) incl. VAT.
Rooms: 59 (7 rooftop studios).
Restaurant: The Zetter Restaurant.
History: The Zetter is housed in a Victorian Grade II listed building. It used to be the Zetter Football Pools Hall headquarters.
X-Factor: There are Elemis products in the bathrooms but, even better, each room has a bright, wool-knit hot-water bottle but, sadly, must stay in the room.
Internet: Broadband 10 GBP per day/WiFi 15 GBP per day.

Preise: ab 205 € (140 GBP) inkl. VAT.
Zimmer: 59 (7 Dachterrassen-Studios).
Restaurant: The Zetter Restaurant.
Geschichte: Das viktorianische Zetter, einst der Hauptsitz der Zetter Football Pools Hall, steht unter Denkmalschutz.
X-Faktor: Badezimmer-Produkte von Elemis. Himmlisch: Jedes Zimmer ist mit einer bunt bestrickten Wärmflasche ausgestattet – leider darf man diese nicht mit nach Hause nehmen.
Internet: Breitbandanschluss für 10 GBP pro Tag; WiFi-Zugang für 15 GBP pro Tag.

Prix : À partir de 205 € (140 GBP) incl. TVA.
Chambres : 59 (7 studios sur le toit).
Restauration : The Zetter Restaurant.
Histoire : Le Zetter se trouve dans un bâtiment victorien classé, autrefois le siège du Zetter Football Pools Hall.
Le « petit plus » : Il y a des produits Elemis dans les salles de bain mais, encore mieux, des bouillottes en tricot dans les chambres que, hélas, on ne peut pas emporter.
Internet : Accès haut débit pour 10 GBP par jour/WiFi 15 GBP par jour.

1

2

3

1   Pub/Pub/Pub

Three Kings
7 Clerkenwell Close
London EC1R 0DY
Tel: +44 20 7253 0483
Tube: Farringdon

You won't notice the Three Kings pub walking around old, industrial Clerkenwell – and they like it that way. The cosy old-school hideaway in a romantic street corner opposite of an old church has a loyal clientele from the local film and fashion houses, who gather outside, to deconstruct the day. Its gypsy-chic look and flair with papier- mâché decorations set it apart from the £10-martini lounges.

Wer durchs alte, industrielle Clerkenwell spaziert, wird den „Three Kings Pub" ziemlich sicher übersehen. So bleibt dieser Pub an einer romantischen Straßenecke gegenüber einer Kirche ein behaglicher, altmodischer Zufluchtsort für die Stammkunden aus der lokalen Film- und Modebranche. Der Zigeunerschick und die Papiermaché-Dekorationen sind ein Kontrastprogramm zu den schicken Lounges, in denen ein Martini locker zehn Pfund kostet.

En vous promenant dans le vieux quartier industriel de Clerkenwell vous ne remarquerez sans doute pas The Three Kings mais sa clientèle de gens du cinéma et de mode l'aime pour ça. Situé dans petit coin romantique en face d'une vieille église, ce pub douillet à l'ancienne a un parfum chic bohème avec des décorations en papier mâché qui le distingue des bars design à 10 £ le martini.

2   Restaurant/Restaurant/Restaurant

Moro
34–36 Exmouth Market
London EC1R 4QE
Tel: +44 20 7833 8336
www.moro.co.uk
Tube: Farringdon

Not many restaurants on this side of town can claim to be a London institution, but Moro was here when this pedestrian market catered exclusively to the council estates that abut it. Sam and Sam Clark opened Moro in 1997 and instantly earned top reviews for their Moorish tapas and Mediterranean comfort food. Execs from the Guardian nearby love it as much as the City glitterati.

Das Moro ist eine Londoner Institution und war bereits hier, als die Straßenmärkte noch ausschließlich die benachbarten Sozialhilfeempfänger bedienten. Sam und Sam Clark wurden bereits kurz nach der Eröffnung des Restaurants 1997 mit Lob von den Gastro-Kritikern für ihre maurischen Tapas und ihre mediterrane Hausmannskost bedacht. Hier verkehren Journalisten der nahe gelegenen Zeitung „The Guardian" genau so wie die Schönen und Gestylten.

Peu de restaurants dans cette partie de la ville peuvent se targuer d'être une institution mais Moro existait déjà quand cette rue piétonne n'était bordée que par des HLM. Dès son ouverture par Sam et Sam Clark en 1997, ses tapas mauresques et sa cuisine méditerranéenne ont été encensés par les critiques. Les rédacteurs du Guardian voisin comme le gratin de la City en raffolent.

3   Pub/Pub/Pub

The Eagle
159 Farringdon Road
London EC1R 3AL
Tel: +44 20 7837 1353
Tube: Farringdon

By most accounts, The Eagle was London's first gastropub, opened by the Eyre brothers in 1991 and it set the precedent for quality British fare in an honest pub. It has a perennial buzz and the excellent food has kept it at the top of the gastropub rankings all these years: comfort food made with fresh seasonal ingredients and a dash of pretentiousness.

The Eagle, Londons erster Gastropub, wurde von den Gebrüdern Eyre 1991 eröffnet und gilt als Vorbild für ehrliche britische Pub-Qualitätskost. Seit Jahren steht das viel beachtete Lokal dank seines exzellenten Essens ganz oben auf der Liste der Gastropubs. Hier gibt's prätentiöse Hausmannskost, zubereitet aus frischen, saisonalen Zutaten.

Ouvert par les frères Eyre en 1991, The Eagle aurait été le premier pub gastronomique de Londres, inaugurant l'ère de la nourriture de qualité dans un pub authentique, brouhaha inclus. Depuis t outes ces années, sa réputation ne s'est pas démentie. La cuisine excellente est à base de produits frais de saison assaisonnés d'une pointe de prétention.

4   Gallery/Galerie/Galerie

White Cube Gallery
48 Hoxton Square
London N1 6PB
Tel: +44 20 7930 5373
www.whitecube.com
Tube: Old Street

Owner Jay Jopling is a voracious gallerist of Young British Artists and man about town. His White Cube, which opened in 2000, is as you'd expect: stout, boxy and whitewashed, a beacon for Hoxtonites. Jake and Dinos Chapman, Gary Hume and Damien Hirst all show here.

Jay Jopling, stadtbekannter Galerist junger britischer Kunst, eröffnete die White Cube Gallery 2000. Wie der Name bereits sagt, markiert sie kubisch und weiß Präsenz und ist eine Bereicherung für Hoxton. Wichtige Künstler wie Jake und Dinos Chapman, Gary Hume und Damien Hirst stellen hier aus.

Jay Jopling est un homme du monde et un galeriste vorace de Young British Artists. Sa vaste galerie, ouverte en 2000 et qui comme son nom l'indique est cubique et blanche, fait la gloire du quartier. Jake et Dinos Chapman, Gary Hume et Damien Hirst y exposent.

4

5

6

---

5 Delicatessen/Delikatessen/Produits
finse

Food Hall
374–378 Old Street
London EC1V 9LT
Tel: +44 20 7729 6005
Tube: Old Street

This upmarket food shop opened in 2004
and has been keeping the Shoreditch
crowd happy since. It offers a selection of
high-end, high-quality food with a concen-
tration on English cheeses (kept in an
extra cooled room), French wine and high-
end Italian products and breads. Drop in
at lunch for one of their home-made fresh
salads or sandwiches with bread from the
in-house bakery.

Dieses edle Lebensmittelgeschäft gibt
es seit 2004, und die Bewohner von
Shoreditch wissen das sehr zu schätzen.
Hier findet man eine Auswahl erstklassi-
ger Lebensmittel mit viel englischem Käse
(sie werden in einem Kühlraum gelagert),
französischen Weinen und edlen italienischen Erzeugnissen und Broten. Zum
Lunch kann man hausgemachte, frische
Salate oder Sandwiches mit Brot aus der
Hausbäckerei bestellen.

Cette épicerie haut de gamme fait le
bonheur des résidents de Shoreditch
depuis son ouverture en 2004 avec son
choix d'aliments de qualité, notamment ses
fromages anglais (conservés dans une
chambre froide spéciale), ses vins français,
les meilleurs produits italiens et son pain
cuit sur place. Passez à l'heure du déjeuner
chercher leurs délicieuses salades et
sandwichs frais.

---

6 Restaurant/Restaurant/Restaurant

Fifteen
15 Westland Place
London N1 7LP
Tel: +44 87 1330 1515
www.fifteenrestaurant.com
Tube: Old Street

This is fine dining Jamie Oliver-style,
meaning the walls are coated with retro
mosaics and the dishes have names like
"Fantastic Salad". The open kitchen (you
may catch Oliver on one of his few days in)
serves a six-course tasting menu and a set
lunch, with vegetarian options. If you're
passing through town without a reserva-
tion, you might get a shot at a table in the
casual main-floor trattoria.

So wird bei Jamie Oliver diniert: Die Wände sind mit Retro-Mosaiken verziert und
auf den Tisch kommen Gerichte mit Namen wie „Fantastic Salad". In der offenen
Küche (mit etwas Glück kann man einen
Blick auf Oliver erhaschen) werden das
sechsgängige Tasting-Menü und ein
Lunch-Menü mit vegetarischer Alternati-
ve zubereitet. Ohne Tischreservation wird
man am einfachsten in der schlichten
Trattoria im Hauptgeschoss einen Platz
finden.

L'esprit de Jamie Oliver règne partout : les
murs sont tapissés de mosaïques rétro, les
plats portent des noms genre « la salade
fantastique ». La cuisine ouverte (vous y
apercevrez peut-être Oliver en personne)
offre un menu dégustation de six plats ou
des menus simples avec options végéta-
riennes. Si vous n'avez pas réservé, tentez
quand même d'obtenir une table à la charmante trattoria.

Personal Finds/Eigene Entdeckungen/
Découvertes personnelles:

Museums & Others

© 2006 TASCHEN GmbH
Hohenzollernring 53, D-50672 Köln
www.taschen.com

© 2006 Maps by Michael A Hill/Mapsillustrated.com

Compiled, Edited & Layout by
Angelika Taschen, Berlin

General Project Manager
Stephanie Bischoff, Cologne

Design
Eggers + Diaper, Berlin

French Translation
Philippe Safavi, Paris

German Translation
Simone Ott Caduff, California

Lithograph Manager
Thomas Grell, Cologne

Printed in Italy
ISBN-13: 978-3-8228-2409-2
ISBN-10: 3-8228-2409-7

Frontcover: Floral Silk Wallpaper
Page 2/3 St James Trellis Wallpaper
from Cole & Son (Wallpapers) Ltd
Manufacturers of Fine Printed Wallpaper since 1875
www.cole-and-son.com

We cannot assume liability for any inaccuracies which may be contained in
the information provided. / Für die Richtigkeit der mitgeteilten Informationen
können wir keine Haftung übernehmen. / Nous ne pouvons etre tenus
responsables de la véracité de informations communiquées.

To stay informed about upcoming TASCHEN titles, please request our
magazine at www.taschen.com/magazine or write to TASCHEN,
Hohenzollernring 53, D-50672 Cologne, Germany, contact@taschen.com,
Fax: +49-221-254919. We will be happy to send you a free copy of our
magazine which is filled with information about all of our books.